BONUS 99 SPEARO RECIPES VIDEO PLAYLIST

Check our curated video playlist at:
www.noobspearo.com/99-spearo-recipes-videos

DISCLAIMER

The information contained in this guide is for informational purposes only.

Not all of us are professional chefs so any cooking advice that we give is based on our opinions and personal experience. You should always seek the advice of a professional before acting on something that we publish or recommend.

All of the recipes in this book have been written in good faith. This means that they have shared recipes that have worked for them. BUT, you are cooking your own meal and should take care and use your own instincts when it comes to what you eat and prepare for others. Bottom line is good fish is very good, bad fish can be very bad.

This process starts with the fish as soon as it is caught. Despatch it quickly, store it on ice or in a chilled environment, and prepare it cleanly. There are a range of recipes in this book which use raw fish. These should be prepared with fresh fish (caught that day) or the instructions for ageing should be followed carefully. Similarly, some recipes can be refrigerated or frozen. Use your own judgement—a couple of days in the fridge is probably okay—a week or two on the bench over summer isn't the best place to store fish! Take extra care with these ideas.

Overall, use your senses and common sense with these recipes—if it doesn't look right, feel right, smell right or taste right maybe choose something else to eat. Stay safe and have fun.

The publication of such Third Party Quotes and information does not constitute my guarantee of any information, instruction, opinion, tips or services contained within the Third Party Material.

No part of this publication shall be reproduced, transmitted, or sold in whole or in part in any form, without the prior written consent of the authors. All trademarks and registered trademarks appearing in this guide are the property of their respective owners.

Users of this guide are advised to do their own due diligence when it comes to cooking. All information should be considered in line with advice from your local government food standards authority.

By reading this guide, you agree that Noob Spearo Pty Ltd is not responsible for your safety in any way relating to the information provided in this guide.

99 SPEARO RECIPES

BY THE NOOB SPEARO COMMUNITY

You picked up this book so I am betting that, like me, you want to become better at cooking. You are not alone as thousands of spearos share the same desire.

To learn culinary skills it takes time and an experimental mindset. It also helps to have some actionable, simple meal guides to help you get past your 2-3 go-to recipes. Well done for picking up this book and having a crack!

Rather than being an overwhelming, complicated, specialist chef's book about seafood, this book is about making good, simple food and slowly punching out of your comfort zone and trying new ways of preparing, cooking, and presenting your catch!

I would love to hear how some of these recipes have improved your cooking, email me at **shrek@noobspearo.com**, tag me **@noobspearo on Instagram** or **Noob Spearo on Facebook** and share your cooking story with **#99spearorecipes**

Like spearfishing, cooking seafood the world over is conducted in similar ways. However, every area of the world has developed specific techniques and styles to suit their local seafood. Recipes in this book come from the temperate waters of the UK, New Zealand, Southern Australia, California, Canada, South Africa, and also into the subtropical and tropical waters of the Bahamas, Australia, Florida, Hawaii, Mauritius, the Pacific Islands and the Caribbean.

If you don't find the specific species used in each recipe, there are often substitute species identified or at least the characteristics of the fish. Research and find out which species in your area are similar and experiment! *Use the fish glossary at the back for this.

Here are more than 150 recipes from spearos just like you that will help you dramatically improve your culinary skills. Make meals for the people you love, with the fish and seafood you love to chase!

Get into it!

Isaac 'Shrek' Daly

Noob Spearo Podcast Host.
@noobspearo

As we all know the ocean is not the same every time we jump in, there are seasons, the snapper and cuttlefish run, winter crays, summer dollies, yellowfin and bluefin or longtail.

Still, there is also the residential drummer, bream, pike and red morwong, we all know we can get a feed but what are you going to do with it once it has a hole in it?

Within these pages are well over 99 recipes to get you started, give you confidence and hopefully get you to give something other than crumbed fillets a crack (don't get me wrong I love a shnitty).

Many of these recipes have a sub species so it doesn't matter where you live, your fish can find an interesting home on the table.

We need to look after our local dive spots and we need to be advocates of sustainable fishing practices and bag limits (as we all know).

Hopefully, this book will give you the confidence to give a lesser quality fish a crack and let some of the more prized species swim another day if you see the numbers in your local dropping.

There is a lifestyle attached to being a spearo, it's not a hobby, it will take you all over the world if you let it, and at its core is food and there is nothing better at breaking down barriers than breaking bread and having a meal together, so go learn some shit, be a better cook ....everyone benefits.

Mark LaBrooy

Husband, Chef, Author, Subsistence Hunter.
@markthreeblueducks

INDEX

06 | FOREWORD

09 | FOOD SAFETY

12 | CONTRIBUTORS

14 | CARING FOR YOUR CATCH

20 | HOW TO DRY AGE FISH

24 | GUIDE TO CURING

28 | RAW, CURED & PICKLED

60 | GRILLED, BARBECUED & FRIED

124 | A GUIDE TO HOT SMOKING FISH

130 | SMOKED

138 | BAKED & ROASTED

168 | GUIDE TO LOBSTERS

176 | STEAMED & POACHED

194 | SOUPS, STEWS & CURRIES

214 | GUIDE TO URCHINS

220 | PASTA & RISOTTO

234 | MIXED BAG

250 | SAUCES & ACCOMPANIMENTS

262 | THE TEAM

264 | ACKNOWLEDGMENTS

268 | FISH GLOSSARY

278 | TERMS GLOSSARY

Photo courtesy of @benrennie_ & @twin_elements

Foreword

ABOUT THE CONTRIBUTORS AND PREFACE

Isaac 'Shrek' Daly records the Noob Spearo Podcast in Brisbane, Australia. Shrek grew up in love with the temperate waters of New Zealand. At first swimming, then lifesaving, then at 17, scuba diving and freediving. Spearfishing became the next natural lifestyle progression after moving to Australia in 2004.

In 2014, he started interviewing spearfishing experts, authorities, and characters from around the world aboard the Noob Spearo Podcast.

Diver - Isaac Daly

ABOUT THE BOOK AND NOOB SPEARO

Spearfishing is a sport that has one of the steepest learning curves imaginable.

"I encountered lots of obstacles getting started spearfishing and so we created the Noob Spearo to help people overcome their own hurdles".

- **Shrek**

NOOB SPEARO'S VISION

1. Reduce spearfishing deaths
2. Develop the next generation of environmentally aware spearos
3. Grow spearfishing by developing community and relationships
4. Shoot fish and have fun

NOOB SPEARO PODCAST

The Noob Spearo Podcast features world-class spearos who share their hard-won wisdom and experiences with us in interviews shared for free at noobspearo.com and also on iTunes, Spotify and wherever you listen to good podcasts. Many of the recipes in this book come directly from spearfishing experts, authorities, and characters from all over the world who have featured on the Noob Spearo Podcast. More than 190 renowned spearfishing men and women have joined us on the show.

NOOB SPEARO BLOG

noobspearo.com is the home of articles on everything from how to get started shore diving to how to hunt, shoot and land spanish mackerel. Guest contributors, feedback from our listeners and community, and our own experiences are fueling an ever growing catalogue of tips, tricks, hacks, DIY guides, and articles for the aspiring spearo.

CORE VALUES

We don't believe in big-noting and speaking to new or up and coming spearos like they are a new kind of bacteria found on Shrek's feet during a hot summer. Forums and social media can be full of spearos abusing and disrespecting one another—we don't go in for that at Noob Spearo.

We like to share a laugh, enjoy our spearfishing, tell real stories, and share lessons learned, while inviting the next generation of divers into a healthy, safe, and sustainable relationship with this epic lifestyle.

GET INVOLVED

If you have a message to share with spearos or want to be part of a healthy community, sign up to the Noob Spearo newsletter and join our community. Contributors are always welcome and some of our best information now comes from spearos like you with helpful information to share.

SEAFOOD AND SUSTAINABILITY

Sustainable is a word that's taken an absolute pizzling. The word sustainable and its meaning has become muddied like Brisbane's Moreton Bay after the summer rains, so I want to present you with my idea (and possibly many spearos') understanding of what sustainable means to someone who likes to spend their time underwater.

Sustainable fishing/seafood gathering means that we take from the ocean only what it can reproduce and replace. Our fishing activities shouldn't negatively impact the environment for the next generation. Our children, their children, and beyond should inherit better fisheries and oceans than we have.

This means that when a local species is under threat for whatever reason (pollution, ocean temperature changes, ecosystem imbalance, over-fishing etc.) we give it a break and encourage others to do so too. It also means that just because a fishery is abundant does not mean that we should take more than we need.

Underwater hunting and gathering should be an intentional activity conducted with the highest levels of ethics and awareness towards the resource, others and yourself.

Some of the recipes in this book refer to certain species as being highly sustainable in their respective areas. Be aware that the same species in your area might not be as sustainable due to different local pressures, regulations, and attitudes.

As you grow in your spearfishing ability, grow also in your knowledge of your local environment and hand on that knowledge to others!

WHAT IS CORNERSTONE CONTENT?

Look out for cornerstone content. It's our aim to introduce you to some really awesome techniques and ideas that will change the way you think about seafood.

Techniques like 'dry ageing' and 'smoking' can seem intimidating and possibly difficult to try.

So these cornerstone content guides have been put together to get you started and on the ladder and reaching for new ways of doing seafood! Some cookbooks like The Whole Fish Cookbook by Josh Niland and Rick Stein's Fish and Shellfish are game changers but can leave you feeling like your missing the basics to get started on the cooking journey.

Both books are inspiring and are changing mindsets around the world about seafood. The problem is that often we need the bottom rungs (the entry level) knowledge before we can stretch out and approach recipes like Josh Niland's Salt and Vinegar Blue Mackerel & Cucumbers with Fried Rye Bread.

If you are reading a recipe that refers to a cornerstone content guide, I recommend you read it as this will help to demystify the broader techniques and get you up and cooking confidently!

CC Recipes that refer to these cornerstone content guides will be represented with this icon. So make sure you check out these guides for comprehensive tips, tricks and preparation techniques.

FISH GLOSSARY

One of the key benefits of this book is the ability to swap out the seafood species used in a recipe with an alternative species which you may have in your local area.

G For the recipes that may have confusing common fish names/families we have represented these with this icon.

We highly recommend you check out the fish glossary at the rear of the book which goes into great detail with species similarities, eating characteristics and much more.

POTENTIAL ISSUES WITH FISH

FOOD SAFETY AND WARNINGS

In this book we pulled together the best recipes our community has to offer. We stand in contrast to most people who obtain their seafood from restaurants (i.e. already prepared) or from fish markets. Being spearo-chefs means that we are essentially fulfilling multiple roles in the "sea to serve" food chain, from seafood supplier, to preparation, to chef, to consumer.

In a commercial setting, quality assurance steps would be undertaken at each stage and most of us are generally accustomed to receiving our food in a safe condition (although many of us have experienced the effects of eating food in an unsafe condition). As such we need to be aware of a number of safety issues around seafood.

S Recipes that refer to seafood with potential food safety issues will all be represented with this icon. Please make sure that you check out this guide for comprehensive tips and preparation techniques to avoid any potential issues.

In the following section are conversations and tips from some of our contributors. The team at Noob Spearo are not experts in this area and we would encourage readers to inform themselves on the risks involved with seafood borne illnesses.

The process of seafood harvest, processing, preparation, and responsible handling should all be done in as clean as an environment as possible with meticulous attention during the processing and storage phase.

To that end, we have pulled together a number of resources from the experts to help.

TIPS FROM 99 SPEARO RECIPES CONTRIBUTORS

Raw Fish

While fully cooking fish with heat will kill parasites, we often want to eat it raw or partially cooked, which poses a risk. To reduce the risk, freezing fish at or below -4°F or -20°C will kill parasites that can be present in a fish's flesh but regular home freezers often won't get cold enough to kill parasites.

If you don't have access to a commercial or deep freezer that can reach these temperatures, the safest home remedy is to put dry ice in the bottom a cooler, put a layer of cardboard over it, then add the fish (vacuum sealed or wrapped in plastic with air removed) then another layer of cardboard, then more dry ice.

Leave it in the cooler for a few days and it should be good to go, but there are a lot of factors at play here.

That being said, I personally eat almost all California fish species raw (even ones with known parasites like the common *Anisakis*) but I have a multi-step routine for meticulously checking each fillet and each morsel and understand that I'm putting myself at risk by not following the FDA Guidelines.

One other caveat, I regularly eat rockfish (notorious for the *Anisakis* worms) raw without freezing it first but have a meticulous inspection process before I do consume it... so it's a risk thing one way or the other.
- Eric Keener

I know many people in Europe always freeze their fish before doing raw dishes like sushi, carpaccio, gravlax etc. I spoke to a sushi chef who runs a restaurant in Rome and it's because of *Anisakis* worms. They always freeze for 5 days before serving to clients.

If you are confident with something like a sea trout or wild caught salmon and can inspect the gut cavity then it's probably ok, but it's still your personal call to make. But, for liability purposes, freezing is recommended in Europe.
- Daniel Mann

Daniel Mann is right. However, to get more specific, the Food and Drug Administration food code states that fish eaten raw should be frozen at -4°F (-20°C) for a minimum of seven days, or for 15 hours at a temperature of -31°F (-35°C). Most home freezers do not get that cold. Most restaurants have commercial freezers that can get very cold.
- Eric Keener

REFERENCES

Food Safety Information Council Australia

Food Standards AU/NZ

US Food & Drug Administration

Food & Agriculture Organisation

Safe Fish Australia

Visit **www.noobspearo.com/references** for more information on food safety and links

FURTHER FOOD SAFETY CONCERNS WITH FISH AND SEAFOOD

CIGUATERA POISONING

Ciguatera fish poisoning is a form of food poisoning caused by the consumption of fish that have accumulated a type of toxin called ciguatoxins. Ciguatoxins are produced by dinoflagellates of the genus *Gambierdiscus* in warm tropical waters. Dinoflagellates are found on algae and coral and are consumed by herbivorous fish species.

As these species are preyed upon by larger predatory species the toxin can accumulate in them to the point where they are toxic to humans. This process is called biomagnification. The symptoms can last from weeks to years.

How to prevent Ciguatera poisoning: Seek local knowledge on which fish should be avoided. Eat small quantities of fish known to carry amounts of Ciguatoxin. If symptoms appear, stop consumption.

For more discussion and info on Ciguatera, listen to the Noob Spearo Podcast episode 25 with Levi Brown who contracted a significant dose of Ciguatera Poisoning.

SCOMBROID POISONING

Scombroid Poisoning symptoms present rapidly (within minutes or a few hours) and are caused by eating spoiled fish usually from the *Scombridae* fish family (tunas and mackerels). Symptoms usually last for approximately four to six hours and rarely exceed one to two days.

To prevent Scombroid poisoning: Cooking, smoking, canning, or freezing will not destroy histamine in contaminated fish. Proper handling of fish is the best preventative. Bleed and immediately store fish in an ice slurry.

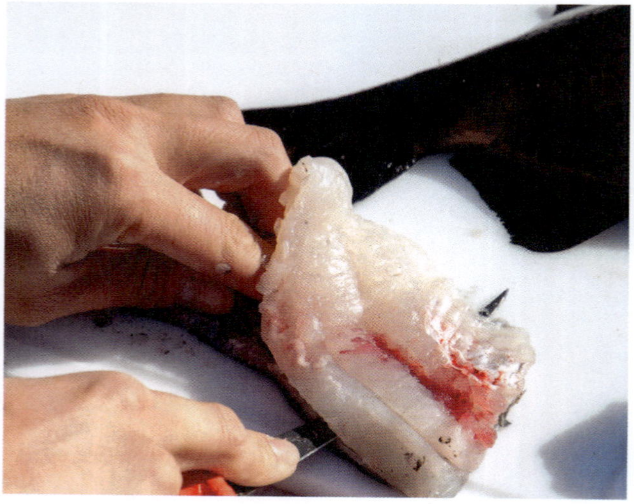

CIGUATERA VS SCOMBROID POISONING SYMPTOMS

CIGUATERA

- Diarrhoea
- Vomiting
- Headaches
- Itchiness
- Muscle Aches
- Paresthesia (reversal in feeling e.g. hot feels cold)
- Dizziness, Vertigo and Nausea
- Weakness
- Bradycardia/Tachycardia (low/high heart rate)
- Hypotension/Hypertension (low/high blood pressure)

SCOMBROID

- Facial flushing/sweating
- Burning-peppery taste in the mouth
- Dizziness
- Nausea
- Headache
- Tachycardia
- Cold-like symptoms
- Can develop into rash/hives on face/body
- Diarrhoea and abdominal cramping

SMELLY FISH

Once a fish has been killed, it begins to break down. This is what causes the smell. Smell is one way we can tell a fish is ok to eat however some fish smell bad quite quickly and yet they can still be ok to eat. This is why fish is often served with lemon or other acidic accompaniment and it can be quite effective. Again, this is up to you to judge for yourself.

MUSHY FISH (SOAPY FISH)

Some fish go mushy as soon as you apply heat and the problem is, that you can't tell they are going to go mushy until you cook them. This problem is caused by a parasite that can live in the fish's gills called *Kudoa thyrsites*. It is not harmful to people but the fish can taste soapy and mushy. Not the result you want for your family and friends. One way to get around this if it happens is to have a backup plan–either another fish or maybe just a good takeout joint nearby.

TESTING FISH

One trick to minimise poor experiences is to cut a small piece of fish off and cook and sample it before cooking and serving the meal to your friends and family. It can be time consuming though and it's not 100% foolproof.

WEIGHTS AND MEASURES CONVERSIONS

Cooking is not speargun engineering. The quantity of panko crumbs for fish tacos is not critical in the way that the diameter of a shaft in a speargun is. The measurements listed for ingredient quantities in many spearo recipes are, in many cases, best guesses. We also have the old Imperial/Metric issue so, where possible, conversions have been provided and you can always use Google when in doubt. Common sense and a healthy dose of experimentation will see you create some spearlicious meals.

RECIPE QUALITY STATEMENT

These recipes have been submitted from spearos just like you and me. Some recipes were provided without precise quantities however the Noob Spearo team have communicated back and forth to try and ensure each and every recipe is able to be replicated with success and ease.

That being said, ingredients are often added to a person's taste preference so please experiment with these recipes until they are the way you like them. If you would like to communicate with the spearo directly, often their social media contact details have been provided.

Go ahead and flatter them and don't forget to add the hashtag **#99spearorecipes** to your social media posts!

CATCH, COOK & SHARE

Don't forget to share your cooking if you decide to recreate one of the recipes from our spearo chefs. Tag the spearo and use #99spearorecipes

About the Contributors

KEY CONTRIBUTORS

Special thanks to the following key contributors for their invaluable advice, guides and multiple recipe submissions which helped make this book possible:

Ben Hohnke | @hohnkeoutdoors	**Jai Gibbons** | @spearochef
Ben Rennie | @benrennie_ & @twin_elements	**James Sakker** | Catch it Grow it Cook it
Captain Dan Walsh | @upfrontcomms	**Josh Bollen** | @bosh.jollen
Daniel Mann | @daniel___mann	**Michael Isbey** | @matakanasmokehouse_nz
Deryck Tan | @deryck.gyotaku	**Sam Clothier** | @wetmammal
Eli Ravines | @Aquaholic173	**Spencer Allen** | @el_spencerino
Eric Keener | @finandforage	**Yianni Barthelmess** | @huntfishgrowcook
Harry Foster | @hazfos	**Plus many more..**

THE SPEARO CHEFS

More than 72 everyday divers from around the world submitted their actionable seafood recipes to help make us all more intentional towards the seafood we harvest! Massive thanks to:

Aaron Kiggins	Damian Dellaca	Jason Harris	Rachel Thomson
Adam Mori	Daniel Mann	Jeremey Smith	Rasmus Björkman
Alex Hamilton	David McGowan	Jeremy Arnold	Renee Taylor
Alyssa Kay	Derek Dunning	Jeremy Karl Day	Rhys Gotje
Amanda Bratton	Deryck Tan	Jon Stenstrom	Ric & Bee Divola
Anthony Thodey	Didrik T. Hurum	Jordan McComb	Ryan Francis
António Cardeal	Eathan Kirkman	Josh Bollen	Sam Clothier
Ashley Clark	Eckart	Keanu King	Sam Rowbotham
Ben Hohnke	Eli Ravines	Mark Cronje	James Beckman
Ben Rennie	Eric Keener	Mark Cronje & Hiroko Ooka	Spencer Allen
Bert Keulder	Gabriella Gerbasi	Mark LaBrooy	Stephen Logan
Brandon Swanepoel	Harry Foster	Matt Bond	Surf-fur
Bret Whitman	Harry Lindley	Max & Ben MacDonald	Sven Franklin
Cameron Jutila	Harry Young	Nick Giannola	Chris Bakon
Cameron Wayne Smith	Henry Hunter	Omar Aljundi	Tim Hall
Captain Dan Walsh	Isaac 'Shrek' Daly	Pat Swanson	Tony 'Taz' Alcock
Christopher Lincoln	Jai Gibbons	Patrick Ryan	Yianni Barthelmess
Craig McNiven	James Sakker	Philip van Zijl	Zac Kenway

The Team

VOLUNTEER EDITORS, PROOF AND BETA READER TEAMS

This recipe book would not have been possible without a passionate team of volunteers who gave their time, expertise, and energy to help edit and proofread each and every recipe multiple times. A huge thank you to Alistair Lean, Martin Hing, Edward Bodkin, Samuel Phillis, John Wood, Eric Keener, Steven Keegel, Andrew Bleakley, Jason Wagnon, Captain Dan Walsh, Daniel Mann, Harry Foster, Livia Cruz, Brandon Swanepoele, and others.

CHIEF ADMINISTRATIVE OFFICER

This project would not have been possible without the impresario-like skills of Livia Cruz. Livia has been a linchpin. Thank you for all your efforts.

EDITORIAL DESIGN & CREATIVE DIRECTOR

Massive thanks to Jason Harris who has undertaken nearly all design related work for the 99 Spearo Recipes project. From the Kickstarter to the finished 99 Spearo Recipe book in your hands, Jason has been instrumental in this book's development.

FISH GLOSSARY TEAM

Martin Hing, Samuel Phillis, and Steven Keegel all contributed towards creating a substitute species table and chapter to assist people to find alternative species to use for every recipe. We sought to create something special and unique that had never really been tried.

Thank you guys for all your work with this!

PHOTOGRAPHY

Huge thanks to all of the contributors for submitting imagery alongside their fantastic recipes.

All their imagery is their own. A massive shout out to the Fin & Forage team for submitting a large number of photos that feature throughout this book.

Visit them at **finandforage.com** and **@finandforage** on Instagram.

CARING FOR YOUR CATCH

Cornerstone Content Guide

Written by Jai Gibbons
@SpearoChef

As spearos, caring for our catch is of the utmost importance—we do this not only out of respect for what we are harvesting, but also to maximise the quality of our catch. When that fish hits the table, we are eating nothing but the best that it has to offer.

There are a few simple steps that we can take to ensure that we're doing our duty as caretakers of the ocean and respecting the life of the quarry we take.

It can often be impractical to do everything to the highest fish butchery standards every time. Implementing as many of the best practices as you can will ensure you have the best quality eating fish.

IKEJIME (AKA BRAIN SPIKING)

The ikejime technique originated in Japan, but nowadays is used worldwide. The basic technique is very simple and involves inserting a sharp object into the brain of the fish as soon as practical. This minimises the fish's suffering and reduces stress in the flesh to preserve the eating qualities.

While every species of fish is anatomically different, there is a simple rule of thumb to locate the brain. Looking down on top of the fish, imagine you are drawing a line between the eyes, then form an equilateral triangle backwards towards the tail of the fish.

The point on the triangle behind the eyes is where the brain is on most fish. When ikejime is performed correctly, the fish will generally give a flick and flare the gills or fins. The absolute telltale is the jaw of the fish will be slack when it has expired.

BENEFITS OF IKIJIME

Not only is ikejime the fastest way to despatch a fish, it results in the lowest levels of stress. This benefits the quality of the fish by improving its freshness, taste, and shelf life

For more information visit: **www.ikijime.com**

BLEEDING

Bleeding your fish is the next critical step to ensure the quality of the meat, and there is never a reason not to do it. A bled fish will have a cleaner and more delicate flavour.

Blood is also the first thing in a fish to start to go off and can give a bitter taste. Removing it will help preserve the best eating quality, especially when ageing the fish for several days or more. A fish's heart will continue to pump after having ikejime performed on it, so you can still bleed a fish after this process.

Cutting a gill is an effective method of bleeding a fish if you don't want to compromise the gut cavity for a process like dry ageing.

If you are processing the fish that day or the next, the better method is to slice the soft jugular area under the gill plate that the gills lay flat against. This leads directly to the heart, and the blood will readily exit the body.

Both bleeding and ikejime are best done in the water, because they are the fastest way to humanely kill the fish and you won't have blood stains to clean off your boat later, so win-win. However, you should also always consider the implications of a pool of blood around a diver, especially in popular areas.

ICING THE FISH

Getting your fish on ice and dropping the core temperature down as quickly as possible is going to ensure that you're eating nothing but the best quality. Fish that are immediately ikijimed, bled, and iced in a slurry will last longer in the fridge and ultimately taste better.

Throwing a fish into an ice box with a frozen water bottle is a start but really just doesn't cut it. A slurry of ice and sea water that covers the fish in a good quality ice box is ideal. Then once back on shore, refrigerate or fillet immediately.

SCALING

Scaling your fish is something you need to do if you want to use the skin of the fish. The skin often carries a lot of flavour and can have a delicate layer of fat just under it. The most common way to scale a fish is to use a scaler. To scale the fish, you scrape against the scales towards the head and the scales flake off. This opens up each skin pocket which can hold moisture.

These skin pockets can harbour bacteria and will decrease the shelf life if left as they are. Scaling with the 'sukibiki' technique means you are essentially cutting the scales along with those pockets away while still keeping the skin intact and keeping all the positives described above.

Cutting the scales off requires a razor sharp knife and can take some practice to get right. This technique is one you can investigate further elsewhere.

Before scaling a fish, consider your options before you start. This will help you maximise the quality and assist in the cooking process.

CONSIDERATIONS INCLUDE:

Holding time—how long will you hold the fish before eating it?
Skin utilization—will you use the skin or just remove it?
Dry age—are you planning to dry age the fish?
Storage—how are you planning to store the fish before use?
Remains/waste—do you (or your partner) want to get scales all over your kitchen?

ADDING UNNECESSARY MOISTURE TO THE SKIN WILL GREATLY AFFECT HOW THE SKIN PERFORMS IN THE PAN

If you have decided to scale the fish, it's important to prepare the area. You need a dry and clean working environment.

You do not want to introduce water if the goal is to utilise the skin, as the water will inhibit the cooking process by introducing unwanted bacteria into the skin. This is especially important if you are planning to keep the fish for an extended period of time or dry age the fish.

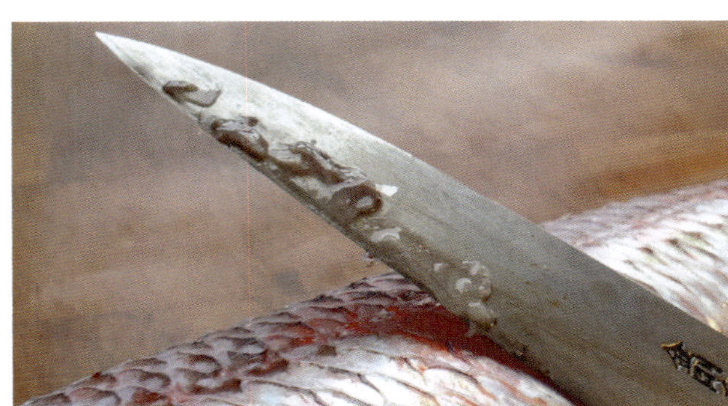

Adding unnecessary moisture to the skin will greatly affect how the skin performs in the pan, either by grill or blowtorch.

After removing the scales, it's a great idea to gently scrape the skin in the same way the scales were facing to remove any excess moisture and then wipe with paper towels.

GUTTING THE FISH

Removing the gut contents is a very simple thing to do, but also very easy to do badly. The most common way is to make a very shallow incision from the anal cavity up towards the head. Try not to pierce the stomach.

Cut between the ventral fins and all the way to the throat. Grasping the gills, you can pull back down towards the tail of the fish and remove the gut contents and gills in one motion.

There is likely to be some extra bits still inside the cavity, like congealed blood, so be sure to remove that. If you are only planning on filleting the fish, gutting isn't absolutely necessary.

STORING YOUR CATCH

The most important part of the "caring for your catch" puzzle is how you store the fish after you catch it. There are three fundamentals to take into consideration:

Temperature

Get and keep the internal temperature of the fish cold as quickly as possible.

Moisture

Remove as much moisture as possible from the environment in which you plan to store the fish.

Time

Allow the fish to go through rigor mortis (going stiff) before preparation and let the fish firm up.

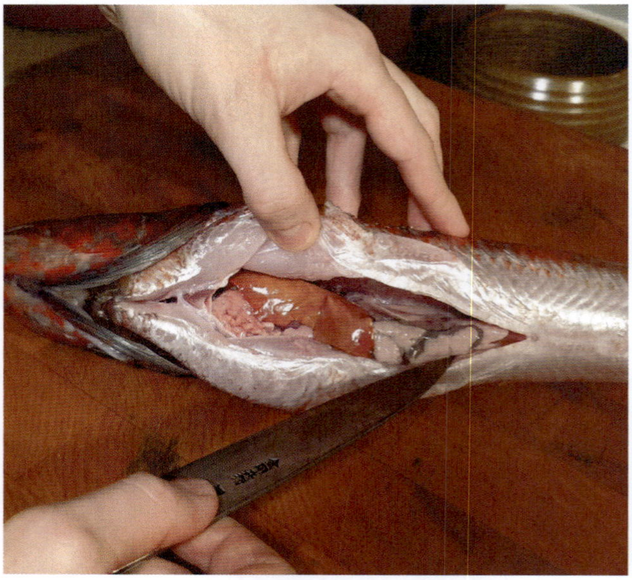

When storing your catch, getting the fish cold is the first priority. The best way to achieve this when diving is to put the fish straight into a cooler/esky/chilly bin. The cooler should have a salt water and ice mix called a slurry.

Do not use fresh water as it will spoil the fish. There needs to be enough slurry in there to cover the fish. You could consider putting each fish in a plastic bag in the slurry, as this will keep them cold but drier.

You should try to keep the fish with scales intact, and leave the guts inside the fish unless you have pierced the gut cavity, as this reduces any chance of contamination.

When you get home it's important to decide what you are going to use the fish for. Start with the decision to either scale the fish or leave the scales on.

Then remove the guts and get the fish as dry as possible. Use clean towels or paper towels.

After this, pack the gut cavity with fresh paper towels to soak up any excess moisture. Next place the fish on a tray with either a towel, silicone mat or plastic wrap underneath and over the top.

In most circumstances, you do not want air to dry out the fish. If done correctly, the fish will not decompose past edibility for up to a week, as long as you replace the towel daily.

POST RIGOR GLORY

The last (and optional) step is to wait. Allowing your fish to rest for at least 8 hours will mean a much higher quality fillet. The fish will also become much easier to fillet.

Your fish should feel slightly soft and springy unless it has been in the ice for too long. If you fillet the fish too early, the protein in the fish will not have gone through rigor mortis and the flesh will often have a wetter, less appealing texture and behave poorly when heat is added, often curling in the pan.

A dead fish will start to stiffen up after some time. It will often bend and warp. This is the rigor mortis process.

Explained simply, this is caused by a chemical change in the muscle which causes it to gradually harden, usually from the tail towards the head. The flesh is very unappealing at this point and needs more time to allow the flesh to relax.

When the fish has relaxed and the muscle is not hard but firm (much firmer than it was before rigor), the result will be a much higher quality fillet.

It will also behave better when heat is added, and have a nicer, firmer, cleaner texture which will aid in filleting and improve mouthfeel, especially when eating the fish as sashimi.

This is the optimal result. Often this process takes between 8-24 hours depending on the size of the fish.

| Written by Jai Gibbons, @SpearoChef

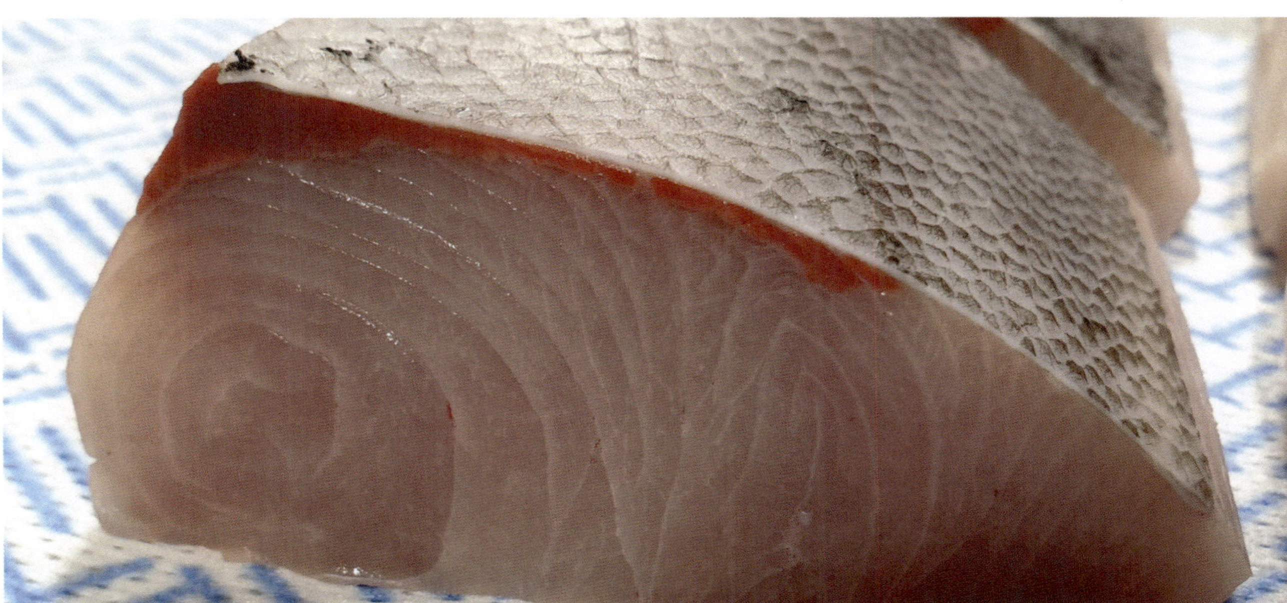

HOW TO DRY AGE FISH

Cornerstone Content Guide

Written by Eric Keener, Fin & Forage
@finandforage

It's common to assume that "fresh caught" fish, straight out of the water will offer the highest quality meat, but eating fish the day it was caught does not actually equate to a better eating experience.

Similar to beef at the butchers, ageing fish requires careful knife technique, a controlled environment, and a few steps to ensure the fish remains clean. Aged fish not only tastes better, but the texture changes as well.

WHY?

Before we talk about how, let's visit the reason why we would want to do this.

You're probably aware that steaks are aged for months before they're sold to be thrown on the grill.

This time allows chemical reactions to occur and as a result, the natural flavour and texture of the delicious meat are developed. Most species of fish dry age the same but with fish, there are added benefits.

"By day 3, the meat takes on a denser but firmer texture from water loss. The enzymes in the meat's muscle cells begin to break down the meat's proteins, fats, and glycogen—a carbohydrate into amino acids, fatty acids, and sugars. There's also a dramatic increase in glutamate—the key ingredient that produces umami flavour." - Michelin Guide.

At Fin+Forage, we LOVE umami!

HOW?

STEP 1: PROPER HANDLING

Before you can age the fish, you have to catch the fish, or in our case, spear it. Make sure to only age fish that you have a true stone shot (spear through the brain or spine that does not pierce the stomach cavity or fillets, as that will introduce bacteria).

Once you have possession of the fish, you may be hunting on the water for a few more hours, so if you're interested in reading the best way to dispatch a fish and keep it in the best quality while diving visit finandforage.com or keep reading. Once you have bled and brained your fish, packed it on ice in your cooler for the drive home, it's time to prep it.

STEP 2: PREPARATION.

Important note: When you're processing the fish it is imperative that you know how to carefully fillet it. You certainly want to avoid puncturing the belly cavity and organs which will expose the meat to bacteria. Carefully remove the guts and discard any offal you don't intend to use—you can use the discarded bits to make fertilizer for your garden.

Do not at any point let fresh/tap water touch the fish meat as it causes rapid destruction of the cells and causes it to spoil quickly. Use heavily salted water to clean the gut cavity then remove the gills and any bloody bits.

Keep the fish intact—skin, head and fins on—pat the entire fish dry with a paper towel, wrap it in a clean paper towel, stuff the belly cavity with paper towels, then place in a tightly wrapped plastic bag.

Bury the fish in ice, in a good cooler. Depending on the size of the fish, I usually let it stay buried for 48-60 hours. Be sure to rinse the fish in salted water every day, pat it dry, check for foul odor (discard if unpleasant aroma forms), change out the towels, put back in the bag and bury it again.

STEP 3: KNIFE WORK

Depending on how you intend to prepare the fish for your meal, you can scale it or remove the skin as called for by your recipe. This could be where you stop your process, or you could do one more additional step which really seals the deal for a wonderfully flavourful fillet.

To demonstrate the maximum flavour of the meat, I'll use this step in the example of sushi. When you bring the fish out of the bag and before you place it on the clean cutting board, pat it dry again. Make sure your fillet knife is sterile and clean, then:

1. Fillet one side of the fish. Try your best not to let the fillet touch the outside of the fish or the cutting board.
2. Remove the fillet and pat it dry before placing it exposed on a small baking rack with a plate or towel beneath it.
3. Clean the knife, and fillet the other side.

As mentioned previously, NEVER rinse fillets in tap water. Water spoils fish fast and ruins the taste. At this point, you can keep the bones and head to make fish stock/fumet/dashi or you can send it back down to the depths of Davy Jones' locker for other animals to enjoy.

Once both fillets have been patted dry and placed on the cooking rack, check for parasites by holding up the fillets towards the sun or bright light and looking for any dark spots. They are typically visible and appear like very thin coiled worms. If you see one, you should plan on cooking the fillet and not eating it raw.

Assuming you don't have a large commercial fridge, the next best option is to place the rack uncovered in your fridge. There should be air flow to both the top and bottom of the fish. From here it's a matter of preference how long you keep it refrigerated.

For thicker fillets, you might consider leaving it in there for up to 24 hours. For thinner fillets, 5-10 hours should work well.

STEP 4: INSPECT

Now that it's out of the fridge, it's time to slice it up. If there are any hard thin pieces around the outer edges from the drying process, you can trim it up. Once I trim my pieces and slice them to the desired size and width, I do another candle light test on each piece to inspect for parasites. Please know this is NOT a guarantee that you won't get a food borne illness—the risk can still be present, we are just mitigating that risk by keeping everything clean and inspected.

STEP 5: GET WEIRD!

The meat is ready to eat. Play with your food! I recently dry aged a Californian sheephead, where I tried multiple flavour combinations with the meat. It was a blast. I highly recommend using a culinary torch to burn some lemon and rub it on top of the fish. The flavour is amazing. Other flavours I played with were jalapeño, yuzu, cilantro, ponzu, gochujang, sriracha, and miso paste.

Written by Eric Keener, @finandforage

KOBUJIME CURING TECHNIQUE

Cornerstone Content Guide

Written by Spencer Allen
@el_spencerino

Kobujime is a Japanese method of seaweed curing your catch. Not only does it add complexity and umami flavour, but I've found it a fantastic, inexpensive and simple way to get into curing.

KOBUJIME

Kobujime is a Japanese method of seaweed-curing your catch. Not only does it add complexity and umami flavour, but I've found it a fantastic, inexpensive and simple way to get into curing.

In this case I've used Sheepshead *Archosargus probatocephalus*, as I find it a fantastic sashimi fish, and it's what I had on hand for the photographs and the meal. My absolute favourite way to turn out an amazing meal from a dive with the least amount of work is crudo.

It's culturally transcendent, as it can include some variation of ceviche, sashimi, tartare, carpaccio, or poke, and it's easy to experiment if you follow a basic fundamental structure.

STRUCTURE

That structure is generally comprised of some mix of:

- a fresh, raw, carefully inspected and prepped saltwater-based protein source such as fish or scallops
- a source of acid such as citrus or vinegar
- a source of sweet flavour such as tomato, peaches, melon, etc
- an aromatic/spice/bitter flavour such as onion, raddish, ginger, hot pepper
- a fatty buffer such as olive, chili, coconut, avocado, or sesame oil
- an optional salad or garnish component such as daikon, jicama, cilantro, or cabbage

The combination and presentation options are pretty endless, but I usually find they work best with ingredients prepared in either a minced/chopped and mixed manner, or a thinly sliced and arrayed manner.

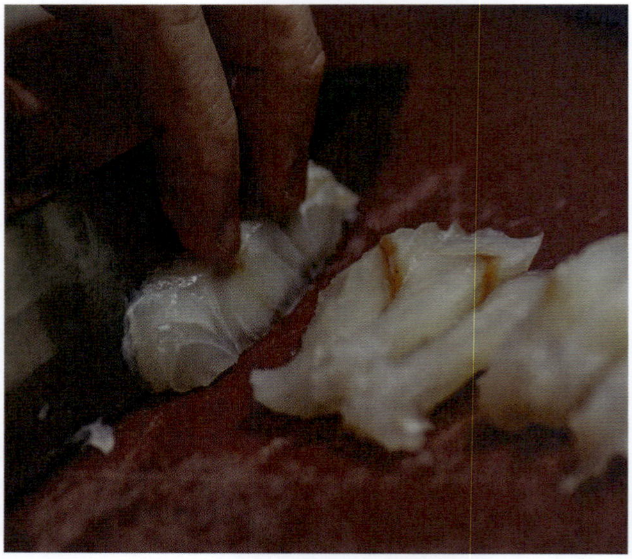

As a rule, I tend to carefully inspect my fillets for any parasites, and often vacuum seal and store in a deep freeze below -4°F (-20°C) if I'm not eating immediately.

TOOLS:

13 x 9in (33 x 23cm) quarter sheet baking tray
1 roll plastic cling wrap
1 small spray bottle or basting brush

NOT ONLY DOES IT ADD COMPLEXITY & UMAMI FLAVOUR, BUT I'VE FOUND IT A FANTASTIC, INEXPENSIVE & SIMPLE WAY TO GET INTO CURING

INGREDIENTS

12-16oz (340g-450g) fillet of any fresh saltwater fish
2 sheets kombu nori
1 small bottle of sake (alternately a 1:1 mix of distilled water and rice wine vinegar)

TRIED CURING FOR YOURSELF?

Make sure to post your recipes and don't forget to add the hashtag #99spearorecipes to your social media posts

METHOD

Fill your spray bottle (or if you're going to use a brush, a small bowl) with sake or the vinegar mixture. You'll need just enough to lightly coat and dampen one side of each sheet of kombu nori.

The idea is that you'll sandwich your fish between the two pieces, directly in contact with the sake, to allow the seaweed flavour to infuse more readily.

Slice your fillets at an angle, across the grain, into sashimi pieces roughly 1/2 inch (1.25cm) in thickness. Place the pieces next to one another on the first sheet of nori, in contact with the sake.

Take the second piece of nori, and place it on top of the sashimi slices, sake side down.

Wrap the entire sashimi nori sandwich tightly in cling wrap and place on the tray. Note: you can place the cling wrap down prior to the first steps to make this process easier.

Refrigerate for 4-6 hours Serve as sashimi.

RAW, CURED & PICKLED

'Cooking' seafood doesn't have to involve heat. The seafood spearos have access to is so fresh and of such high quality that it can often be eaten raw in several different ways.

Very fresh seafood suitable for eating raw is often called 'sashimi-grade' and while spearos couldn't catch seafood any fresher, we sometimes don't quite treat our fish in ways that bring out the best quality, aka sashimi grade. Before reading this chapter, it's highly recommended that you read Jai Gibbons' 'Caring For Your Catch' chapter to get the absolute best quality from your fish and seafood.

Also please read the food safety stuff because Listeria, *Vibrio parahaemolyticus*, and Salmonella, *Staphylococcus aureus* are no joke.

WET MAMMAL'S BONITO POKE BOWL

This is a quick, easy, and amazing seafood dish. It's my modern take on a poke bowl with some avocado slices and is Insta-worthy. I formed this recipe through trial and error and borrowing ideas from other people's poke bowls.

Other fresh fish can replace the bonito, but some species definitely work better than others. Making it is pleasurable and when I don't skimp on ingredients, it's delicious for just me and my friends.

COOK TIME 20 MIN | SERVES 2
Bonito

INGREDIENTS

1 bonito
Soy sauce
Rice wine vinegar
Sesame oil
Chilli flakes
Sesame seeds
Dried seaweed flakes
Alg seaweed rainbow seasoning (similar to Furikake seasoning)
1 cucumber
1 avocado
1 carrot
1 cup rice (cooked/warm)
200g (7oz) cooked edamame beans
Bunch of watercress

METHOD

MARINATED FISH

The amount of marinade needed will depend on the size of your fish!

Fillet, skin, debone, and cube the fish into bite sized pieces.

Mix 4 parts soy sauce, 2 parts rice wine vinegar and 1 part sesame oil in a bowl.

Add chilli flakes, sesame seeds, seaweed flakes and rainbow seasoning to taste.

Place fish cubes in the marinade bowl and mix. Ensure fish is well coated.

Marinate for 15 minutes—check flavours after 5 minutes and adjust to taste.

VEGETABLES

Slice the cucumber and avocado. Grate the carrot.

CREATE THE POKE

Put the cooked rice in the base of a bowl.

Arrange the cucumber, avocado, carrot, and edamame beans around the edge of the bowl.

Leave a space in the centre.

Place the marinated fish in the centre of the bowl.

Garnish with fresh watercress and a few chilli flakes.

> **"POKE [PRON. POH-KAY] MEANS TO SLICE OR CUT AND ORIGINATED IN HAWAII AS A SALAD MADE FROM RAW OR MARINATED FISH AND RICE."**

SPEARO CHEF

Sam Clothier
@wetmammal

ALTERNATIVE FISH

Skipjack, salmon, yellowtail kingfish

BONITO AND URCHIN TOSTADAS

This is a good dish for sharing with friends. You can either assemble and serve it for them restaurant style or put each item in individual bowls and allow your friends to do it themselves!

Whenever I get a bonito, I'll always grab a couple of urchins on the way in. I know I'll be doing some sort of raw dish and the urchin roe pairs so well with the bonito.

COOK TIME 20 MIN | SERVES 2
Bonito and 3 urchins

INGREDIENTS

1 red onion
100ml (3fl oz) apple cider vinegar
100ml (3fl oz) water
50g (2 oz) caster sugar
Salt
2 bonito fillets, skinned and deboned
30ml (1fl oz) olive oil
½ tsp cumin
½ tsp smoked paprika
Pepper
2 avocados
1 lemon
¼ cup chopped coriander (cilantro)
3 sea urchins, aka uni or kina
1 bag tostada (tortilla) chips
Raw abalone slices (optional)

METHOD

Thinly slice the red onion and place in a bowl.

Bring the vinegar and water to the boil in a saucepan.

Add the sugar and a teaspoon of salt. Stir until dissolved.

Pour the vinegar mix over the onions and leave to cool.

Cut the fish fillets into approximately 0.5cm (0.2in) cubes and put in a clean bowl.

Add the olive oil, cumin, and paprika to the fish. Season with salt and pepper. Mix well and set aside.

Roughly mash the avocado in a bowl and mix with the juice of half a lemon and the coriander (cilantro). Season with a little salt and pepper.

Open the urchins and remove the tongues of roe and set aside.

Assemble the tostada as a stack in any order. I like the tostada chips with avocado on the bottom, followed by onion, bonito, and topped with urchin roe. Enjoy however you like!

SPEARO CHEF

Yianni Barthelmess
@huntfishgrowcook

ALTERNATIVE FISH

Tuna, goatfish, snapper, yellowtail kingfish

CHARRED DRY AGED BONITO

The recipe is an easy, fun way of preparing bonito and seeing the difference between fresh caught and dry aged fish. Dry aged fish has its advantages.

You can keep fresh fish on hand for the whole week, sometimes even longer. It develops a more concentrated umami flavour throughout the dry ageing process. Moisture has left the fish and flavour has become concentrated in the flesh.

COOK TIME 10 MIN | SERVES 2-4
Bonito | Prior preperation req.

INGREDIENTS

1 bonito, caught fresh and aged for 5-7 days

EQUIPMENT

String or hook for hanging the fish
Sharp knife
Blow torch

SUGGESTED ACCOMPANIMENTS

Sesame and sea salt
Soy and wasabi
Hot sauce
Lemon
Lime
Sea salt
Extra virgin olive oil
Any dipping condiments/sauces you desire

METHOD

Clean and dry the bonito extremely well.

Leave the bonito in the fridge on a wire rack or hang for up to one week.

Check the quality every day and if needed, wipe away any moisture.

Fillet one side of the bonito. Cut out the bones and blood line to make two quarter fillets.

Tip - You can leave the other fillet on the bone in the fridge to use another time later in the week. This way you can see the difference the dry ageing processes makes throughout the week and determine how best you like your fish aged.

With a blow torch slowly move up and down on the skin of the bonito until it is nicely torched without cooking the flesh too much. Then quickly chill in the fridge.

With a long sharp knife cut the fillet into thin (5mm/.2in) slices.

Dip in whatever sauce you like or throw over rice. The possibilities are endless!

SPEARO CHEF

Eli Ravines
@Aquaholic173

PASSIONFRUIT CEVICHE

I thought I'd share with you my very own Wet Mammal ceviche recipe. I'm a big fan of ceviche and have been experimenting with it for years. I've tried many traditional Peruvian and South American versions , which are epic, but I just felt like flaring this dish up a little.

I've also had great success with using a traditional recipe and then just adding some diced watermelon as well. It's a pretty basic ceviche but has a passionfruit punch to it!

COOK TIME 30 MIN | SERVES 2
Blue morwong

INGREDIENTS

1 Blue morwong
Limes
Passionfruit
Sea salt
Cucumber
Green pepper (capsicum), any colour is ok but I like the green for taste
Tomatoes
Avocado
Olive oil
Chilli (pick your heat)
Fresh coriander (cilantro)
Fresh mint
Garlic

METHOD

Bowl 1: So first off juice a couple of limes and scrape out a passionfruit or two into a bowl. Crack a fair whack of salt into the mix (Don't worry you won't be eating all of this). Cover and place in a fridge to chill.

Bowl 2: Remove all skin and bones from the fillets and dice the fish into 1cm (0.4in) cubes. Place into a bowl, cover, and put back into the fridge.

Bowl 3: Chop the following into similar sized bits : tomatoes, cucumber, green pepper (capsicum) and avocado. Add to a bowl with some olive oil, chopped chilli, chopped coriander, and chopped mint. Even add some crushed garlic and crack some pepper on top, then mix together with your hands.

Pro tip: I premix this before adding the fish to reduce the bruising on the fish flesh and to prevent the fish falling apart.

Once you are nearly ready to serve, pour the contents of bowl 1 (lime juice and passionfruit mix) over bowl 2 (the cubed fish). The acidity of the lime juices will begin to poach (cook) the fish.

Leave the fish in the lime mixture for no more than 5 minutes and be sure to move it around a couple of times.

Remove the fish from the juice and place it into bowl 3 for a light mixing. Garnish with some more chopped mint and coriander.

Bingo! Awesome ceviche!

This dish originates from Peru and can be used with a wide range of fish. Get experimenting and let me know what you think! I've tried this with plenty of Sydney's famous 'poor eating fish' and they've tasted great!

Best used with fresh fish or fish that are frozen after cleaning. You can cure the fish for longer in the lime juice but you'll lose some of the awesome texture and the unique fish flavour.

SPEARO CHEF

Sam Clothier
@wetmammal

LIME COCONUT CEVICHE TORTILLA BOATS

This recipe is one of my go-to recipes for camping because it is easy to make. It needs no cooking and doesn't require many ingredients that need to be chilled. You can use dried or powdered herbs in place of the fresh herbs—meaning more room for beers in the fridge! It is a fresh and tasty dish with a tangy, tropical twist which has evolved over time. It is light and refreshing, making it the perfect dish to be enjoyed on a hot summer night. It can be served as a meal on its own. However, I tend to enjoy it as an entrée or tapas style, served in little tortilla boats that I make in the oven or over the fire if I'm camping. I hope you enjoy this refreshing recipe as much as my friends, my family and I do.

COOK TIME 15 MIN | SERVES 4
Firm white skinned and boned fish fillets

INGREDIENTS

500g (20oz) firm white fish (coral trout used in recipe)
¼ cup fresh lemon juice
½ cup fresh lime juice
¾ cup cucumber, diced 1cm (0.4in)
¾ cup red onion, diced 1cm (0.4in)
¾ cup cherry tomatoes, diced 1cm (0.4in)
¾ cup red capsicum (pepper), diced 1cm (0.4in)
2 cloves garlic, minced
½ cup fresh coriander (cilantro), finely chopped
½ cup fresh mint, finely chopped
½ red chilli (optional)
½ green chilli (optional)
1 tsp fish sauce
1 tbsp sweet chilli sauce
Hot sauce (optional)
1 cup coconut milk
1 tsp lime zest
1 packet of jumbo tortillas or 1 packet of mini tortillas—depending on which tortilla boat you need

SPEARO CHEF

Rachel Thomson
@lifesshort_staymoist

METHOD

CEVICHE

Dice fish fillet into small half inch (1.25cm) cubes and place in a bowl.

Juice the lemons and limes removing pulp and seeds. Keep 1 lime peel for zest garnish at the end.

Pour the lemon and lime juice over the top of the fish.

'Cook' the fish by resting in the juice for 15 minutes.

Stir every few minutes to ensure even coverage of the fish.

Add the cucumber, onion, capsicum and tomato.

Stir through the fish.

Add the garlic, chilli, coriander and mint. Stir again.

Pour over the fish sauce and sweet chilli sauce. Add hot chilli sauce if you enjoy it. Stir thoroughly.

Finally, add the coconut milk and top with the lime zest to serve.

TORTILLA BOATS 2 WAYS

Method One: Perfect for tapas style serving of the ceviche as it makes for perfect bite size serving amounts. You will need jumbo tortillas and circular egg rings.

Preheat the oven to 180°C (356°F).

Using a cup that is slightly larger than the circumference of the egg ring, cut the tortillas out into smaller circles. Usually 3 smaller circles to one jumbo tortilla.

Place the egg rings on a baking tray and fit the small tortilla circles into each ring pushing them down slightly in the middle to create a slight lip.

Bake for 10-15 mins or until the tortillas have become firm and crispy.

Serve ceviche in the tortilla boats you have created in the perfect bite size amounts.

Method Two: Better if you are choosing to serve as a main meal as it makes larger tortilla boats. You will need mini tortillas and a muffin tray.

Preheat the oven to 180°C (356°F).

Turn muffin tray upside down and push the tortillas down in between the muffin holes.

Bake for 10-15 mins or until the tortillas have become firm and crispy.

Spoon ceviche into the tortilla boats and serve.

ALTERNATIVE FISH

A firm or semi-firm lean white fish

"COCKTAILS OR COLD BEVERAGES AS AN ACCOMPANIMENT ARE ESSENTIAL"

Harry Foster

CORAL TROUT & MANGO CEVICHE

This dish is the quintessential taste of the tropics! Fresh coral trout from the Great Barrier Reef, paired with local in-season mangoes and a mixture of fresh herbs and citrus. Serve fresh, chilled and in good company—cocktails or cold beverages as an accompaniment are essential.

COOK TIME 20 MIN | SERVES 4
1 fillet of coral trout

INGREDIENTS

1 coral trout fillet, skinned and deboned
1 red onion
1 bowen mango
1 pack of yellow cherry tomatoes
Fresh coriander (cilantro)
1 red chilli
1 lime
Good quality olive oil
Salt and pepper
1 green chilli
1 pack round white tortilla chips
Cos lettuce/betel leaf or similar leafy greens to serve

METHOD

CEVICHE

Prepare your trout fillet by slicing it into 3-4mm (0.1in) slices—start from the tail end and work your way up.

Dice the red onion and mango. Quarter the tomatoes. Finely shred some of the coriander and slice the red chilli (very thinly!).

Juice the lime and use this to combine all the ingredients together in a bowl with a generous glug of olive oil. Season with salt and a good hit of cracked pepper.

Add the fish and toss through the ceviche. Let sit for 10-20 mins to let the fish cure. The longer you leave it, the more cured the fish will become.

Put your ceviche in a serving bowl, garnish with fresh green chilli and more coriander. Serve with a bowl of tortilla chips. Alternatively, it can be presented in some cos lettuce cups for a stylish starter or with betel leaf as seen in the pics.

SPEARO CHEF

Harry Foster
@Hazfos

ALTERNATIVE FISH

Kingfish or similar firm fleshed white fish

ARIKI CEVICHE

Here is a bastardised ceviche recipe that I like to make on the boat. It's always the first thing on the menu when I have friends over and probably the best nacho accompaniment known to humankind. I think it's possible to make good ceviche with a broad range of fish and I'd encourage you to try squid, crayfish or spanish mackerel as well as the coral trout I used here.

I followed a recipe which has gradually evolved into a base of red onions, garlic, ginger, cumin and whatever crunchy vegetables are at hand. For the citrus it's usually lime but anything with citric acid is possible, grapefruit and blood orange came out pretty amazing with crayfish a while back.

COOK TIME 15 MIN | SERVES 4
Coral trout

INGREDIENTS

1.5 fillets of coral trout
1 medium red onion
½ cucumber
15 cherry tomatoes
1 banana pepper
As many hot chillies as you like
3 cloves of garlic
A thumb-sized piece of ginger, grated
Ground cumin
2 limes
Salt and pepper
A handful of fresh coriander (cilantro)
Olive oil
A bag of good corn chips

SPEARO CHEF

Henry Hunter
@henbomb86

METHOD

Prepare the fish. First stage is at sea; ikijime and bleed the fish as soon as possible. Ice it immediately.

Fillet and skin the fish. Dice the fish fillet, and put aside in a bowl.

Note: The size of the chunks will determine how long the citrus takes to react with the flesh, just like cooking with heat—so don't make them too big. I like cutting across the grain and making my dice more like slithers. Which is great for scooping onto corn chips.

In a separate bowl finely add chopped onions, cucumber, cherry tomatoes, banana pepper and chillies.

Add the crushed garlic, grated ginger and ground cumin. Mix thoroughly.

Squeeze your two limes over the diced trout and mix. Try not to "overcook" the fish, which can happen if you use too much lime or leave them in for too long. I find two limes for 500g (1.1lb) of fish works great. 5 minutes max, afterwards discard the excess lime juice.

Roughly mix everything together, add salt, pepper, coriander and a few glugs of olive oil.

Serve with the corn chips and probably a cold beer or two.

ALTERNATIVE SPECIES

Anything from squid, crays, mackerel, tuna. Squid ceviche is a really delicious alternative

CAST

RENNIE POKE BOWL 2 WAYS

The Rennie poke bowl has fast become a staple meal following a big day out on the water. Using simple ingredients and being fast to prepare, it makes an ideal tucker for the crew to share after the clean up and filleting is complete. We tend to prepare all the ingredients and everyone adds their favourite toppings depending on personal preference. It is an incredibly filling and refreshing meal that hits the spot after a big day of diving.

This recipe is well suited to most pelagic fish including rainbow runner, kingfish, silver trevally, jobfish, wahoo and various tuna species. For those that prefer their seafood cooked, marinated fillets or BBQ crayfish makes for a great alternative.

COOK TIME 15 MIN | SERVES 4
1 fillet of spanish mackerel

INGREDIENTS

MARINATED FISH

500g (1lb) fish fillets and/or crayfish tail (per person)
Sriracha mayonnaise
Rice wine vinegar
Sesame oil

Note: quantities of marinade ingredients will need to be adjusted for quantity of fish. Just ensure you have enough to coat all the pieces and taste as you go.

POKE BOWL

1 cucumber
1 bunch spring onions
1 bunch of radish
3 carrots
1 chilli
3 avocados
1 sheet of nori/seaweed
Pickled ginger
½ cup brown rice (per person)
1 lime

METHOD

Chill your fillets then cut into 2-3cm (approx 1in) cubes. Mix several teaspoons of Sriracha mayonnaise, a splash of rice wine vinegar and several drops of sesame oil in a bowl.

Add the raw diced fish and cover with the marinade. Leave these to marinate in the fridge while the vegetables are prepared.

Finely dice cucumber, spring onions, radish, carrot, chilli, and avocado.

Set aside some shredded nori (sushi seaweed) and pickled ginger to use as garnish.

Steam or microwave brown rice.

Assemble the poke bowl by adding steamed rice to a large bowl. Top with fish and vegetables. Garnish with shredded nori and pickled ginger, a drizzle of the remaining marinade and lime juice. Hook in!!

Note: If you prefer your fish cooked, simply prepare your chosen fish or crayfish by marinating with a teriyaki marinade. Grill, then flake the flesh over the rice in place of the raw fish.

SPEARO CHEF

Ben Rennie
@benrennie_

ALTERNATIVE FISH

Jobfish, wahoo, kingfish, tuna (most pelagics with a firm white flesh)

> "MANY MACKEREL SPECIES ARE HIGHLY SUSTAINABLE. THEY CAN BOAST RAPID GROWTH RATE, CHARACTERISTIC OF MANY PELAGIC SPECIES AND REACH REPRODUCTIVE MATURITY AT A YOUNG AGE."
>
> *Ben Rennie*

GRAVLAX ON AUSSIE SALMON

Gravlax is a very old recipe from Scandinavian cuisine. In Sweden, it's often served on a smorgasbord during traditional festivities such as Christmas, Easter and Midsummer gatherings. Most commonly eaten with potatoes or on bread with butter. If you want to get traditional, try Hovmästarsås mustard sauce, which is also a great addition to this dish. This is an easy recipe that will serve many people.

COOK TIME 15 MIN | SERVES 2-4
1 fillet of Australian salmon

INGREDIENTS

1-1.5kg (2-3lbs) fillet of Australian salmon, skin left on.
½ cup sugar
½ cup rock salt
1 handful of chopped dill

METHOD

Remove all the bones from the fish. Dry and clean with a paper towel.

To make the cure, mix the rock salt, sugar and dill. You can also add other herbs or spices, such as peppercorns to taste.

Place a layer of the mix in the base of a sealable container. Place the fish skin side down on the mix. Use the rest of the cure mix to cover the fish. Cover the container and chill in the fridge.

The fish is cured and ready to eat in 1 or 2 days. The longer you leave it, the stronger the flavour.

No water or liquid is added. The liquid is simply a result of osmosis from my understanding and should just be disposed of once the meat is cured.

As usual, proper handling of the fish from when you catch it is important to ensure the best outcome. In Sweden we always freeze the salmon before doing this recipe to kill any parasites but from my understanding that's less of an issue in the southern hemisphere. **Refer to page 8-9 for important seafood safety information.**

SPEARO CHEF

Rasmus Björkman
@rasbjo

ALTERNATIVE FISH

Any salmon but also possible with species such as cod

TREVALLY CARPACCIO

I was first introduced to this recipe by Fabio Bertin, an Italian friend - and a pretty handy spearo. I liked the fact that it was quick to make, adaptable, delicious, and very much respected the fish. You can construct a small plate for yourself, or giant platters for your friends. A perfect entrée, accompanied by a beer or white wine. Handy hint - have plenty of crusty bread on hand to mop up the juices (the best part!).

COOK TIME 15 MIN | SERVES 2-4
Fresh trevally

INGREDIENTS

Fresh trevally fillets, skinned and boned
Lemons, juice and zest
Garlic
Capers
Flat leaf parsley
Salt
Pepper
Extra virgin olive oil
Crusty bread to serve

Trevally is an under-utilised table fish. Amazing as sashimi, especially if left for a day, it develops a beautiful sweet flavour.

In New Zealand there is only one species, but it is fairly widespread. In Australia and beyond, you are spoiled for choice with trevally or jack species.

A great bonus species for spearos when looking for pelagics.

METHOD

Thinly slice your fish (2-3mm or 0.08-0.1in) and place it in a single layer on a large plate or platter. Doesn't matter if the fish is a little "scrunched".

Zest the lemon and sprinkle over the fish (it doesn't have to be perfectly even—this is a rustic dish).

Mince the garlic and sprinkle over the fish.

Sprinkle with the capers and parsley. Season with salt and pepper.

Squeeze some lemon juice over the fish.

Drizzle olive oil liberally over the fish—don't be shy with it!

Leave for 10 minutes for the flavours to develop—best at room temperature.

Dig in! Forks, chopsticks, fingers—it doesn't matter.

Mop up the juices with the bread. Job done!

SPEARO CHEF

Pat Swanson
@occasional.spearo

ALTERNATIVE FISH

Any firm fleshed fish - kingfish, kahawai (Australian salmon), snapper

"URCHIN ROE MAKES A DELICIOUS GARNISH TO THIS DISH."

Spencer Allen

YUZU PONZU DRESSED SHEEPSHEAD SASHIMI

Sometimes sashimi can be really acidic and my wife for one, tends to get a bit overloaded by too much acidity. So this mix was especially created for her. It uses a classic Japanese sauce that combines sesame, yuzu ponzu, ginger, and scallion. The jicama adds a subtle sweetness while the radish and dandelion greens bring a bitter balance to the mix. This sized portion serves two.

COOK TIME 15 MIN | SERVES 2
1 fillet of sheepshead

INGREDIENTS

6-10oz (170-300g) fillet of fresh sheepshead
½ a jicama, julienne sliced (possible substitutes are water chestnut or daikon radish)
2-3 red radishes, thinly sliced
¼ cup dandelion greens, finely minced

DRESSING:

2 tbsp yuzu ponzu
2 tsp toasted sesame oil
1 tsp fresh peeled and grated ginger
1 tsp finely minced scallion

METHOD

Create a thin layer of julienned jicama on a plate to make a bed for the fish.

Thinly slice the fish fillet, sashimi style across the grain, between ⅛-¼in (3-6mm) thick.

Lay out the thinly sliced fish on the jicama.

Mix all of the dressing ingredients in a bowl and vigorously blend with a fork or whisk. Evenly spoon the sauce over the fish.

Slice the radish crosswise as thinly as possible. Lay it out evenly over the fish.

Mince the dandelion greens and garnish generously before serving.

Note: urchin roe makes a delicious garnish to this dish. See the Guide to Sea Urchins.

SPEARO CHEF

Spencer Allen
@el_spencerino

ALTERNATIVE FISH

Kingfish or similar firm fleshed white fish

UNI TOAST

Sea urchin, uni or kina is prized all over the globe for its tasty gonads or roes, ranging from bright yellows to deep oranges with a creamy, briny flavour. They are found in every ocean around the world and are definitely one for the adventurous as they can be quite a daunting beast to tackle. Luckily the steps to process them are not too difficult.

My favourite is to have them on the rocks straight after a dive but urchin can also be stored on ice for a trip home. You can do lots with urchin but it is amazing on bread with a little seasoning. It is important to note that uni quality varies season to season and it helps to learn what seasons are best in your area.

COOK TIME 15 MIN | SERVES 1-2
1 sea urchin

INGREDIENTS

Sea urchin
Sourdough, or other crusty bread
1 nori sheet
Chives
Sesame seeds
Salt

UTENSILS

Nylon gloves (dive gloves are perfect)
Kitchen scissors/shears
Small sharp knife (paring knife or other slim knife)
2 spoons
2 bowls of iced water

SPEARO CHEF

Josh Bollen
@bosh.jollen

METHOD

TO EXTRACT THE ROES

Flip the sea urchin upside down so you can see the mouth. Using the knife, cut around the mouth and separate it from the rest of the shell.

Use the kitchen scissors to make a cut/crack each side of the hole, from here you want to start trying to pry the urchin apart.

You can stick two spoons into the hole to try to lever open the shell, you can pull it apart with your hands (best for smaller ones) or even insert the kitchen scissors and try opening them inside the urchin.

Once the urchin is cracked in half you want to look for the yellow/gold fleshy segments inside. Be careful not to break them as they can be very delicate. Use a spoon to scoop the uni into the ice water.

Once you have pried all the roe out, gently wipe away any stray bits of urchin.

Clean segments can be placed in the second bowl of water. Place the pieces onto a plate, eat or store them in the fridge.

TO CREATE THE TOAST

Cut up bread into pieces and lightly toast under the grill/in the oven.

Rip up nori sheets into small pieces, a food processor or blender will speed up this process. Finely chop the chives.

Take your uni out and cover each piece of toast with some.

Sprinkle with nori, sesame seeds and chives. Add a pinch of salt or try some dressing, like ponzu or soy sauce to season to your taste.

ROCK SCALLOP WATERMELON AGUACHILES

Among my favorite things to forage in the Southern California kelp forests is the rock scallop. When the visibility isn't especially great, or it's not the fishiest day, you can always find a few to bring home, and they make for amazing table fare. A fantastic flavour combination is watermelon and basil.

I love raw scallops, but have also tried to find a counterpoint to the rich creamy flavours and textures they can have. The sharpness of the serrano and brightness of the champagne vinegar are especially appropriate to achieve this.

COOK TIME 15 MIN | SERVES 4
Fresh rock scallops

INGREDIENTS

3-6oz (100-150g) fresh rock scallops white meat
1 serrano chilli pepper
1 ripe nectarine
Watermelon
3 tbsp watermelon juice
1 tsp olive oil
1 tbsp champagne vinegar
1 tbsp minced basil

SPEARO CHEF

Spencer Allen
@el_spencerino

METHOD

Cut your nectarine lengthwise around the pit into sections, about 1/8-1/4in (3-6mm), and remove the pit.

Place in a conical, fanned array in the center of a serving plate, peaked in the centre and splayed out like a flower. Using a very sharp knife, slice your scallops crosswise as thinly as possible. Arrange these around the nectarine on the serving plate.

Cut the watermelon to produce rectangles the same size as the scallops and place over each piece of scallop. Take some of the remaining watermelon and press it through a sieve with a spoon to make juice.

Mix this with the basil, olive oil and champagne vinegar to create a dressing. Spoon generously over the scallops.

Slice the serranos as thinly as possible at a 45 degree angle, and distribute evenly. Add as many as you like, but be careful as serranos can be hot!

CATCH, COOK & SHARE

Don't forget to share your cooking if you decide to recreate one of the recipes from our spearo chefs. Tag the spearo and use #99spearorecipes

ALTERNATIVE FISH

Any salmon but also possible with species such as cod

RUBY RED VERMILLION ROCKFISH CEVICHE

Whenever I'm making ceviche, I always consider what might be interesting departures from the traditional pico de gallo ingredients. So far this is my favorite variation. I find the grapefruit cuts the tartness of the lime and adds an interesting bitter component. My preference isn't to "cook" the fish by letting it marinate for too long, but you can add marination time to your own preference.

I also find when making a chopped crudo that it's super fun to present it by pressing it into a dome shaped teacup to form the dish rather than just spoon into a bowl.

COOK TIME 20 MIN | SERVES 2
Vermilion rockfish

INGREDIENTS

1 grapefruit
1 peach
16 oz (450g) fresh, raw rockfish fillets
2 scallions
1 jalapeño
1 tbsp fresh lime juice
1 tsp avocado oil
1 tbsp minced cilantro (coriander), plus a sprig for garnish
Furikake flakes for presentation

METHOD

Cut the peel off the grapefruit and, with a sharp knife, cut out each section and remove the white pith.

Cut the peach away from the pit and remove the skin.
Chop grapefruit, peach, rockfish, scallions and jalapeño into ¼-½ in (3-6mm) chunks.

Mix thoroughly in a bowl with lime juice, avocado oil, and minced cilantro. Leave to marinate for up to 15 minutes, depending on how much you like the lime to "cook" or cure the fish. I personally prefer to serve as soon as mixed—the longer you leave it, the firmer it will get.

Press mixture into a dome shaped teacup with your spoon until firm. Place the serving plate over the top of the filled ceviche mould and while holding the two together, flip to the plate right side up.

Gently tap the mould as you lift it off the plate, with some practice you'll achieve a very easy, restaurant level presentation of your ceviche.

Sprinkle the ceviche with furikake for an added, fancy presentation.

SPEARO CHEF

Spencer Allen
@el_spencerino

ALTERNATIVE FISH

Most pelagics with a firm white flesh

KINGFISH BOTTARGA

A take on the classic Italian bottarga, which is a cured mullet roe. I've tried using kingfish roe sack a number of ways and nothing gets the same special results as this recipe. It's easy to prepare but takes time and patience.

The results can be used as a condiment or to garnish anything from a cephalopod bolognaise to just lightly shaved over your toast for breaky. It can be kept for ages when vacuum sealed in the fridge.

INGREDIENTS

1 large kingfish roe sack
Sea salt for curing (you will need a lot!)

METHOD

This recipe relies on patience and precision. So be prepared to work for it!

Clean the roe sack from the rest of the organs. You must keep it whole, so be very gentle!

With a small pin and coin clean and press the remaining blood from the roe sacks. Be gentle and very careful not to rupture the sack. Pat the roe dry.

Salt the entire roe sack generously with sea salt.

Place uncovered in the fridge for at least a few hours.

Repeat, until the roe has shrunk in size to about a 5th of its original size and has little to no moisture left.

This could take 5-12 times depending on the size of the roe. Just keep changing the salt.

Once the roe has hardened up a bit, brush off the excess salt.

Transfer it onto a wire rack and let dry until it firms up even more.

How long this takes depends on the size of the roe. This entire process can take several days but the reward makes it all worthwhile!

When ready it should be easy to finely slice or grate over toast, pasta or whatever you please.

Peel the skin back before you grate it!

"I LOVE THIS RECIPE BECAUSE IT MAKES USE OF A PART OF THE FISH THAT WOULD NORMALLY BE DISCARDED. "

SPEARO CHEF

Eli Ravines
@Aquaholic173

ALTERNATIVE FISH

Mullet roe, any other large roe sacks

CALICO POKE BOWL WITH JICAMA ROSES

The calico bass is appropriately named. I never fail to find myself awestruck by the iridescence and complexity of their colours. They somehow embody the magic of a sunrise over the California kelp forest, yet manage to blend into the blue water almost seamlessly.

Truly gorgeous to look at and at the same time a damn pitbull of a fish. They are remarkably challenging to stalk. If you take one on a pole spear in decent visibility, you know you did something right. This is a no frills dish that doesn't overdo it on flavours, but gives the fish itself room to shine.

COOK TIME 15 MIN | SERVES 2-4
Calico bass fillet

INGREDIENTS

¼ jicama (water chestnut and/or daikon radish can be substituted)
½ cup cherry tomatoes
1 large cucumber
16oz (450g) raw calico bass fillet
1 tsp toasted sesame oil
1 tbsp rice wine vinegar
2 tbsp fresh squeezed orange juice
2 tbsp furikake
¼ cup cilantro

METHOD

Peel and thinly slice jicama lengthwise. The idea is to have strips of jicama, roughly 2-3in (5-7cm) long, 0.5-1in (12-25mm) wide, and ⅛in (3mm) thick.

Wrap 2-3 strips around each cherry tomato to form a rose flower shape.

Peel and roughly chop the cucumber into ½in (1cm) cubes and place in a bowl.

Roughly chop the calico fillets to similar proportions and add to the bowl.

Add the oil, vinegar, orange juice, furikake, and cilantro. Mix well.

Spoon into bowls, and serve alongside the jicama roses.

CATCH, COOK & SHARE

Don't forget to share your cooking if you decide to recreate one of the recipes from our spearo chefs. Tag the spearo and use #99spearorecipes

SPEARO CHEF

Spencer Allen
@el_spencerino

ALTERNATIVE FISH

Most pelagics with a firm white flesh

SIMPLE CEVICHE

This is a simple recipe for ceviche. Any white fish will do but I choose to use hogfish because of its sweet, and mild flavour. Hogfish live in the western Atlantic Ocean, in a region stretching from the north coast of South America to North Carolina.

Hogfish, a type of wrasse, are common throughout the Caribbean and Gulf of Mexico. They live near coral reefs and open bottoms in depths of 10 to 100ft (3 to 30m).

COOK TIME 15 MIN | SERVES 2-4
2 hogfish fillets

INGREDIENTS

1lb (450g) raw hogfish fillets
2 lemons
3 limes
1 tbsp salt
1 tbsp pepper
1 cob sweet corn
1 large tomato
1 large white onion
1 large cucumber
1 mango
1 bundle cilantro (coriander)
1 red chilli pepper
3 jalapeño peppers
3 serrano peppers

METHOD

First, ensure your raw fish is extremely dry before chopping the fillets into thumbnail-sized cubes.

Put the chopped fish in a bowl and add the juice from the lemons and limes.

Mix in the salt and pepper and place in the refrigerator for later. The fish will begin to 'cook' in the juice. There is no minimum time for the fish to cure. While the fish is curing, begin chopping the rest of your ingredients to thumbnail size.

Boil the corn and remove the kernels from the cob. Be sure to seed the peppers or your ceviche will be extremely spicy. I also like to seed the cucumber.

Combine all chopped vegetables in a large bowl and add the cured fish with all of the juices. Mix well.

Ceviche can be enjoyed immediately, but like any good dip or salsa, I think it tastes better the next day after all the ingredients and flavours have had time to blend.

SPEARO CHEF

Jeremey Smith
@Adventure_Explorer_

"THIS CAN BE EATEN WITH A SPOON, WITH CHIPS, OR MY FAVORITE WAY, ON AVOCADO TOAST FOR BREAKFAST. "

ALTERNATIVE FISH

Any white fish

SHREKVICHE

I 100% stole this recipe and adapted it for my personal tastes (@fed.by.chef.julian on Sammy Hitzke YouTube Channel). I love the texture and sharpness of spring onions and feel that it kicks arse with the finger lime/ passionfruit threat. I recommend using finger limes but I used passionfruit in this recipe and it worked a treat. The beauty of ceviche is that it's super-fast, super-yum, and suits a fish like trevally, yellowtail kingfish, smaller mackerel, or even less highly rated eating fish such as amberjack or even rainbow runner. In this recipe, I use surgeon fish but you can experiment and remember that cooking doesn't have to be elaborate to be fun. A simple dry age for 2-3 days will turn a tough fish into optimal eating quality and the lime does the rest of the legwork!

COOK TIME 15 MIN | SERVES 2-4
2 fillets of fish

INGREDIENTS

500-700g (18-25oz) of fish
3 limes
4 passionfruit (preferably 6-8 finger limes as they are small)
2-3 chillies
2 tbsp of fish sauce
2 tbsp brown sugar or palm sugar
1 tsp of water
Bunch of spring onions (scallions in the US)
Bunch of coriander (cilantro)
4-5 fresh or dried kaffir lime leaves
Handful of mint
1 avocado

METHOD

Slice fish into thin sashimi-like slices. Set aside on a paper towel in the refrigerator to remove excess moisture.

Juice the limes into a bowl. Finely grate 2-3 teaspoons worth of lime skin into the bowl.

Cut the passionfruit (or finger limes) into halves, spoon the seeds, pulp and juice into the lime juice.

Cut the chilli (or dice it up finely if you prefer) and add to the lime juice. If you are using dried kaffir lime leaves, dice and add these as well - if they are fresh, leave them till last.

Add the fish sauce and the sugar into the bowl (soften palm sugar first by placing it into a small bowl with a teaspoon of water and microwave for 30 seconds). Slice the spring onions, chop up coriander to taste and add these to the bowl.

Lastly, add the sliced fish into the bowl. Let it sit while the fish is 'cooking/curing', begin preparing additional elements. Don't allow the fish to sit beyond 10 minutes, as the lime juice can overcook the Shrekviche.

Finely slice the fresh kaffir lime leaves, break mint leaves off, spoon the avocado out and cut into small pieces.

Finally, drain the lime juice, add the finely sliced kaffir lime leaves, mint and avocado and serve. Enjoy the Shrekviche immediately. I love to eat Shrekviche with corn chips (Doritos as usual!)

SPEARO CHEF

Isaac aka Shrek
@noobspearo

"A SIMPLE DRY AGE FOR 2-3 DAYS WILL TURN A TOUGH FISH INTO OPTIMUM EATING QUALITY AND THE LIME DOES THE REST OF THE LEGWORK!"

Isaac aka Shrek

ALTERNATIVE FISH

Parrotfish, trevally, tuskfish

SOUTH OF THE BORDER LIONFISH CEVICHE

Raw fish recipes are a global phenomenon but ceviche was originally developed in South America. It has been slightly modified from region to region. This one is more of a Mexican style, however, ingredients can easily be introduced to suit your taste buds! So make it a good fit for you and your area.

COOK TIME 15 MIN | SERVES 2-4
2 lionfish

INGREDIENTS

2 medium lionfish
2 limes
2 cloves of garlic
2 roma tomatoes, without the heart
1 jalapeño
1 green or yellow capsicum
½ red onion
1 bunch of cilantro (coriander)
1 medium avocado
Sea salt to taste
Corn tortilla chips to serve

METHOD

Carefully remove the venomous spines from the lionfish, before filleting and skinning.

Dice the fillet into small pieces, making them as even as you can. Marinate the fish in the lime juice, along with finely minced garlic and lime zest, for 1 hour in the refrigerator.

While the fish is marinating, brunoise (finely chop to 3mm) the vegetables. For the tomatoes, ensure you first quarter them and remove the heart.

Drain the lime juice from the fish and stir in the vegetables. Gently slap the cilantro in the palm of your hand to bring out the aromas, roughly chop to desired size.

Spoon out the avocado and cut into cubes, gently toss the avocado and cilantro through the ceviche when ready to serve.

Season with salt to taste and enjoy with corn chips.

> **"THIS FISH NOT ONLY TASTES AMAZING BUT ITS VENOM PACKS A BRUTAL PUNCH, WITH SOME REFERRING TO THE TOXICITY AS THAT OF A COBRA. "**

SPEARO CHEF

Patrick Ryan
@deepwaterdreamin

ALTERNATIVE FISH

Any firm white fleshed fish

STINKY PIKE SASHIMI

Wet Mammal (Sam Clothier) had mentioned on his channel that pike were good as sashimi. I thought back to all the pike I'd caught on lures and how badly they smelt with that grim slime. I decided that this pommy bloke was a few sandwiches short of a picnic, but eventually I decided to give it a try. That night, back at camp I cut it up and tried it raw, and to my absolute horror he was right, this overlooked and misunderstood fish made good sashimi.

COOK TIME 30 MIN | SERVES 1-2
1 pike. Prior preperation req.

INGREDIENTS

1 cup sushi rice
1.5 cups of water
1 avocado, sliced
1 pike, filleted
2 tbsp of rice vinegar
2 yaki nori sheets

OPTIONAL:
Pickled ginger
Soy sauce
Wasabi
Kewpie mayo

METHOD

First cook your sushi rice (see cornerstone content pertaining to this).

While the rice is cooking, slice up your avocado and pike fillets into long strips.

After the rice is done, mix in the rice vinegar.

Place a sheet of yaki nori onto a sushi mat.

Lay down a thin layer of the sushi rice, add the avocado and fish. Kewpie mayo is good in this step as well.

Roll up the sushi and slice.

Serve with the pickled ginger, soy sauce and wasabi.

LET IT SET

Let the meat set! Fresh doesn't mean you need to eat it straight out of the ocean.
@tommy_dozz

SPEARO CHEF

Ben Hohnke
@hohnkeoutdoors

ALTERNATIVE FISH

Kingfish, goatfish, any fish suited to sashimi

ALTERNATIVE FISH

Other tuna species

TUNA TARTARE IN SESAME GINGER SAUCE

My friend shared this tartare recipe with me after I devoured it a few months ago. He wasn't even done preparing it and I had already eaten half of it! It's delicious, easy and simple to prepare.

This portion serves 2 people. I would recommend it as an appetizer or snack served with Stacy's Simply Naked chips or as a side with sushi. You can also mix the tuna with the sauce and serve it as a poke bowl.

COOK TIME 15 MIN | SERVES 2
2 fillets of fish

INGREDIENTS

SAUCE

2 cloves of garlic, minced
1 tbsp grated ginger
2 green onions, chopped
2 tbsp soy sauce
1 tbsp sesame oil
1 tbsp rice vinegar
1 tbsp honey to taste

TARTARE

300g (10oz/about 1 cup) of sushi grade tuna, cut into small cubes approx ½in (1cm)
4 green onions, finely chopped
2 tbsp toasted sesame
1 avocado, chopped into small pieces approx ¼in (½cm)
½ cup diced cucumber approx ¼in (½cm)
1 handful of cilantro (coriander), chopped
1 tbsp lime juice
Pinch of salt & pepper

METHOD

Put all the sauce ingredients into a bowl and mix together. Set aside in a refrigerator.

Once chilled, add the cut up tuna, green onions and sesame seeds directly to the bowl of sauce and mix until combined. Refrigerate until ready to serve.

In a separate bowl, mix together the finely chopped avocado, cucumber, cilantro, lime juice, salt, and pepper.

Presentation is key to this dish, so plate your tartare by using a mould or a circular ramekin. Make a layer of the tuna mix in the mould first, so it will be on top once flipped.

Add the cucumber and avocado mix. Repeat these layers until the mould is full.

Place a plate on top of the mould and flip.

Garnish with additional sesame seeds, green onion and/or cilantro. You could also use spicy mayonnaise or tartare sauce.

SPEARO CHEF

Gabriella Gerbasi
@ggerbasi

DIY CANNED TUNA

This is my first attempt at doing a DIY canned tuna. This is perfect for those who wish to prolong the life of their tuna species caught and allows you to ensure no fillets go to waste. It gives another use to self-caught tuna and it can last up to 3 years in the jar in the pantry and once opened can be stored in the fridge. Experiment with adding additional flavours to the batches to create something that you and your family can enjoy. I really enjoyed using tomato relish and caramelised onion, we also tried beetroot and mustard relish. Canning your own caught tuna allows you to break-free from store bought, canned tuna!

COOK TIME 60 MIN | SERVES 1-4
2-3 tuna steaks. Prior preparation req.

INGREDIENTS

2-3 steaks of raw tuna
Relish (jarred)—pick your own flavours

EQUIPMENT

Pressure cooker
Screw-top jars—ensure jars are sterilised prior to use

METHOD

Cut up all the raw tuna into small chunks, this can be done from fresh or frozen fillets. Best results are from fresh as the meat will darken if frozen. Add all of the cut-up tuna into a large mixing bowl.

Start by adding 2-3 heaped tablespoons of tomato relish and 2 tablespoons of caramelised onion relish to your batch and mix. You can always add more depending on your batch size if it looks like you need more.

Add a good splash of olive oil over the batch and mix through. Add your salt and pepper to the batch and continue to combine the flavours together.

Next it's time to jar your tuna mix, add your tuna to the jars so they are relatively full, pack it too full and it can crack. Don't allow anything to touch the edges of the screw top.

Fill the pressure cooker half full with water and sit the jars in the base of the pressure cooker but do not stack jars.

Close up the pressure cooker and put it on a high heat. Once the pressure cooker has reached max temp and is venting steam move onto a low heat for an hour.

After 1 hour on low heat, open the pressure cooker carefully (Please follow the instructions for opening the pressure cooker) and remove jars of tuna and allow them to cool to room temp.

Enjoy!

SPEARO CHEF

Harry Young
@offshore__adventures

ALTERNATIVE FISH

Bonito, albacore, bluefin, skipjack, longtail

CURED URCHIN BUTTER

This is a recipe I used to use while cooking in NYC at a two Michelin star restaurant—so it's time consuming but delivers a unique and delicious result. The butter tastes like a cheese. No joke. You can use it in so many ways - spread it on toast, toss it through pasta or melt it over sautéd veggies to serve - just a few examples.

Think of it as a finishing product that will raise your cooking to the next level!

COOK TIME 15 MIN | SERVES 4
Sea urchin

INGREDIENTS

300g (10.5oz) cleaned washed sea urchin roe
400g (14oz) salt
80g (3oz) sugar
250g (9oz) unsalted butter

EQUIPMENT

Muslin/cheese cloth

METHOD

Taste urchins before processing. This is important as this dictates the taste of the butter. Sometimes they can taste extremely metallic and minerally - these should be avoided.

Clean and rinse the roes/tongues and pat them dry. Set them aside. Mix salt and sugar together. In an appropriate container (glass or plastic is best) sprinkle half of the curing mix on the bottom of the container.

Place cloth over the cure mix. Place the roe on cloth, cover with the other piece of cloth and put the remaining cure mix over the top.

Cure for 4-6 days (If you don't have 300g, cut this time in half or even less. Less urchin will take less time to cure. Some moisture will come out, this can be poured off, and the roe then left to continue to cure in the cooler. Gently remove the roe sacks. They will have shrunk by about half.

In a food processor add the butter and roe and blend until smooth and fully incorporated. Store in an airtight jar or container.

I wouldn't keep it in the fridge for more than a month (up to six months in the freezer). This can obviously change depending on the storage conditions and temperatures.

*Butter should be soft to the touch but not too soft.

Enjoy!

SPEARO CHEF

Eli Ravines
@Aquaholic173

GRILLED, BARBEQUED & FRIED

It seems reasonable to assume that man's first cooking was done over open flame, grilling is an ancient cooking technique often revolving around dry, direct, radiant heat.

On the other hand, frying is a very different cooking technique utilising a form of fat to partially or fully submerge the food in and cook it at a very high temperature.

When deciding which technique to use, it is important to think about what type of fish you are using and what mode of cooking would suit it best. An oily fish such as tuna, bonito, or mackerel would benefit more from dry, radiant heat that the grill provides. An oily and delicate fish will also dry out when too much heat is added, so hitting the outside hard while keeping the inside protected and less cooked will ensure you get the most out of the fish.

A less oily fish such as flathead, snapper or red rock cod will benefit a lot from being coated and submerged in fat. Or even just fried directly in oil. These types of fish don't carry huge amounts of fat so adding fat will increase how succulent and delicious they are. This also enables quick cooking with maximum surface area. This will create a crust that locks in all the moisture avoiding the overcooked, dry result that less optimal cooking causes.

Both techniques require a reasonable amount of skill to master. Adjusting to get the right amount of heat. Predicting the right amount of time. These skills once mastered, will reward you and your family with perfect, moist, flavoursome fish.

SEARED & BASTED LEMON PARSLEY BUTTER ROCKFISH

Cooking is a bit of alchemy. Sometimes you combine ingredients that complement each other, so that their sum is greater than their collective parts. This is absolutely true, in my experience, with the combination of parsley, lemon and butter. I find it especially true when applied to most firm, flaky, white fish.

What's more, the Maillard browning effect and the seared crisping of fish skin act as a perfect complement. My favorite fish to hunt for this in California, is the rockfish. Ideally with a 6-8oz (170-225g) fillet, scaled with the skin on. This is a ridiculously simple way to cook fish fillets, and a great way to start out. This pairs quite well with cooked pasta tossed in the skillet with the remaining butter/parsley/lemon.

COOK TIME 15 MIN | SERVES 2
Vermilion rockfish

INGREDIENTS

6-8oz (170-225g) fillet of vermillion rockfish, scaled, skin on
1 tbsp ghee (or clarified butter)
2 tbsp butter
1 tbps lemon juice fresh squeezed
2 tbsp minced parsley
Grill weight for more consistent crispy skin (optional)

> **"VERMILION ROCK COD CAN OFTEN BE FOUND HIDING IN PALM KELP OR AMONG BOULDERS."**
>
> *Spencer Allen*

METHOD

Make sure your fillet is thoroughly dry. Pat down with a paper towel. To be sure it's dry, wrap it, and let it rest a while to absorb any leftover excess moisture.

Heat a cast iron skillet or heavy frying pan, on high heat, to around 350°F (180°C). Evenly coat the base of the pan with ghee.

Carefully place the fillet in the skillet, skin side down and press it down evenly with spatula or grill weight to ensure the skin sears and crisps evenly.

Allow to cook for 2-3 mins, until the skin is a golden brown. Usually it will release from the skillet with the spatula once it's ready. Lower the heat, then add butter, lemon, and parsley to the skillet and stir.

There are two schools of thought for the next step. One, is to lift and tilt the skillet gently so the liquid pools, and baste with a spoon over the fish to finish cooking.

The other, and my preferred method is to carefully flip the fish and let it cook further for 1-2 minutes, then spoon the remaining lemon/butter/parsley mixture over the crispy skin.

Let rest 3-5 mins on a plate before serving.

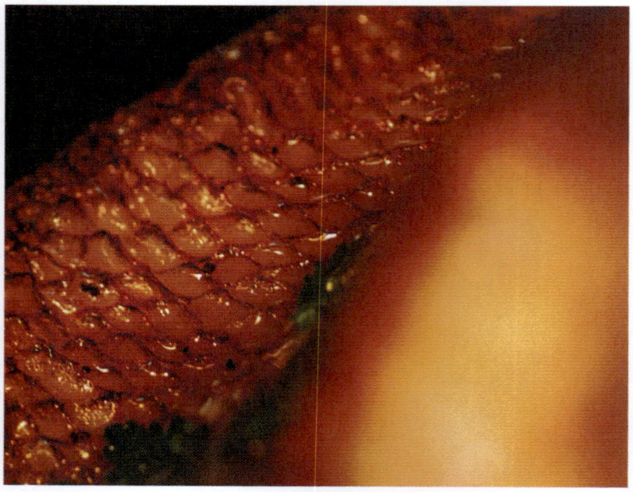

SPEARO CHEF

Spencer Allen
@el_spencerino

ALTERNATIVE FISH
Parrotfish, trevally, tuskfish

> "I SEE IT HAPPEN ALL TOO OFTEN. A FISHER TAKING THE FILLETS OFF THEIR CATCH AND THROWING THE REST OF THE FISH AWAY. NO! DON'T BE THAT PERSON — THE WINGS ARE ARGUABLY THE BEST PART."

Harry Foster

TANDOORI FISH WINGS

I see it happen all too often. A fisher taking the fillets off their catch and throwing the rest of the fish away. No! Don't be that person—the wings are arguably the best part.

Fish wings are the taste equivalent of a chicken thigh. The meat is darker, flavourful and when cooked right, perfectly flakes off the bone into bite sized pieces. This recipe is a fantastic use for those wings that could otherwise end up in the scrap bag, and it will soon become a favourite.

COOK TIME 15 MIN | SERVES 4
4 fish wings

INGREDIENTS

3 tbsp tandoori paste
3 tbsp natural yoghurt
½ lemon, juiced
Olive oil
4 fresh fish wings scaled and split butterfly style

GARNISH

Tandoori spice
Natural yoghurt

SPEARO CHEF

Harry Foster
@hazfos

METHOD

Mix the tandoori paste, yoghurt, lemon juice and a good glug of olive oil in a bowl or ziplock bag.

Add your fish wings to the bowl or bag and ensure they are covered in the marinade. This can be for any length of time—you can cook right after covering in marinade but a bit longer, even overnight, is better.

Heat the coals or a grill plate on a barbecue to a high heat. Drizzle with olive oil and cook the wings until charred and the skin is crispy.

Turn as required, but be cautious as they can become delicate. The burnt bits on the edge are crucial so don't be afraid to take them a little further than you usually would!

Garnish with tandoori spice, a little yoghurt and a generous squeeze of lemon.

Serve with rice, naan and side dishes such as raita, kachumber, Indian mint chutney or pickled red onion.

ALTERNATIVE FISH

Most species

GRILLED STUFFED BURRITO

We had a blast paddling out in our new kayaks and after covering some serious ground, we decided on a spot to start spearfishing. While Zach was chasing a lingcod, I spotted a huge fish in a cave. A California sheephead! I try to only take about one of these fish per year because they are good for the Northern California area since they eat purple urchin, which is currently a huge problem. I knew I wanted to enjoy this one to the fullest, so we made burritos and ceviche!

If you are pressed for time or simply want a rad meal that takes next to no time to make, this one's for you. It doesn't require much work and certainly won't challenge you as a cook, but sometimes we just want to relax and not sweat over a delicious meal. You can skip the pickled habanero entirely if you really are pressed for time, but we recommend making it a day or two before.

COOK TIME 30 MIN | SERVES 2
2 fish fillets

INGREDIENTS

PICKLED HABANERO

White wine vinegar
Red wine vinegar
2 habanero peppers (hot chilli), thinly sliced
2 shallots (spring onions) thinly sliced
carrots, peeled and sliced ¼in (approx ½cm) thick
10 peppercorns
3 juniper berries
3 bay leaves
Oregano
1 tbsp olive oil

BURRITOS

Mexican rice (off the shelf, in the box or sachet)
White fish fillets, sliced into 1in (2.5cm) wide strips
Mexican (taco) seasoning
Canola or peanut oil
1 tin black beans
1 sweet white corn
Pico de gallo (fresh salsa)
Sour cream
XL tortillas
Red cabbage, thinly sliced
Avocado, sliced
Spicy nacho doritos, crushed
Cilantro (coriander), chopped

SPEARO CHEF

Eric Keener
@finandforage

METHOD

PICKLED HABANERO

Mix 1:1 parts vinegar and water. Enough to cover all the ingredients in the container you will use to store them.

Add all the remaining ingredients to a small soup pan. Include habanero seeds if you want it extra spicy.

Bring the mix to a boil, then reduce the heat to medium low for 10 minutes to simmer.

Remove from the stove and let the mixture cool. Place in a clean container. Cover and store in the fridge for at least 24 hours.

BURRITOS

Cook the rice according to the instructions.

Warm a non-stick pan over medium heat.

Dust the fish fillets with the Mexican seasoning. Add some high smoke point oil (canola or peanut oil) to the pan once hot.

Add the fish strips to the pan and don't move them for several minutes until the bottom has developed a nice brown crust. While the fish is cooking, warm up your beans and corn.

Flip the fillets and cook for about half as long on the other side. It is important to only flip the fillets once. Remove the fillets from the pan and set aside. Keep the pan on the heat.

Mix the pico de gallo and sour cream, sprinkling in a little mexican seasoning.

Layer all of the ingredients on the tortilla, reserving some avocado, pico de gallo mix and cilantro for garnish. Roll the burrito up tight, folding the ends. Place in the warm pan used for the fish.

Cook for 1-2 minutes until brown on one side. Roll the burritos over and brown the other side. Remove from the pan and garnish with remaining avocado, pico de gallo mix and cilantro. We recommend serving with the pickled habanero which can be made a few days in advance. Boom. Massive meal, massive flavour, in next to no time flat.

ALTERNATIVE FISH

Any white fleshed fish

CRISPY FISH WINGS

Ladies and gentlemen, I present a tasty crispy fish wings recipe! Fish wings are absolutely delicious and a great way to use more of your catch, reducing waste. Honestly, once you start eating fish wings, you won't go back.

The best thing I find to do, especially if there is a big sporting event and you are entertaining, is to freeze your fish wings until you have 12 pairs or more. This is a super easy, quick meal everyone can enjoy.

COOK TIME 20 MIN | SERVES 4
Fresh fish wings (collars)

INGREDIENTS

2 free range eggs
10 fish wings, scaled-in this recipe I've used blue morwong, flathead and bream wings
1 cup white flour
Smoked paprika
1 tbsp sea salt
1 tsp black pepper
1 tbsp garlic granules
Chopped or dried chilli - pick your heat!
200ml (7fl oz) vegetable oil
Kewpie mayo
Sriracha sauce
Peri-peri mayo
2 limes

SPEARO CHEF

Sam Clothier
@wetmammal

METHOD

Firstly, ensure all scales have been removed. Nothing more annoying than getting stuck into your fish wings and keep coming across fish scales.

Begin by cracking an egg or two into a big bowl and whisk it up. You want enough egg to cover over your wings. You can always start with 1 egg and see how that goes. One egg should do 4-6 wings, depending on how big your wings are. Let them have a soak for 10 minutes or so.

What's in the flour mix? Well let me tell you! Start off by putting plain white flour into a bowl. Add paprika, salt, pepper, garlic granules and chilli to your own desire. It's trial and error to your own taste buds and unfortunately, like most of my cooking, I don't measure it out. I just eye it in.

Remove your wings one by one from the eggy soak. Let the big gloppy bits of egg drip off. Coat the wings in the flour mix.

Bring a frying pan with vegetable oil up to heat. Sprinkle a tiny amount of flour mix into the oil, it should bubble instantly. Reduce the heat if it's burning the oil.

Now to fry your wings up. Using tongs, place your wings into the oil. Try to only flip them once! Keep them face down, and only flip when perfectly crispy.

Place some kitchen roll (paper towel) onto a plate and place the freshly fried wings onto the plate. This will absorb excess oil to ensure extra crisp.

You can add additional salt on top. In most cases I don't. Once all your wings are completed, place them onto a serving board and complement with kewpie mayo, sriracha, peri-peri mayo and limes for a little something something.

ACTIONABLE TIP

When cleaning fish, ensure the workplace is kept clean and dry where possible. Avoid introducing excessive water to fish flesh, and pat dry before storing or freezing. @benrennie_

ALTERNATIVE FISH

Common reef demersal fish

MY OH MY MAHI!

Mahi-mahi are an exceptional target species for spearos. They are abundant, grow fast, are curious and easy to hunt. Not only that, but they are also stellar tasting. This recipe is easy and great for lots of guests. Much of it can be prepared in advance, such as the salsa and marinade, so the cook doesn't miss any of the fun. The epic nature of the mahi-mahi with the salsa and rice will guarantee your guests sing songs of your hunting and cooking prowess!

Mahi-mahi is the first species I've ever had to fight a shark to keep my catch, so this dish is near and dear to my heart!

COOK TIME 15 MIN | SERVES 4
Mahi-mahi steaks

INGREDIENTS

SALSA

½ a pineapple, chopped into small chunks
3 tbsp red onion, diced
3 tbsp red bell pepper (capsicum), diced
1 jalapeño or habanero pepper, minced
1 lime, juiced
3 tbsp coriander (cilantro), chopped
1 pinch of cayenne pepper

FISH MARINADE

1 tbsp pineapple juice
1 tbsp orange juice
2 tbsp organic honey
3 tbsp balsamic vinegar
3 tbsp soy sauce
3 tsp olive oil
Dark sesame oil
2 tsp grated fresh ginger root
3 cloves garlic
1 tsp crushed red pepper (chilli) flakes
5 mahi-mahi steaks, about 6oz (170g) each
Cooked rice to serve
Canola oil
Sea salt

METHOD

SALSA

Prepare the day before your meal.

Mix the pineapple, onion, red pepper (capsicum) and jalapeño in a bowl.

Stir in the lime juice, coriander (cilantro), cayenne pepper and cover. Refrigerate until you are ready to serve.

FISH MARINADE

Pour the pineapple juice, orange juice and organic honey into a bowl. Add balsamic vinegar, soy sauce, olive oil and stir to combine.

Heat a frying pan and use the sesame oil to fry the ginger, garlic and red pepper (chilli) flakes. Once sauteed, add these to the liquid in the bowl. Stir to combine.

Place the frying pan aside for later. Do not clean it!

Place the fish in the marinade and refrigerate for at least 30 minutes.

COOK AND SERVE FISH

Prepare the rice. Reheat the frying pan to a medium heat with some canola oil.

Add the marinated fillets. Do not crowd the pan or move the fish. Allow a crust to form on the underside.

Flip the fish and lightly cook the non-crusted side. The mahi-mahi should be barely cooked through.

Serve the fish, crusted side up on a bed of cooked rice with a little of the marinade.

Drain the liquid from the salsa and serve alongside.

SPEARO CHEF

Eric Keener
@finandforage

ALTERNATIVE FISH

Any white fish

“MAHI-MAHI IS NOT CONSIDERED ENDANGERED, AND IS CITED AS AN ENVIRONMENTALLY-FRIENDLY FISH FOR CONSUMPTION DUE TO THEIR RAPID REPRODUCTION RATE”

Gabriella Gerbasi

BONFIRE GRILLED MAHI-MAHI WITH GARLIC CILANTRO LIME SLAW

This is my go-to fish taco recipe, and I love how quick and easy it is to prepare. I've shared it with people who usually don't like cooked fish and they loved it. Just writing about this recipe is making me crave that sweet cilantro lime taste. Here's to many warm-weather nights with tons and tons of fish tacos in your future!

COOK TIME 15 MIN | SERVES 2
2 fillets of fish

INGREDIENTS

2 Mahi mahi fillets
Olive oil
Cilantro
Salt and pepper to taste

GARLIC CILANTRO LIME SAUCE:

¼ cup (80ml/3fl oz) oil
¼ cup (80ml/3fl oz) water
½ cup chopped green onions (spring onions)
½ cup cilantro leaves (coriander)
2 cloves garlic
½ tsp salt
2 limes, juiced
2 cup (160ml/6fl oz) sour cream or full-fat Greek yoghurt

CABBAGE SLAW:

1lb (500g) thinly sliced or shredded cabbage (green and purple is nice)
½ tsp kosher salt, more to taste
¼ cup thinly sliced red onion, more to taste
½ cup chopped cilantro (packed coriander), about ½ of a large bunch
½ of jalapeño, finely chopped
¼ cup (80ml) fresh lime juice, more to taste
2 tbsp olive oil

METHOD

SAUCE

Pulse all the sauce ingredients in a food processor or blender until smooth.

SLAW

Place the shredded cabbage in a medium bowl. Toss with the salt. Add the onions, cilantro, jalapeño, lime juice, olive oil and toss well.

Adjust lime, salt, and jalapeño, adding more to taste–you want this to taste tangy and flavourful. Toss most of the sauce (not all) with the cabbage. Use the leftover sauce to top the tacos.

FISH

Pat the fish dry with paper towels and drizzle with a little olive oil, cilantro salt and pepper.

Use aluminum foil over the grill and grill each side of the fish for a few minutes.

Cook until the desired doneness and squeeze with a little lime juice. Grill the tortillas, brushing with olive oil if you prefer.

TACOS

For the prettiest and easiest-to-eat assembly, go in this order: smashed avocado, slaw, and fish. Finish with cotjia cheese, lime wedges, and extra sauce.

ALTERNATIVE FISH

Fish that have a moderately firm texture and large, moist flakes such as grouper, black sea bass or snapper.

SPEARO CHEF

Gabriella Gerbasi
@ggerbasi

WHOLE CHARRED FISH WITH PEANUT CURRY SAUCE

This has to be one of the easiest fish recipes to have in your repertoire. Just a few ingredients, a whole fish and you're laughing. A few garnishes to boot and you've got a really impressive and delicious dinner from barely anything. The hardest step is choosing your fish. You need to use a fish that has a nice firm texture and is of a size that can fit in your BBQ. Basically, any smaller reef fish and also coastal species work great!

COOK TIME 15 MIN | SERVES 4
1 whole fish

INGREDIENTS

1 whole fish, gutted, gilled and scaled
120g (4oz) green curry paste
200g (7oz) coconut cream
2 tbsp tamarind puree
2 tbsp fish sauce
1/2 lime, juiced
2 tbsp peanut butter

GARNISHES

Thai basil
Fresh chilli
Kaffir lime leaves-very finely sliced
Sesame seeds
Coconut rice to serve

METHOD

Heat the BBQ to a high heat.

Prepare the fish by scoring the flesh and rubbing it with half the green curry paste. Make sure it is well coated.

Place the fish on the BBQ, it will take 8-12 minutes on each side. Start cooking your sauce once you have flipped the fish.

While the fish is cooking, start preparing the sauce.

Heat the second half of the curry paste to a medium temperature.

Add the coconut cream and reduce this until it thickens.

Add the tamarind, fish sauce and lime juice. Adjust the flavours to your taste.

Add the peanut butter, turn off the heat and stir until well combined.

Check that the fish is cooked using a skewer, it should pass through easily. Rest the fish for 5 minutes before serving.

To present the dish, dress the fish with the sauce, garnish with Thai basil, chilli, kaffir lime leaves and sesame seeds. Serve with coconut rice.

SPEARO CHEF

Harry Foster
@hazfos

ALTERNATIVE FISH
Coral trout, morwong, drummer

BACON WRAPPED GROUPER CHEEKS

Grilled bacon-wrapped grouper cheeks are a party favorite. They are extremely easy to make. The hard part is harvesting the cheeks. Cheeks can be harvested from a variety of grouper species. We spear them in the Gulf of Mexico so our cheeks are from gag, red, or black grouper. All have identical taste and texture.

If you wish, you can also grill the cheeks without the bacon.

COOK TIME 15 MIN | SERVES 2
Gag grouper

INGREDIENTS

Bacon (thin sliced)
Grouper cheeks
Barbeque sauce

METHOD

Lightly cook the bacon in a pan.

Wrap each grouper cheek with 1 layer of bacon.

Place wrapped cheeks on a skewer.

Brush each side of cheeks with barbeque sauce.

Grill on the barbeque at 400°F (205°C) for approximately 6 minutes each side.

SPEARO CHEF

Alyssa Kay
@alyssakayPT

ALTERNATIVE FISH

Most species

BUTTERFLIED BEAUTY

This is a quick and easy recipe that is great as a starter or snack to pick at for yourself or with friends, so you only need a couple! I made it after going out on a little shore dive with the goal to get dinner. Went out for a butterfish or kahawai, and came back with some old fishing line, a golf ball as well! I'd never cooked with it before so I was stoked to try a new species. I'm always a fan of underdog species, especially small bait fish, I love them! With the increase in recreational seafood hunters it takes the pressure off the popular fish. Usually I whole fry small fish but I thought I'd try something new. With the help of the internet, and some inspiration from the "Eat What You Kill" group, this tasty treat came to fruition.

COOK TIME 20 MIN | SERVES 1
kahawai

INGREDIENTS

1 kahawai per person (or bait fish of your choosing), scaled, gutted and gilled
Olive oil
Salt and pepper

DRIZZLE:

One finely chopped chilli (to your preferred level of ring stinging)
Splash (1 tbsp) of fish sauce
Splash (1 tbsp) of olive oil
One clove of finely chopped garlic
Little knob (thumb size) of finely chopped ginger
1 tbsp of honey
Juice of 1 lime plus its zest
Splash (1 tbsp) of sesame oil

METHOD

Mix all your drizzle ingredients together in a bowl. Taste and add more of what you like to your preference.

Butterfly your kahawai and score the skin side with a sharp knife.

Brush with olive oil on both sides.

Season with salt and pepper.

Heat your grill plate or barbeque to high heat.

Blister your fish for a few mins on each side until cooked through. Get those grill lines burned on and crisp the skin up to your liking.

Remove from heat and spoon the drizzle over the top.

Pair with some steamed rice and you're good to go!

While butterflying the fish, save any scraps for a fish stock at a later date. A charcoal barbeque is the best option for flavour I reckon, but a hot plate or gas type will get the job done also.

SPEARO CHEF

Renee Taylor
@reneestaylor

ALTERNATIVE FISH

Blue mackerel, any small oily fish, think bait fish!

ABADABAS

Abalone (or abs) can be as tough as old boots, but if done right, they can be as soft as scallops. For this recipe I use green or brown lip abalone which are easy enough to come across in South Western Australia. Greens can be found around most headlands or islands, generally along cracks and seams. Browns are found under ledges, often upside down. Both can be hard to spot but once you have your eye in, it's on!

COOK TIME 30 MIN | SERVES 4
Abalone

INGREDIENTS

16-20 (5 x 5mm/0.25 x 0.25in) strips of cheese (tasty, cheddar or your preference-haloumi to be flashy)
16-20 strips of thinly cut bacon
2 abalone (140mm/5.5in)
¼ cup (35g/1.2oz) flour
1 beaten egg
1 cup (135g/5oz) breadcrumbs
16-20 pickled jalapeño slices
16-20 toothpicks
Beer, for drinking

*Note quantities depend on size of abalone

QUICK FRY TIP

When frying seafood, aim to use oils with a high smoke point such as canola, vegetable and rice bran oil.

METHOD

Cut cheese into 5 x 5mm (0.25 x 0.25in) squares. Place to the side.

Cut bacon into 2cm (0.75in) strips and lay them down next to each other on a flat board or plate.

Trim the beard and the foot off the abalone. Slice the abalone into 5mm (0.25in) thick pancakes. Cut the abalone on a horizontal plane to make a slice resembling pancakes.

Tenderise the pancakes with a mallet. Cut the pancakes in half.

Put flour, egg and breadcrumbs into 3 plates next to each other. Place an abalone 'half pancake' into the flour, then turn it over ensuring good coverage of flour.

Take the floured abalone pancake and submerge it in the egg, again making sure you have good coverage.

Place the abalone pancake into the breadcrumbs, turn it over ensuring good coverage. Place the abalone on top of a bacon strip, put cheese and jalapeño on top of the abalone.

Roll up and secure in place with a toothpick. Repeat steps 3-12 for remaining Abalone.

Heat oil in a deep fryer or pan. Deep fry all the abadabas for 1 minute. Enjoy (with beer)

SPEARO CHEF

Damian Dellaca
@dami.0606

ALTERNATIVE SPECIES

Any species of abalone

ABALONE SCHNITZEL

Abalone schnitzel is a simple recipe for abalone which can be found in the colder waters of Australia. In California though, you'll have to wait until 2026 to start chasing the famed giant red abalone again. The style of this dish makes it great as a snack after diving. It's a great treat as it lets you feed a lot of people with a small catch—making it really sustainable.

COOK TIME 20 MIN | SERVES 1
Abalone. Prior preparation req.

INGREDIENTS

Ingredient quantities will vary depending on the number and size of abalone.

1 medium abalone per person
¼ cup plain flour
1 egg
¼ cup breadcrumbs or panko crumbs
⅓ cup canola or peanut oil
Lemon wedge
Salt

METHOD

Shuck the abalone from the shell and remove the gut. Trim the tough frill from the edge of the abalone with a knife.

Cut a series of 5mm (0.2in) thick strips in the longest direction of the abalone.

Use a meat tenderizer to carefully pound out the strips into schnitzel steaks about 2mm (0.05in) thick.

Set out flour, egg (lightly whisked), and bread crumbs in separate bowls.

Coat each schnitzel in flour, dip in egg and then press into bread crumbs.

Set in the fridge for 30-60 mins—this will help the crumb stay on.

Shallow fry in hot oil on each side until just brown, usually only a minute each side.

Serve with lemon wedge and pinch of salt plus your favourite cold beer.

SPEARO CHEF

James Sakker
Catch It Grow It Cook It

ALTERNATIVE SPECIES

White fish fillet

SLOW FRIED TASMANIAN BLACK LIP ABALONE

Abalone has a reputation to be one of the hardest seafoods to cook properly. This is due to the 'tough' muscle that makes up the edible parts. My recipe has been developed over many abalone cook ups whilst trying a variety of techniques. In the end it was laziness that proved to unlock the secrets.

No more slicing and dicing, no more messy and time consuming flour, egg, crumb preparation. Just back to basics and doing everything everyone goes against. We are going to cook this very slowly and very easily. This recipe is with a side salad, but once the abalone has been cooked, it can complement a fresh wrap, be placed over a rice dish, mixed through pasta or even used as a tasty breakfast side with eggs.

COOK TIME 20 MIN | SERVES 1
Abalone

INGREDIENTS

1 Tasmanian black lip abalone
1 cup bread crumbs
2 tbsp of lemon herb seasoning
1 tsp of salt
1 tsp of pepper
1 tsp of garlic powder
1 tsp of paprika
½ cup of rice bran oil
1 handful of fresh rocket lettuce
1 small carrot
½ of a red onion
Garlic aioli
1 lime

SPEARO CHEF

Tassie Adventure Man (Chris Bakon)
Tassie Adventure Man

METHOD

Collect, shuck and tenderise your abalone.

Place breadcrumbs, herbs and spices in a ziplock bag. Mix thoroughly. You can use this mix as a base—feel free to experiment and add your own twists.

Put the abalone in the bag and cover with the crumbing mix. Pour Rice bran oil in a pan on low heat. Vegetable oil can also be used. Have enough oil to shallow fry, around 10 mm (0.4in) deep.

Once the oil is hot, place the whole abalone in the pan. It should be bubbling a little in the oil but not like a normal fry up.

Cook on one side for 10 minutes, turn over and cook for another 10 minutes. Tip: If the oil gets too hot or is too hot to start, just take the pan off the heat and lower the heat source. The oil will drop in temperature very quickly.

Prepare a dish with salad. I use a simple salad of rocket lettuce, thinly sliced carrots, and thinly sliced onions, all tossed together with a dressing of garlic aioli. This is something you can change to whatever your imagination can see. Once again, explore different sides and combinations or check out my videos where I make wraps with wasabi aioli.

Remove abalone from the pan. Place on a paper towel to drain excess oil. Slice the crumbed abalone in approx 5mm (.2in) wide strips. Serve alongside the salad. Finally, squeeze some fresh lime over the abalone and tuck in.

ALTERNATIVE SPECIES

Green lip abalone and paua (New Zealand)

THAI GREEN MANGO SALAD FRIED WHOLE FISH

A super easy, fresh dish to make with minimal prep, but an extremely delicious dish. The green mango is a key ingredient. The recipe originally comes from Thailand, close to my ancestral home of Cambodia. I grew up eating this dish whenever green mangoes were available, and my mum taught me how to make it. Everyone who tries it instantly wants to make it. Every bite is refreshing and packed with flavour.

COOK TIME 20 MIN | SERVES 2
Black spot goatfish

INGREDIENTS

1 green mango, grated
1 green apple, grated
2 small chillies, diced
2 garlic cloves, crushed
2 tbsp fish sauce (Squid brand is best)
1/4 cup sugar
1 bunch coriander (cilantro), finely chopped
1 lemon, juiced
100-150g (3.5-5oz) cashew nuts, crushed with a few left whole
Whole fish for frying
Vegetable oil

METHOD

Mix all the ingredients, minus the fish and vegetable oil, in a big bowl and set to one side.

Add enough oil to pan-fry the fish and bring up to heat.

Add the fish whole or filleted (fillets should have skin on and scored sides to prevent curling). Cook until crispy on both sides.

Remove fish from pan and place the fish onto a plate of paper towel to absorb some of the oil.

Move the fish onto a serving plate and top with the mango salad mixture. Garnish as you please and serve.

SPEARO CHEF

Johnnie Marm
@Johnnie_marm

ALTERNATIVE SPECIES

Snapper, barramundi, red morwong, blue morwong, gilthead bream, black bream, bream

FISH KARAAGE

This recipe came about due to my love of chicken karaage and the availability of good fresh fish as a spearo. However, the usual karaage marinade had to be changed as it was too strong in flavour for most fish. The idea of using pickle juice came from fellow spearo, Ryan Myers, who has used it several times for his catch and cooks.

This recipe has great flavours and it suits fish like silver drummer (*Kyphosus sydneyanus*) but could use any fish you choose. It can be served with aioli, mayonnaise, pickled ginger or vegetables like samphire (*Tectcornia arbuscula*) or pigface (*Carpobrotus rossii*).

COOK TIME 15 MIN | SERVES 2
2 fillets of fish

INGREDIENTS

MARINADE

400g (14oz) of firm white fish fillets
2 cloves of garlic
1.5cm (½in) chunk of ginger
300ml (10fl oz) juice from a jar of dill pickles, enough to cover the fish-add more if necessary
1 tbsp soy sauce

COATING

150g (5oz) cornflour
50g (2oz) plain flour
Pinch of salt
Pinch of pepper
Vegetable oil to fry the fish

METHOD

MARINADE THE FISH

Fillet, skin and roughly chop the fish into 4-5cm (1.5-2.0in) pieces.

Crush the garlic, grate the ginger and mix with pickle juice and soy sauce. Adjust flavours to taste.

Place the fish in a bowl with the marinade. Cover and leave for 3-5 hours in the fridge.

COAT AND FRY THE FISH

Mix the cornflour, plain flour, salt and pepper in a clean bowl.

Coat the marinated fish pieces in the flour mixture.

Fry the fish pieces.

Drain the fish on paper towels before serving with your chosen sides.

Note: The fish pieces can be shallow or deep fried. Shallow frying will need more flipping. Deep frying should be done in batches to avoid the oil temperature dropping, which will affect the texture.

SPEARO CHEF

Ryan Francis
@rdmfrancis

ALTERNATIVE SPECIES

Firm white flesh

GREEN THAI FISH CAKES

We found a basic recipe for fish cakes online, and thought we'd spruce it up a bit! So we added some crushed ginger, lemongrass, dill, and the kicker—a handful or two of baby spinach leaves. Hence the "Green" Thai Fish Cakes, because they turn out green! The beauty of this recipe is that you can add in more or less of whatever flavours you like, and use whatever fish you have available.

COOK TIME 20 MIN | SERVES 2-4
Mackerel

INGREDIENTS

Vegetable or olive oil for cooking
500g (1lb) of fish
1 egg
¼ cup (34g/1.2oz) corn flour
1 tbsp fresh ginger, crushed or grated
1 tbsp lemon grass paste
½ cup coriander (cilantro) leaves or 80g (3 oz) tube of coriander (cilantro) paste
2 tbsp fish sauce
2 tbsp sweet chilli sauce
3 shallots (scallions or spring onions)
1 tsp dill paste
2 handfuls of baby spinach leaves
50g (2oz) green beans
Squeeze of lime

METHOD

Pour enough oil into a large fry pan to cover the bottom to 8-10 mm (⅓ - ⅜in) and place over medium heat.

Process the remaining ingredients in a food processor until smooth. Transfer the mixture to a large bowl.

Make palm sized patties and place in the pan a few at a time.

Cook each side for 4-5 minutes or until golden brown.

Place on paper towels and keep warm until the rest are cooked.

Serve with salad, top with mayo, sweet chilli, Asian salad dressing—whatever you fancy.

If you don't like the idea of eating fish cakes that are green, you can leave out the spinach. Either way, the Thai fish cakes are still outstanding!

SPEARO CHEF

Stephen Logan
@stephenisland

ALTERNATIVE SPECIES

Any white fish

YELLOWTAIL KEBABS

This recipe was passed on to me from an old spearo friend Peter Fricke. It is super simple to make and tastes awesome. You can make as many kebabs as you need for the mouths you have to feed. Multiply the ingredients as needed. You can add or replace the ingredients to your liking. Use 3-4 cubes of fish per kebab. Generally larger class fish give you bigger blocks of meat. Yellowtail kebabs are best served at a braai (barbeque). Braai on a low heat to cook evenly, hot coals will cook the fish faster than the vegetables.

COOK TIME 15 MIN | SERVES 4
Kingfish fillet

INGREDIENTS

1 yellowtail fillet—quantity varied to amount of people
Honey mustard basting sauce of your choice
1 red pepper
1 yellow pepper
1 green pepper
1 onion
250g (9oz) white button mushrooms
250g (9oz) punnet of cherry tomatoes
Pack of kebab/skewer/sosatie sticks

METHOD

Skin, debone and cut fillets into 1in (2.5cm) cubes. Place in honey mustard basting to marinade.

Cut red, yellow and green peppers into squares the same size as the cubes of fish.

Cut white onion into squares the same size as the cubes of fish.

Wash the mushrooms and cherry tomatoes.

Assemble the kebabs—begin with a piece of onion and cherry tomato, then a piece of fish, then a piece of pepper and mushroom. Continue until the kebab is appropriately full, with 3-4 pieces of fish per kebab.

Put kebabs over coals on a low heat and cook slowly for 10-15 minutes until the veggies are cooked.

SPEARO CHEF

Derek Dunning
@dmdfins

ALTERNATIVE SPECIES

Any gamefish with firm meat

WINTER KINGFISH BELLY SATAY

Winter kingfish belly satay skewers are easy, simple and delicious. All of this dish can be prepared ahead of time and simply grilled or fried to be enjoyed, which makes it great to have with company. Often people don't utilise the belly and just discard it. Give this recipe a go and I guarantee your friends and family will be begging you to bring the whole fish home.

COOK TIME 15 MIN | SERVES 4
Kingfish belly. Prior preperation req.

INGREDIENTS

1 thick yellowtail kingfish belly cut into 1cm cubes and put onto skewers

MARINADE

1 tbsp sunflower oil
1 garlic clove (crushed)
1 long red chilli (chopped)
1 tsp white pepper (ground)
1 tbsp ground coriander (cilantro) seeds
1 tsp ground nutmeg
1 tbsp ground cumin
1 tsp shrimp paste or fish sauce
1 tbsp light soy sauce
1 tbsp kecap manis (Indonesian sweet soy sauce)

SAUCE

1 tbsp peanut oil
1 garlic clove (crushed)
1 Asian eschalot (red, finely chopped)
2 small red chillies (thinly sliced)
¼ cup (60ml/2fl oz) smooth peanut butter
½ cup (125ml/4fl oz) light coconut milk
2 tbsp kecap manis (Indonesian sweet soy sauce)
1 tsp Worcestershire sauce
1 tsp light soy sauce
Salt
50g (2oz) unsalted roasted peanuts (crushed)
½ lime
¼ cup (125ml/4fl oz) water

METHOD

MARINATED KINGFISH SKEWERS

Create the marinade in advance as it needs to be cooled to coat the skewers.

In a wok or small pan heat the sunflower oil. Add the garlic and chilli. Fry lightly.

Add the spices, pepper, coriander, nutmeg and cumin. Continue to fry until smells and flavours are released.

Add the fish sauce and both soy sauces. Cook for 5-8 minutes until it thickens. Remove from heat and allow to cool.

Cut the kingfish into bite sized chunks, skewer them on bamboo or metal rods.

Coat the kingfish skewers in the marinade (between 20 minutes and 4 hours). This can be done in advance of cooking. Chill until required.

SPICY PEANUT SAUCE

Again, this should be created in advance. Heat the oil in a small saucepan over medium-high heat.

Add garlic, eschalot and chilli. Fry until softened.

Add peanut butter, coconut milk, kecap manis, Worcestershire sauce, soy sauce and a pinch of salt. Reduce the heat.

Gently simmer, stirring occasionally for 10 minutes, until the ingredients are combined.

Add crushed peanuts, lime juice and ¼ cup (125ml/4fl oz) water, then return to a simmer and cook for a further 2 minutes until reduced slightly. Remove from heat and set aside to cool.

FINISHED DISH

Cook the marinated kingfish skewers on the BBQ, in a frying pan or under the grill.

Serve with steamed jasmine rice and asian greens.

Serve the spicy peanut sauce as a dip or poured over the top of the skewers.

SPEARO CHEF

Jai Gibbons
@SpearoChef

ALTERNATIVE SPECIES

Leatherjacket

ZESTY PARSLEY KINGFISH

This recipe was inspired by an awesome Sydney based spearo—Justin Ewan who is an absolute kingfish magnet. I first saw this marinade recipe posted by him which utilised spicy red chillies. I decided to substitute the red chillies for a jalapeño and lime to give a fresh and zesty taste.

This marinade would pair well with a range of fish as sweet as yellowtail kingfish, amberjack or trevally. A quick recipe that is sure to impress.

COOK TIME 15 MIN | SERVES 2
2 yellowtail kingfish cutlets. Prior preparation req.

INGREDIENTS

2 yellowtail kingfish cutlets, bone in.

MARINADE

2 lemons
1 jalapeño
2 garlic cloves
½ bunch of parsley
1 lime
100ml (1/3 cup/3fl oz) olive oil

METHOD

Grate the zest of the lemon and place your jalapeño, lemon zest, garlic and parsley into a food processor.

Add the lemon and lime juice and olive oil, and process until very smooth.

Place 90% of the marinade in a large container or bowl, then add the cutlets, turning them to coat thoroughly.

Cover and refrigerate for at least 20 minutes, marinating longer if time permits.

Place remaining parsley mixture in a small bowl and set aside as a garnish.

Heat a barbecue or grill plate on medium-high heat. Cook fish for approx 2 minutes on each side or until charred.

Plate up with your favourite side and top fish with remaining zesty parsley mixture and serve.

SPEARO CHEF

Jason Harris
@JaceDives

ALTERNATIVE SPECIES

Amberjack, trevally or similar lighter flesh fish

THE MANGO KING

The mango king is perfect for a warm summer's day when you have a few fresh mangoes ready to go after a perfect dive. It will work with a range of species, especially those that hold together well on an open grill. Kingfish cook very quickly, especially around citrus so make sure to undercook rather than overcook it. Once you have the all important charing marks, it's time to take it off. Pair this with a fresh salad and a refreshing drink.

COOK TIME 15 MIN | SERVES 2
2 yellowtail kingfish cutlets. Prior preparation req.

INGREDIENTS

2 large kingfish cutlets (bone in)
1 mango, peeled, diced
3 limes
¼ cup (60ml/2fl oz) extra virgin olive oil
2 tbsp light soy sauce
2 tbsp sriracha sauce
2 cloves of garlic, crushed
1 tsp ground turmeric
Salt and pepper

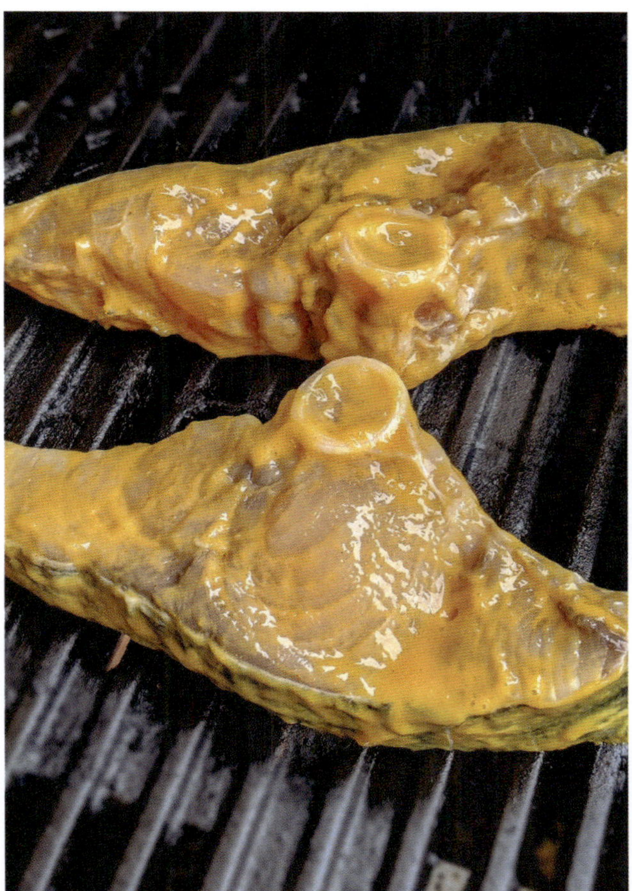

SPEARO CHEF

Jason Harris
@JaceDives

METHOD

Place mango, juice of 1½ limes, oil, soy, sriracha, garlic and turmeric in a food processor, then season with salt and pepper. Process until very smooth.

Place half the mango mixture in a large bowl, then the fish, turning to coat.

Cover and refrigerate for at least 20 minutes, marinating for longer if time permits.

Place remaining mango mixture in a small bowl and set aside.

Heat a barbecue grill on medium-high heat. Cook fish for 2 minutes on each side or until charred.

Whilst cooking the fish, grill remaining lime halves, cut-sides down, until charred. Transfer the fish to a large plate when finished.

Top fish with remaining mango mixture and grilled limes, and serve with fresh salad and a refreshing drink.

ALTERNATIVE SPECIES

Amberjack, trevally or similar lighter flesh fish

SPICED KINGFISH CUTLET WITH POTATO ROSTI, WARM CHICKPEA SALAD AND MINTED YOGHURT

By using a cutlet you can cook the fish evenly and to perfection - something you can't do easily with a whole fish. This recipe is a great example of how cooking fish on the bone helps to keep the moisture and flavour while maintaining temperature control. Just like cooking a thinner, more delicate piece of fish.

COOK TIME 30 MIN | SERVES 2
2 fillets of fish

INGREDIENTS

POTATO ROSTI

1kg (2lbs) desiree potatoes
100g (4oz) of ghee or clarified butter
Salt and pepper

MINTED YOGHURT

½ clove garlic
½ bunch of mint, finely chopped
¾ cup plain Greek yoghurt
¼ of a lemon, juiced

WARM CHICKPEA SALAD

30ml (1fl.oz) of olive oil
1 clove garlic, finely diced
1 tin (400g or 14oz) of chickpeas, strained and rinsed
½ bunch of kale, spinach or silverbeet leaves, chopped roughly
Salt

SPICED KINGFISH CUTLET

1 large kingfish cutlet or 2-3 small ones
2 tbsp of toasted lightly crushed cumin seeds
2 tbsp of toasted lightly crushed coriander seeds
1 tsp of smoked paprika
Salt
30ml (1fl oz) of rice bran oil

SPEARO CHEF

Jai Gibbons
@SpearoChef

METHOD

POTATO ROSTI

Preheat the oven to 160-170°C (320-340°F).

Rinse and grate the potato into a tea towel. Squeeze out as much of the moisture as you can. Transfer potato to a mixing bowl.

Heat 80g (2.8oz) of ghee or clarified butter and mix through the potatoes until coated. Add a pinch of salt and pepper to taste.

Heat a nonstick or cast iron pan to a moderate heat and add the remaining ghee to the pan. Swirl it around so the pan is coated. Gently place all of the potato into the pan and press it down to form an even layer.

Cook for a few minutes on the stove and then place the pan into the oven for 15-20 minutes until golden.

Set aside and get ready to cook the rest of the dish. You can reheat the rosti if necessary.

MINTED YOGHURT

Finely dice half a clove of garlic. Mix with mint, yoghurt and lemon juice. Add salt and pepper to taste. Set aside.

WARM CHICKPEA SALAD

Preheat a heavy based frypan to a moderate heat.

Add olive oil and garlic. Fry until golden and fragrant. Add the can of drained chickpeas. Heat for a few minutes.

Add chopped kale, spinach or silverbeet. Remove once this has wilted. Place in a serving bowl, season lightly with salt.

SPICED KINGFISH CUTLET

Place the cold kingfish cutlet on a tray or plate. Mix the cumin, coriander seeds and paprika with a small pinch of salt. Gently press the kingfish cutlet into the spices and coat it thoroughly.

Let it sit for at least 5 minutes to come up to room temperature.

Preheat a heavy based or cast iron pan to medium heat and add 30ml (1fl oz) of rice bran oil.

Place the kingfish cutlet into the pan. Avoid moving it around too much as this will cause the spices to come off and ruin the presentation side of the fish.

After a minute or so gently check to see if the spices are starting to turn golden.

Once golden, flip the cutlet and continue to fry until it is just cooked through to the bone in the centre.

Remove and let it rest for 1 minute before putting onto your serving board or plate.

ALTERNATIVE FISH

Australia salmon, any oily fish and medium to large fish

APPLE CIDER BATTERED FISH WRAPS

This meal has always been a hit with the girls and good mates alike. I like to serve it with a bit of salad and lemon on the side. I came up with this recipe while I was living on a small sailing boat and a neighbor told me to chuck a bit of beer together with flour and fry the fish. But I've made a few modifications to the mix and it's still easy as. Feeds 2 but with more ingredients you can make heaps—I've served 15+ people with this recipe in one go!

COOK TIME 30 MIN | SERVES 2
Flathead fillets

INGREDIENTS

1 cup canola oil
Approx 500g (18oz) of fresh fish fillets, skin left on.
4 tortilla wraps
50g (2oz) of ready made 4 leaf salad mix
2-3 tomatoes or you can use equal quantity of baby tomatoes
Sauces to taste—mayonnaise, tartare, aïoli, kewpie (your choice)

BATTER AND CRUMB

Adjust amounts based on the number of portions
1 cup plain flour
A bottle of cider (alcoholic is better, but non-alcoholic cider can be used)
200-220g panko breadcrumbs
Salt and pepper
2 tbsp garlic powder
1 tbsp chilli powder

METHOD

Mix the flour and cider together to make a soft paste. When it sticks to the spoon you know it's the right consistency.

Pour the panko breadcrumbs onto a separate plate.

Add salt, pepper, garlic powder and a touch of chilli powder to the panko crumbs. Mix it up.

Heat a frying pan with about 1cm of oil on a low-medium heat. Test the oil when the oil is hot—if you place a crumb into it and it bubbles, it's perfect.

Roll your fish into the batter and coat well then into the crumbs until fully covered. This will get messy!

Immediately place the crumbed fish into the oil as the crumbs tend to go soggy if left too long. Place the fish skin side down, laying away from you. This avoids splashing oil toward you.

Cook until fish pieces are golden brown on the underside. Flip over and repeat.

Once cooked, place the fish onto some paper towels to let the oil drain.

Place a portion onto a wrap with a bit of lettuce and tomato. Add your sauces. Fold up wrap.

Climb to the front of the boat and watch the sunset with a mate. Nothing better in my opinion.

SPEARO CHEF

Keanu King
@Kkeanu25

ALTERNATIVE SPECIES

Snapper, calamari also works well

MULE'S SURE FIRE GRILLED LOBSTER

This is a great one to impress friends, family and especially first dates! It's quick and easy to cook. Add some chips and salad for an awesome light feed for two people per lobster. The beauty of serving up lobster is that it always impresses the non-diving fraternity. I came up with these flavours after a bit of trial and error and I'm happy with the result. Once you have cooked it a few times, throw your own spin on it by adding some thyme, chives, mustard or anything else you think will compliment the dish into the mix. Serve with chips and salad or my favorite, a warm salad of roast sweet potato and beetroot, spinach, charred pine nuts and feta cheese topped with balsamic reduction.

COOK TIME 30 MIN | SERVES 2
Lobster

INGREDIENTS

GRILLED LOBSTER

1 lobster
1.5 tbsp butter
1 tbsp minced garlic (fresh is best)
2 tbsp shredded parmesan cheese
3 tbsp bread crumbs
Parsley leaves for garnish

SALAD

1 raw beetroot
⅓ sweet potato
Olive oil
1 tsp salt
¼ cup of natural pine nuts, almonds or walnuts
Small bag of baby spinach leaves
½ cup feta cheese cubes
Balsamic reduction to serve

SPEARO CHEF

Sam Rowbotham
Facebook.com/Mulsey

METHOD

GRILLED LOBSTER

Cut the lobster in half lengthways and clean out the gut and poop chute. For added flavour the mustard (tomalley) in the head can be left and spread over the meat.

Soften the butter in a bowl and mix the garlic into it. You can add extra herbs or spices here if you like (thyme, chives, mustard can work well.)

Spread the garlic butter mix over the lobster halves.

Heat a pan to moderate to high heat, place the lobster halves into a pan cut side down and cover. Cook for 5-10 minutes depending on the size of the lobster.

Heat the grill to high heat.

Remove the lobster halves from the pan and sprinkle a mix of parmesan and breadcrumbs evenly over the open side of the lobster.

Grill for 3-5 minutes until the topping is crispy and golden.

Garnish with parsley.

WARM ROAST VEG SALAD

Cut some beetroot and sweet potato (skin on) into rough cubes around 2-3cm² (0.75-1.25in²) and place on a baking tray with a drizzle of oil and salt.

Place in a preheated oven at 180°C (355°F) for approx 40 min until soft and just starting to crisp up.

Remove from the oven and set aside for 5 min.

In a hot pan, fry the nuts in olive oil until just starting to char on edges, around 5-8 min.

In a large bowl place the spinach leaves, the still warm roast veges and still warm nuts.

Mix together and transfer to serving plates.

Crumble feta over the salad and drizzle a good amount of balsamic reduction over the top.

GUIDE TO LOBSTERS

If your looking for more information make sure to check out the Guide to Lobsters on pg. 168 for everything from finding them to preparing them.

TAIWANESE POPCORN SPINY LOBSTER

Lobster is a pretty amazing table fare. You can usually just steam the tail and melt some butter. No need to gild the lily.... Or is there? This recipe is pretty much a 1:1 take on Taiwanese popcorn chicken. It's also pretty simple!

Lightly starch dredged, deep-fried, and seasoned with the magic of Chinese five spice. For those of you not familiar, Chinese five spice is a powdered mix of fennel seed, star anise, cinnamon, cloves, and in this case sichuan peppercorn. That last ingredient has an amazing, tongue-numbing, almost metallic quality to it. This can also be done with an air fryer if you're not especially keen on the mess and hazard of a boiling pot of frying oil.

COOK TIME 30 MIN | SERVES 2
California spiny lobster

INGREDIENTS

FOR FRYING

1 spiny lobster tail (roughly 8oz/200g), cut into 8 even sections
High smoke point oil, such as highly refined coconut, peanut, or avocado oil
1 cup tapioca starch (can also substitute cornstarch or sweet potato starch)
Handful of Thai basil leaves (optional for garnish and aroma)

MARINADE

2 cloves of garlic, minced
1 tsp minced ginger
1 tbsp light soy sauce
1 tsp sugar
1 tsp Chinese five spice

FINAL SEASONING

1 tsp Chinese five spice
1 tsp sugar

METHOD

Combine marinade ingredients in a dish and set aside.

Take the meat from the lobster tail, cut it into 8 even sections and place them into a mixing bowl with the marinade ingredients. Evenly coat every piece. Place in the refrigerator for 15-30 mins.

Pour your oil into a pot that is large enough to place the lobster in without it being crowded. Heat it up to 350°F (180°C).

Dredge (lightly coat) the marinated lobster in starch and carefully place it into the hot oil for 3-4 minutes, until golden brown.

Remove the pieces with a slotted spoon or tongs and drain well on paper towel or a wire rack.

Generously sprinkle with the seasoning mix.

To create the garnish, carefully drop a handful of Thai basil leaves in the hot oil and quickly cover. Be careful, as they will pop and splash in the oil.

Fry for 1-2 minutes until just translucent. Remove them with a slotted spoon, drain, and toss with the lobster.

SPEARO CHEF

Spencer Allen
@el_spencerino

ALTERNATIVE SPECIES

Any lobster species

LOBSTER TAGLIATELLE WITH CHAMPAGNE AND VANILLA CREAM

In the year 2000 there was a movie called "Dinner Rush" set in a New York restaurant. In one scene, the chef creates a pasta dish for his girlfriend. I loved that movie and the scene cooking the dish really stuck with me. So this is my quick interpretation of that dish. The presentation is striking and the dish is an absolute banger.

COOK TIME 30 MIN | SERVES 2
Eastern rock lobster

INGREDIENTS

1 eastern rock lobster
Olive oil
½ onion
2 garlic cloves
100ml (3fl oz/2 cup) champagne
2 vanilla pods (split and scrape the seeds to use)
300ml (10fl oz/1.5 cups) cream
50g (2 oz) peas
250g (10 oz) tagliatelle
10g (½ oz) chives
Lemon zest
Salt and pepper

METHOD

Boil the lobster for 5 minutes then stop the cooking and put the lobster in iced water.

Remove the tail from the body. Chop the shelled tail meat into chunks.

Heat a large frying pan with a little olive oil and sear the lobster meat on one side until you get a little colour. Remove the lobster from the pan.

Let the pan cool slightly, add a little more olive oil and cook the onion and garlic until it softens.

Add the champagne and vanilla seeds. Allow the alcohol to cook off. Use the liquid to deglaze the pan—scrape off any bits of lobster or onion that have been caught on the bottom of the pan.

Add the cream and peas. Reduce the heat to a very low simmer to thicken the sauce.

In a separate pan, cook the pasta.

Once cooked, add the pasta to the pan and toss it through the sauce.

Return the lobster meat to the pan and mix again.

Garnish with chives and lemon zest. Perch the lobster head on top for the grand finale!

SPEARO CHEF

Yianni Barthelmess
@huntfishgrowcook

ALTERNATIVE SPECIES

Bugs and even prawns will work

OLD MAN BLUE TACO

This should feed 4 people or 2 hungry spearos and it's a nice easy dish to make. It could be shared by a vegetarian (minus the crayfish!). We love the idea of everyone making their own food and this taco/burrito wrap with crayfish is a really nice way to sit down after a good cray dive with your family and friends.

COOK TIME 20 MIN | SERVES 4
California spiny lobster

INGREDIENTS

2 crayfish (lobster) tails (approx 1kg or 35oz), cubed into bite-sized pieces
200g (7oz) mushrooms, sliced
40 pitted kalamata olives
200g (7oz) haloumi cheese, cut into cubes
2 handfuls baby rocket
1 cucumber, sliced
2 small tomatoes, sliced
1 ripe avocado, sliced
200g (7oz) grated cheese
½ red pepper, sliced
Burrito sauce
4 soft burrito wraps
8 large taco shells
4 tbsp extra virgin olive oil
55g (2oz) salted butter
Salt flakes and cracked black pepper
4 cloves of garlic, finely chopped
Mixed italian herbs (to taste)
Curry powder (to taste)
Smoked paprika (to taste)
Vegita brand stock powder (to taste)

METHOD

Prepare the lobster, salad and other ingredients before you start cooking. Place the ingredients in bowls ready for cooking and/or on the table for serving.

Heat the oven to the recommended temperature to warm the burrito wraps and taco shells.

Heat half the olive oil and butter in a large frying pan over high heat and add the sliced mushrooms.

Cover with a lid and sauté until liquid comes out of the mushrooms. As the mushrooms are sautéing, put a large frying pan over a high heat and add the cubed bite sized pieces of lobster.

Toss until meat turns white and then add the finely chopped garlic, mixed herbs, curry powder, smoked paprika and salt flakes and cracked pepper.

Cook on high heat until the lobster turns golden brown.

Remove from the pan and place in a bowl. Remove the lid from the mushrooms, add the bite-sized pieces of haloumi, sliced olives, vegeta and mixed herbs.

Toss until liquid evaporates and the mushrooms and haloumi are golden brown. Remove and place in a bowl.

To serve, place all ingredients on the table and assemble to your personal taste.

SPEARO CHEF

Bert Keulder
@oldmanbluedive

ALTERNATIVE SPECIES

Crab

THAI LOBSTER CAKES

In this recipe green lobster tails are used, but any species you can grab will do. We tend to use the tougher, less flavourful ones like the tropical species in this recipe as there are a lot of other flavours going on. It is very easy to make and very forgiving. If you don't have all the ingredients, don't worry, they will still taste great. The results are great as a snack or an entree or a light summer meal with steamed rice or a salad.

COOK TIME 20 MIN | SERVES 2
Lobster

INGREDIENTS

1 clove garlic
1 in (2.5cm) ginger
8 kaffir lime leaves
1 lemongrass stalk
2 green lobster tails
1 egg
1 can Maesri red curry paste (1-4 teaspoons depending on how spicy you like it)
75g (3oz) snow peas or green beans
Peanut oil
2 limes

DIPPING SAUCE (or serve with sweet chilli sauce)

1 tbsp sweet and sour sauce
1 tbsp sweet chilli sauce
1 tbsp apple cider vinegar
1 tbsp chopped coriander
1 tsp tamarind puree
½ lime juiced

METHOD

Finely chop the garlic, ginger, lime leaves and lemon grass and put them in a food processor.

Remove the meat from lobster tails and add to the food processor.

Add the egg and 1-4 teaspoons of curry paste, depending on how spicy you like it. Blend to a fine paste.

Roughly chop the snow peas or beans and add to the mix.

Using your hands, take a palm sized amount of the mix and press into a cake, continue until all of the mix is used. Heat the peanut oil in a pan and shallow fry until the cakes are golden brown.

Drain them on absorbent paper. Serve with dipping sauce and lime wedges.

SPEARO CHEF

James Sakker
Catch It Grow It Cook It

KARAAGE CRAYFISH

This recipe uses southern rock lobster (*Jasus edwardsii*). This is a really quick and easy meal that is a sure crowd pleaser. It can be served in snack size bites, or you can even chuck them into a wrap. Warning! This is highly addictive but will make you the MVP (most valued player) at any dinner party.

COOK TIME 30 MIN | SERVES 2
Southern rock lobster. Prior preperation req.

INGREDIENTS

1 knob of ginger
3-4 finely diced cloves of garlic
4 tbsp cooking sake
4 tbsp soy sauce
Crayfish/lobster (or other appropriate seafood)
2-3 cups of corn flour (more if necessary)
Rice bran oil for shallow frying
Choice of your favourite dipping sauce (my go-to is chipotle aioli)

ACTIONABLE TIP

When looking for crayfish, be persistent and check every crack and ledge, even if it's in shallower water. The biggest crayfish I find are usually in the first 5m (15ft) of water of water.

METHOD

Finely dice the ginger and garlic and add to a large bowl with the cooking sake and soy sauce.

Dice crayfish/lobster into bite sized pieces.

Add diced crayfish/lobster to the bowl and mix thoroughly with your hands.

Cover the bowl and place in the fridge for 30 min-1 hour.

Remove the bowl from the fridge and lightly coat each piece of crayfish in corn flour.

Add oil to a deep pot for shallow frying and bring heat to approx 160°C (320°F).

When the oil temperature has reached 160°C (320°F), add pieces of crayfish to the pot. Depending on the pot size, I usually do 8-10 pieces at a time.

Try not to overcrowd the pot. If you put too many pieces in the oil, the oil temperature will drop quickly and crayfish will end up absorbing too much oil and become soggy.

Fry for around 2-3 minutes or until the outside of the crayfish is golden. Gently agitate the pieces to stop the bottoms from burning on the bottom of the pot.

If the crayfish changes colour too quickly, then the oil temperature is too high. Either put a few more pieces of crayfish in the oil or lower the heat. Controlling oil temperature at all times is very important for shallow frying.

Once golden, remove pieces and allow them to dry on a wire rack or a piece of paper towel to help drain excess oil.

Serve the karaage crayfish hot with your choice of dipping sauce and a slice of lemon.

SPEARO CHEF

Sven Franklin
@svenjamin_franklin

ALTERNATIVE SPECIES

Any crayfish/lobster species. Also fish as long as the flesh is firm, and squid goes amazing too

TROUT CRACK

When I say these things are like crack.... I truly mean it. Salty, crispy, delicious. You can eat them straight up or as a garnish over so many fish dishes.

COOK TIME 30 MIN | SERVES 2
Coral trout

INGREDIENTS

2 skins from a coral trout
Salt
Rice bran oil
Flavoured seasoning optional

METHOD

At the time of filleting, set aside your trout skins—scales on.

Remove all the flesh and sinew off the skin by scraping it with a knife or spoon.

Cut into strips approximately 2.5cm (1in) wide and 10cm (4in) long.

Place in a bowl or ziplock bag and sprinkle with a couple pinches of salt.

Cure for 20 minutes to an hour. The salt will remove moisture from the flesh and give you a crispier result.

Pat the skins entirely dry with a paper towel once cured.

Fill a small pot with rice bran oil to approximately 2cm (0.75 in) deep and bring to a medium-high heat (180°C or 355°F).

Place the trout skins in the oil in two separate batches (repeat previous step as needed)..

Fry until golden and crispy then let them cool down on a paper towel.

You can eat them at this point or alternatively, season them with a Moroccan (or other) seasoning for added flavour.

These also work as a great garnish to add texture to other fish dishes.

SPEARO CHEF

Harry Foster
@hazfos

TAKOYAKI

Takoyaki or octopus balls are from Osaka, Japan and are something a little different to try with your octopus. These bite-sized balls are quick to make with the right ingredients. For this recipe you will need a cast iron takoyaki pan, available from eBay or Amazon.

COOK TIME 30 MIN | SERVES 2
Octopus. Prior preperation req.

INGREDIENTS

½ a poached octopus
1 egg
¾ cup (100g/4oz) general purpose flour
350ml (1.5 cups/12fl oz) octopus broth (from poaching octopus)
1 tsp soy sauce
Bonito flakes (katsuobushi)
Salt
3 spring onions
60g (2oz) Chinese cabbage (wombok) leaves
Pickled ginger
Okonomiyaki/takoyaki sauce
Kewpie mayo

EQUIPMENT

Takoyaki pan
2 skewers

METHOD

Tenderise and boil the octopus until it is soft enough to push a fork into. This will be at least 20 minutes so keep checking from that point onwards.

Mix the egg, flour and octopus broth in a bowl. Add soy sauce, a sprinkle of bonito flakes and a pinch of salt to the batter.

Chop the octopus into small chunks, as close to the size of a pea as possible. Chop the spring onions and the Chinese cabbage very thinly. Oil the takoyaki pan and put on a medium heat.

Pour the batter into the dimples. It's okay for the batter to slightly overfill the dimples.

Quickly and evenly add a few pieces of octopus, some spring onions, cabbage and ginger to each dimple. Sprinkle bonito flakes on each dimple.

Watch you don't overload the dimples as all these ingredients will need to be pushed into the balls.

As the batter begins to form a light crust, use skewers to start separating the balls from the pan, and shaping them around the dimples of the pan.

Once you have separated each of the balls and a golden crust is forming, turn the balls over with the skewers to start shaping into a ball. Turn them 90 degrees each time to create the ball-shape.

Push any loose batter into the space left in the dimples. If you need, you can top up with any remaining batter.

Once the balls have fully formed and there is a consistent crust forming a ball, remove from the pan.

Drizzle the takoyaki sauce and kewpie mayo over the top.

Garnish with bonito flakes and sprinkle any remaining spring onions over the top.

Enjoy!

SPEARO CHEF

Josh Bollen
@bosh.jollen

CATCH, COOK & SHARE

Don't forget to share your cooking if you decide to recreate one of the recipes from our spearo chefs. Tag the spearo and use #99spearorecipes

PAELLA

Paella is a rice dish from the region of Valencia in Spain. Traditionally, the dish is made very simply, cooked by farmers inland and fishermen on the coast for lunch. Inland they made use of rabbit or duck and seasonal vegetables, while coastally they added numerous ingredients from the sea. As a result it is a great dish for using up all kinds of seafood. Cooking times are important, you may need to stagger adding certain ingredients if you vary the ingredients but this isn't too hard. Saffron is also a huge part of this dish, however, if you don't have access or the budget for it you can still make a tasty rice dish.

COOK TIME 20 MIN | SERVES 4
Abalone & red rock cod

INGREDIENTS

1-2 tbsp olive oil
Sea salt
1 rock cod, broken down into fillets, wings, split and flattened head, frame
3 cloves of garlic
1 brown onion
1 abalone
1.25 cups of grated tomatoes or tomato paste
300g (11oz) short grain bomba rice (alternatively, risotto rice, arborio or japanese sushi rice)
1 tsp sweet paprika
1l (34fl oz/4 cups) fish stock (alternatively chicken stock)
Saffron

METHOD

Heat enough oil to cover the bottom of the pan on medium heat and season with sea salt.

Drop in the fish frames, wings and head to crisp up and flavour the oil. Once the pieces have started to brown, remove them from the pan.

Place wings and head on a plate to be used later, discard the frames.

Add garlic, onion and abalone. If using squid, octopus or cuttlefish add them at this time. Sauté ingredients until the onions begin to caramalise.

Pour in tomato puree and stir through allowing it to bubble lightly in the pan. Add your rice. Stir the rice through sauce for a couple of minutes while adding the paprika.

Pour in your stock and saffron. Then evenly distribute rice around the pan. From here on out you won't be mixing the pan anymore as this will disturb the cooking of the rice.

After 5 min place fish wings, chopped fish meat and head in the pan and add any other seafood you might be using.

Simmer on medium heat for another 15 min or until rice is cooked. Add additional stock if necessary

Check to see if a crust has formed under the rice. If it hasn't, cook on high for another minute. Take the pan off the heat and cover in tin foil or cloth for 3-4 min.

Serve straight out of the pan for an authentic Spanish experience.

SPEARO CHEF

Josh Bollen
@bosh.jollen

ALTERNATIVE SPECIES

Any seafood you would like to try

ARCTIC FREEDIVER'S FRIED FISH

This is a recipe from the late Didrik T. Hurum and was shared on his Instagram in August 2020. Didrik was a hugely loved and popular member of the spearo community. An exceptionally talented spearo able to comfortably fish at 30m (100ft). He was regularly pulling up fish that people would put on their bucket lists.

We hope that this recipe will be a tangible reminder of the person he was and the impact he had on our community.

COOK TIME 20 MIN | SERVES 2
Coral trout

INGREDIENTS

1 cup rice
2 cloves of garlic
Thumb sized knob of ginger
1-2 spring onion, white and green sections
1 red chilli (depending on your tolerance for spice)
1 handful of coriander (cilantro)
Butter
Fish fillets (any white flesh fish you like to eat fried in a pan)
Salt and pepper (to taste)
Seasoned soy sauce
Peanut oil

METHOD

Cook up the rice.

Dice the garlic, slice the ginger, spring onion, chilli and coriander.

Pan fry the fish fillets in the butter. Season with salt and pepper. Optional—add any spices you like, adjust to taste.

Put some of the chilli and garlic in the pan with the fish to give some taste.

When rice is ready, keep it hot until the fish is cooked.

Put the rice on a plate and top it with the fish, spring onion and chilli.

Pour seasoned soy sauce over the fish and rice.

Bring the peanut oil to frying heat. Put slices of ginger and garlic in the frying peanut oil.

When the ginger and garlic is fried, pour this over the fish.

Garnish with fresh coriander on top.

Ready to go with some white wine, beer, or whatever you prefer.

SPEARO CHEF

Didrik Thorun Hurum
@arctic_freediver

ALTERNATIVE SPECIES

Any white fleshed fish

SUPER SIMPLE MEXICAN BREAM

Yellowfin bream (*Acanthopagrus australis*) are prolific fish along much of the NSW and QLD coastline. I grew up catching them on pipis and beach worms but now enjoy catching them with the straight hook. This recipe came about on the spur of a moment while needing to cook a nice bream with limited time. Looking in the pantry, I saw a packet of mexican spice mix and a lime in the fridge. I wasn't expecting the amazing results, I was just time poor and really hungry. It has turned out to be my favourite way of cooking them. Just flake all the meat off and serve in soft tacos with the usual sides. One fish will feed two people comfortably.

COOK TIME 30 MIN | SERVES 2
Bream

INGREDIENTS

1 bream (scaled and gutted)
1 pack of Mexican spice or taco mix (you could make your own as well, but this is the quick way)
1 lime, sliced
Soft tacos
Salad

KEEP IT CLEAN

When cleaning fish, ensure the workplace is kept clean and dry where possible. Avoid introducing excessive water to fish flesh, and pat dry before storing or freezing.
@benrennie_

METHOD

Make a series of slices across the fish, through the skin about an inch (2.5cm) apart.

Rub the spice mix into the skin and gut cavity of the fish.

Insert some lime slices into the gut cavity, and lay some across the skin of the fish.

Place the fish into a fish grilling cage.

Cook over a high heat on a charcoal BBQ, turning regularly.

When cooked, the skin should be nice and crispy and bubbling with the odd bit of fat.

Serve whole and eat straight off the fish, or scrape meat off into tacos with the usual side dishes.

SPEARO CHEF

Ben Hohnke
@hohnkeoutdoors

ALTERNATIVE SPECIES

Whiting, goatfish, snapper or any tasty plate sized reef fish

ASSAM KING PRAWNS

Assam paste, also known as tamarind, can be bought at Asian supermarkets and is a traditional flavour that works well with seafood. Coupled with fresh king prawns and a light salad, this dish is a perfect entree for two. Obviously, you could also increase the quantities and serve as a main course with steamed rice or any other side dishes of your choice.

COOK TIME 30 MIN | SERVES 2
King prawns

INGREDIENTS

50g (2oz) Assam paste
150ml (5fl oz) warm water
1 tbsp vegetable oil
Half an onion, sliced
4 cloves of garlic, diced
1 tsp dark soy sauce
1 tsp sugar
6 large prawns
Sliced chilli, spring onions and coriander

METHOD

Soak Assam paste in 150ml (⅔ cup) warm water for 10 minutes. Loosen paste and remove the seeds.

Drain excess water into a cup for use later.

Heat a wok or pan on high heat.

Add vegetable oil and heat.

Add onions, frying until they turn translucent.

Add garlic, stir until light brown.

Stir in Assam paste, dark soy sauce and sugar.

Continue to heat the sauce until it has thickened slightly. If it is too thick or sticky, add some of the water used earlier to loosen the paste.

Add the prawns and stir.

Remove the wok from the heat as soon as prawns turn red, serve quickly.

Garnish with chilli, spring onions and coriander.

ACTIONABLE TIPS

As soon as you have brained your fish (ikijime), reload your gun and then scale, gut and gill the fish. This improves eating quality as well as brings in potential targets. Nothing worse than having a prized fish come in to investigate and have your gun unloaded.
- Deryck Tan @deryck.gyotaku

SPEARO CHEF

Deryck Tan
@deryck.gyotaku

ALTERNATIVE SPECIES

Any other types of prawn

SOTONG BAKAR (BARBEQUED SQUID)

This is an Indonesian-style barbeque dish. The most important ingredient is kecap manis, a sweet soy sauce. If all other ingredients are not available, kecap manis on its own will still result in an outstanding dish.

COOK TIME 30 MIN | SERVES 2
Squid

INGREDIENTS

1 medium squid
Salt
1 shallot or onion, diced
2 cloves of garlic, minced
1 lemongrass stalk, pounded
1 small piece of ginger, minced
½ tbsp turmeric powder
½ cup (125ml) kecap manis (sweet soy sauce)
1 tbsp tamarind pulp (optional)
Olive oil
3 calamansi limes (Citrofortunella microcarpa) or 1 lime
Bunch of coriander (cilantro)
Red chilli

METHOD

Clean the squid (removing the beak, gladius/pen, and guts) and rinse with water.

Make a series of horizontal slices through the bell, so that one side is sliced but the other is intact to create a series of "ribs".

Season with salt.

Mix all other ingredients (except the lime, chilli and coriander) in a bowl and marinate the squid.

Oil the BBQ plate and heat it up.

Grill the squid until opaque and slightly charred.

Remove from the grill and squeeze the calamansi lime over the squid.

Garnish with coriander and sliced chilli.

SPEARO CHEF

Deryck Tan
@deryck.gyotaku

ALTERNATIVE SPECIES

Cuttlefish or any squid species

"SQUID GROW INCREDIBLY FAST, BREED AND THEN DIE. THEY ARE A GREAT ANIMAL TO SPEAR FROM A SUSTAINABILITY PERSPECTIVE AND LAST WELL IN THE FREEZER."

Daniel Mann

CHORIZO STUFFED SQUID

Squid is synonymous with having a pint at the pub and receiving a greasy bowl of deep fried calamari. I recently speared this 900g squid and wanted to try something a little bit different. I stuffed it with chorizo, squid pieces and onion although you could add in other things like pieces of feta and tomato if you like.

COOK TIME 30 MIN | SERVES 2
Large squid

INGREDIENTS

1 large (1kg/35oz) squid
1 brown onion
1 chorizo sausage
1 lemon
1 tbsp of high heat oil (rapeseed or vegetable)

GREEN SAUCE
1 clove of garlic
1 cup of flat leaf parsley leaves
1 lemon, juiced
¼ cup of olive oil
1 tbsp of capers
Salt & pepper to season

SPEARO CHEF

Daniel Mann
@daniel___mann

METHOD

PREPARE THE SQUID

Start by cleaning the squid. Remove the head from the tube and cut the tentacles off in front of the eyes (to remove the beak). These tentacles crisp up perfectly and really help with presentation. The rest of the head and guts can be saved to thread on a hook in hopes of turning it into fish. It makes great bait.

Inside the tube there will be a translucent piece of cartilage that you can pull out and remove.

Next slide a finger under the wings to gently peel those off each side. Remove the skin on the wings by sliding a finger under it and peeling it off. Slice into squares.

Remove the skin on the main tube and begin to turn the tube inside out like a sock. With larger squid this is more difficult but easy enough. Once inside out, you can peel away the rest of the guts and give it a rinse.

The squid I speared was too large for two people so I cut the tube in half for the stuffed section. The forward part of the squid, I simply lozenged (cross scored), and cut into strips. Flash fry the squid in some high smoke point oil with a squeeze of lemon to finish. Beautiful.

CHORIZO STUFFED SQUID

Finely dice the onion and chorizo then add to a medium heat pan. Chorizo has a lot of oil in it so you don't need to add anything else to the pan. Cook until the oil is released from the meat and the onions have become translucent and taken on the red color of the chorizo.

Remove the mix from the pan but leave the remaining oil in there. Turn the heat up and quickly fry the cubed squid wings, for only a minute or so.

Mix together the chorizo, onion & wing pieces and stuff inside the tube. Seal off with a toothpick. Don't overfill the tube as like most meats, squid will shrink once cooked and may burst if packed too tightly.

Cook for two minutes on each side. For best results, grill the squid tube on a hot barbeque. You want intense heat for a short period to stop the squid getting tough and chewy. I don't have a barbeque, so a hot pan with a snifter of high heat oil like grapeseed will get color on the tube quickly. Also toss the front tentacles in for presentation later. Place the tube on your serving tray. Slice halfway through several times to reveal the stuffing.

I topped mine with a green parsley sauce. Nothing too technical, a big handful of parsley, stalks and all, clove of garlic, juice of a lemon, big splash of olive oil, a few capers and salt & pepper. Throw it all into a blender and voila, green sauce.

Bon appétit!

CORAL TROUT WING IN A TEMPRA SAUCE

This is a Nonya recipe I learned from my mother back home in Malaysia. Nonya is a spicy Singaporean cuisine consisting of a combination of Malay and Chinese ingredients and techniques.

COOK TIME 20 MIN | SERVES 2
Coral trout wings

INGREDIENTS

Coral trout wings
Salt and pepper
Rice flour
Rice bran oil
½ onion, sliced
1 tbsp diced garlic
¼ cup (60ml/2fl oz) light soy sauce
½ cup (120ml/4fl oz) water
1 tbsp sugar
2-3 calamansi limes or 1 green lime
Red chilli
Spring onions (scallions)
Coriander (cilantro)

METHOD

Pat the coral trout wings dry.

Season with salt and pepper.

Dust with rice flour.

Deep fry in rice bran oil until golden brown and crispy, before removing from the pan.

Heat a pan and add a tablespoon of oil.

Add sliced onion and stir until translucent.

Add diced garlic and stir until golden.

Add light soy sauce, water, sugar and squeeze in lime juice. Adjust to taste.

Pour tempra sauce over fried wings and garnish with sliced chilli, spring onions and coriander.

SPEARO CHEF

Deryck Tan
@deryck.gyotaku

ALTERNATIVE SPECIES

This recipe works for most reef fish. Small fish can be fried whole. Fillets of large fish can also be used

SWEET AND SOUR BUFFALO BREAM

Sweet and sour fish is a very popular dish in Chinese restaurants. It also works well if you use sliced pork instead of fish. Do not tell your guests you are serving buffalo bream until after the meal. Most people will be impressed if you do it right!

COOK TIME 30 MIN | SERVES 2
Buffalo bream

INGREDIENTS

1 buffalo bream
Salt and pepper (to season)
Corn flour (to dust)
Rice brain oil
½ onion cut coarsely
½ carrot, cut into ovals
½ capsicum, cut into diamonds
¾ cup (150g/5oz) pineapple chunks
1.5 tbsp cornflour mixed with 1 tbsp water
¾ cup (175ml/6fl oz) pineapple juice
2.5 tbsp red wine vinegar
⅓ cup (80ml/2.5fl oz) water
¼ tsp salt
2 tbsp sugar
Spring onions
Coriander
Chilli

METHOD

Fillet and skin the buffalo bream. Cut the fillets into bite sized cubes.

Season with salt and pepper and dust with the corn flour.

Shallow fry in rice bran oil until golden brown.

Drain and set aside.

Heat 1 tbsp of oil in a pan. Add onions and stir until translucent.

Add carrots and stir until soft. Add capsicum and pineapple chunks.

Mix the cornflour and 1 tbsp water into a paste.

Add pineapple juice, red wine vinegar, water, and cornflour paste.

Add salt and sugar to taste.

Pour vegetables on a plate. Place fried fish cubes on top.

Garnish with spring onions, coriander and chilli.

SPEARO CHEF

Deryck Tan
@deryck.gyotaku

ALTERNATIVE SPECIES

Dusky morwong or other undesired fish

CHILLI MUD CRAB

Occasionally, we get mud crabs in the Swan River here in Western Australia. They are a bycatch when we freedive for blue swimmer crabs *Portunus pelagicus* at night.

COOK TIME 30 MIN | SERVES 2
Mud crab

INGREDIENTS

6 tbsp vegetable oil
1 onion, diced
4 cloves of garlic, chopped
2 tbsp cornflour mixed into 4 tbsp of water
2 slices ginger
8 tbsp tomato sauce
4-8 tbsp sweet chilli sauce
2 tbsp light soy sauce
1 egg, beaten
1-1.5kg (2.2-3.3lb) mud crab (cleaved in half and thoroughly cleaned)
Spring onions (scallions), sliced
Coriander (cilantro)
Chilli, sliced

METHOD

Heat vegetable oil in a wok or large pan.

Add onion and fry until translucent. Add garlic and fry until golden.

Mix the corn flour and water into a paste.

Add ginger, tomato sauce, sweet chilli sauce, light soy sauce and cornflour paste.

Stir-in beaten egg.

Add crabs and stir.

Remove from heat as soon as they turn red.

Garnish with spring onions, coriander and sliced chilli.

Serve with steamed rice.

SPEARO CHEF

Deryck Tan
@deryck.gyotaku

ALTERNATIVE SPECIES

Blue swimmer crab, spanner crab

GRILLED TAKO

Octopus (tako = Japanese for octopus) can be a prized bonus catch but are often overlooked because the diver has had a bad experience with tough flesh. This super delicious and easy method will give you an incredibly tender and juicy result and best of all you can sit back and relax for most of it.

COOK TIME 15 MIN | SERVES 2
Octopus. Prior preparation required.

INGREDIENTS

2 lemons
Slices of garlic
2 small octopus (or 1 large)
Olive oil

DRESSING

2 tbsp olive oil
2 tbsp vinegar
1 tsp finely chopped garlic
1 tbsp finely chopped parsley
Salt and pepper

METHOD

Fill a large pot with water and bring to the boil. Once on a rolling boil, add slices of lemon and garlic to add some flavour to the octopus.

Next lower the octopus slowly into the water, the legs should curl up as it enters the water. Let this boil for one hour.

After an hour turn off the burner and let the octopus sit for 45-60 minutes.

To prepare the dressing, mix olive oil, vinegar, garlic, finely chopped parsley, salt and pepper and stir together with a fork to combine.

Remove the octopus from the pot and wash to remove the excess skin from the legs, it should fall away with ease.

Once cleaned, trim the legs from the body or keep them whole if preferred.

Next, toss the octopus in a light coating of olive oil and throw onto a smoking hot grill.

Remove once the grilled marks appear—you don't want to overcook the octopus.

Plate up and drizzle the dressing over the octopus and serve as a side to your favourite seafood dish.

SPEARO CHEF

Jason Harris
@JaceDives

ALTERNATIVE SPECIES

Cuttlefish

MARINATED FLATHEAD SKEWERS

Flathead is one of the most popular table fish in Australia. It can be cooked in a number of ways but this marinade has become a tasty, simple barbecue favourite of mine. It has all the benefits of a spearo dish—quick preparation, easily shared eating and the fish goes great with all your other favorites. We like a pumpkin, walnut and feta salad, making it a fresh, light meal to enjoy.

COOK TIME 30 MIN | SERVES 2
Dusky flathead. Prior preparation req.

INGREDIENTS

1.5 cups of sweet chilli sauce
1 tbsp of diced lemongrass
1 tbsp of powdered ginger
1 tsp of coriander (cilantro)
Salt and pepper
600g (20oz) skinless, boneless flathead
1 red onion
200g (6oz) diced pineapple
Barbecue skewers
1 lemon

METHOD

MARINADE

Pour 1.5 cups of sweet chilli sauce into a small mixing bowl.

Dice approximately one tablespoon of lemongrass and add that to your bowl and lightly mix it through.

Add the powdered ginger, diced coriander and a pinch of salt and black pepper, and mix it thoroughly.

Set this aside while you make the skewers

SKEWERS

Cut your skinless fish pieces into bite sized cubes, thoroughly checking all bones are removed in the process.

Cube your onion into similar sized pieces.

Do the same with your fresh pineapple, making similar size pieces or just use canned pineapple chunks.

Take your barbecue skewers and one piece at a time feed all three ingredients on in a repetitive order, (eg: pineapple, fish, onion, repeat).

Once you have used all of your ingredients, lay the skewers slightly spaced apart in a glass or plastic tray.

Pour the marinade over them, making sure to cover them as much as possible. It helps to use a container that isn't too large so that your marinade doesn't spread out too much.

Place skewers back in the fridge with cling wrap over the top and marinate for roughly 2 hours.

Cook on the barbecue at a medium heat for approximately 12-15 minutes flipping it as you go or until fish flesh appears white and moist.

Serve with a wedge of lemon and a fresh salad of your choosing.

SPEARO CHEF

Eathan kirkman
@eathanwatts

OYSTER OMELETTE

Oysters can be harvested at low tide in northern waters of Western Australia. A big flat head screwdriver and hammer is used to knock them off the rocks. Placed over an open fire, they will pop open negating the need for shucking. Oyster omelette is a popular dish in Asian countries. Each place has its own version, but this one is my favourite.

COOK TIME 30 MIN | SERVES 2
Oysters

INGREDIENTS

WHITE BATTER
2 tbsp tapioca flour
1 tbsp rice flour
125ml (4fl oz/½ cup) warm water

EGG BATTER
2 eggs
1 tsp Chinese wine
1 tsp fish sauce
1 pinch pepper

MAIN INGREDIENTS
1 onion, thinly sliced
3 cloves of garlic, minced
150g (5oz) oysters
3 tbsp vegetable oil
Spring onions (scallions), sliced
Chilli, sliced
Coriander (cilantro), chopped

DIPPING SAUCE
60ml (2fl oz/¼ cup) black vinegar
1 tsp fish sauce
1 tsp sugar

METHOD

Mix the ingredients for the white batter, by pouring the flour into a bowl, making a well in the centre and slowly incorporating the water. Set aside.

Mix the ingredients for the egg batter.

Heat a frying pan or wok, add a tablespoon of vegetable oil.

Pour in a thin layer of the white batter, fry this until it becomes firm.

Pour in the egg batter and fry until firm. Cut into pieces in the pan.

Add the rest of the oil and fry the onions and garlic until translucent.

Add and fry the oysters. They will cook quickly, so be careful not to overdo them.

Garnish with the spring onion, coriander and chilli, and serve with the dipping sauce.

SPEARO CHEF

Deryck Tan
@deryck.gyotaku

ALTERNATIVE SPECIES

Mussels

MULLOWAY STEAK ASSAM PEDAS

Mulloway is quite a rare catch in Western Australia but when I get my hands on one, I make this dish. A bit of effort is needed to process this fish into steaks but it is worth it. I serve this as a main dish with steamed rice.

COOK TIME 20 MIN | SERVES 2
Mulloway/jewfish

INGREDIENTS

1 mulloway steak
Salt and pepper
Corn flour
Rice bran oil
½ onion, sliced
4 cloves of garlic, minced
1 tbsp chopped ginger
4 tbsp tamarind paste, soaked in water and seeds removed
2 tbsp fish sauce
1 tbsp sugar
½ cup (85g/3oz) pineapple chunks
3 tbsp soy sauce
Chilli
Coriander (cilantro)

METHOD

Season mulloway steak with salt and pepper.

Dust with corn flour.

Deep fry in rice bran oil until golden brown.

Heat pan. Add 1 tbsp of rice bran oil.

Add onions and fry until translucent. Add garlic and fry until golden.

Add chopped ginger and continue frying.

Add tamarind paste, fish sauce, sugar, pineapple chunks and soy sauce.

Pour over fried steak. Garnish with chilli and coriander.

CATCH, COOK & SHARE

Don't forget to share your cooking if you decide to recreate one of the recipes from our spearo chefs. Tag the spearo and use #99spearorecipes

SPEARO CHEF

Deryck Tan
@deryck.gyotaku

ALTERNATIVE SPECIES

West Australian dhufish

CUTTLEFISH TOMATO KWAY TIAW

Cuttlefish are an uncommon spearo target but are typically found hiding in caves and can be lured out with flashers. They can be tough if not cooked right. Freezing them for a week helps tenderise them and they must not be overcooked. The key is as soon as the scored pieces curl, they are done.

The other key ingredient here is the fresh flat rice noodles. If they are not available, you can use the dried variety. However, dried noodles need to be blanched first prior to cooking. The frying of the flat noodles requires a very intense, high heat. This is to impart the 'wok hei' or 'breath of the wok' burnt taste to the dish and is a stunning flavour when you get it right.

COOK TIME 30 MIN | SERVES 2
Cuttlefish. Prior preparation req.

INGREDIENTS

350g (12oz) fresh flat rice noodles
4 tbsp vegetable oil
4 cloves garlic, chopped
300g (10oz) bean sprouts
2 tbsp dark soy sauce
1 tbsp sweet soy sauce
300g (10oz) cuttlefish, scored and cut into bite sized pieces (prior freezing required)
1 cup chicken stock
1 tsp oyster sauce
¼ cup tomato sauce
2 tbsp cornflour mixed in 1 cup of water
2 eggs, beaten

METHOD

Manually tease the flat noodles apart, they must be fully separated.

Heat a large wok over very high heat and then add the oil. Quickly fry the garlic until golden but not burned.

Add in the bean sprouts and separated noodles, stirring regularly. Add the dark and sweet soy sauces and stir into the wok until the noodles have cooked. Set aside the noodles on a plate.

Heat more oil in the wok. Pat the cuttlefish pieces dry and then quick fry them. Remember, as soon as they start to curl they are done and can be removed.

Pour the chicken stock, oyster sauce and tomato sauce into the hot wok—stirring regularly.

Thicken the sauce with the corn flour mix. Crack the eggs into sauce and stir until they are cooked.

Mix the cuttlefish pieces into the sauce and serve the sauce over the flat rice noodles, garnish with coriander.

Optional—you can add pickled red and green chilli as an accompaniment.

SPEARO CHEF

Deryck Tan
@deryck.gyotaku

ASIAN STYLE BBQ FISH WINGS

You may not know it, but I am a genuine noob spearo. I live a 4-hour drive from the ocean and have spent my life freshwater fishing and hunting where I live. I came up with this recipe after catching a nice golden perch (*Macquaria ambigua*) at a lake near my home. I had just been reading Josh Niland's "The Whole Fish Cookbook" and was looking to utilise as much of my catch as possible. Tending to my vegetable garden the day after I caught the fish, I saw a few choice veggies, so I got the charcoal grill started and harvested some fresh bok choy and spring onions.

I like this recipe for a solo feed or between two people, there are lots of bones to be careful of so I wouldn't recommend it for young children. If this recipe works well with a freshwater fish, any saltwater fish will be infinitely better!

COOK TIME 20 MIN | SERVES 1-2
Fish wings/collars

INGREDIENTS

1-2 large fish wings / collars
Olive oil
Salt and pepper to taste
4-8 stems of bok choy
Spring onion (scallions) chopped

METHOD

Heat your charcoal grill to a medium-high heat (a gas grill is fine, charcoal will give a better flavour).

Coat the fish wings in olive oil and season with salt and pepper.

Trim the green bok choy leaves turning the stems into spear shapes.

Place the fish wings and bok choy to grill. When the fish skin begins to char, flip once and finish cooking the other side.

Once the bok choy and fish are ready, place the bok choy onto the plate and sit the fish collars on top.

Drizzle soy sauce over the fish and sprinkle spring onions over the top as garnish.

> **"THE BEST PART ABOUT THIS RECIPE IS IT'S ESSENTIALLY A WAY TO BE MORE SUSTAINABLE, AND UTILISES THE WHOLE FISH. SO WHEN YOU'RE TAKING OFF THOSE NICE BIG FILLETS OF YOUR FAVOURITE FISH, KEEP THE WINGS!"**

SPEARO CHEF

Ben Hohnke
@hohnkeoutdoors

ALTERNATIVE SPECIES

Any fish you have already filleted

THE QUICK AND DIRTY WHOLE FISH RECIPE

This recipe can be used with pretty much any reef fish species. I aim for fish around a foot (30cm) or so long. Larger fish can be used as well, just make sure it fits on the grill! Try to stick to species that are easy to scale as this makes eating and sharing easy. The fish used here are mangrove/grey snapper (*Lutjanus griseus*) and a jolthead porgy (*Calamus bajonado*). Both are smaller reef species which grow to about 16-20in (41-51cm) but sometimes up to 36in (91cm).

This whole fish dish is a super easy recipe and I have never really measured ingredients, so feel free to adjust to your own tastes. However my caveat to this is that you want the fish to be thoroughly coated but not caked in seasonings. Cooking fish this way leaves ALL the bones in, so make sure you take care when eating and advise caution with family especially children.

For the fish bone phobic (and extra cautious), when the fish has finished grilling, pull all the meat off the carcass and serve it another way, such as in tacos. This is a great recipe to serve in company as one fish will serve between 3-4 people, along with some nice side dishes.

COOK TIME 20 MIN | SERVES 3-4
Mangrove/grey snapper & jolthead porgy

INGREDIENTS

Fish—whole gutted, gilled and scaled.
1-2 tbsp olive oil (enough to lightly coat fish inside and out)
Salt and seasonings to taste. Black pepper and garlic powder are my go to.

ACTIONABLE TIP

If you can, keep your fish whole in storage! Storing the fish whole on ice for a few days will again better preserve the fillets in comparison to store fillets in plastic wrap or paper towels. Nature makes the best cling wrap!

@aim_2eat

METHOD

To prepare the fish, ensure it's gutted, gilled and the scales are removed. Make slices down the sides of the fish, spaced an inch or two (2.5-5cm) apart and go down to the spine of the fish.

Repeat this on both sides of the fish. Apply a thin layer of oil to both the sides and inside the cavity of the fish.

Generously salt the fish—inside and out. Season with your chosen herbs and spices—a nice even coat, not caked on!

Optional - Stuff the cavity of the fish with fresh herbs, lemon, fresh garlic or jalapeños.

Grill for about 5-10min on each size, timing depends on the size of the fish. Look for the skin to crisp up to a nice golden brown colour.

Once cooked, the skin may stick to the grill, be careful moving the fish to the serving plate.

Serve as is or remove all the meat first to make tacos for the bone phobic!

SPEARO CHEF

Nick Giannola
@nickin_nature

ALTERNATIVE SPECIES

Any smaller reef fish

HONEY BUFFALO FISH WINGS

If you've shot a fish that has a good set of wings, you've earned enough stripes to enjoy this beaut of a recipe. Adapted from a chicken buffalo wing recipe, this is fairly simple and looks damn good when you're cooking it, so it's great for a show. If you want to go all out, you could do some ranch dressing or blue cheese sauce. Regardless, these are definitely going down with a beer for me and all my mates.

COOK TIME 15 MIN | SERVES 2
Blackspot tuskfish

INGREDIENTS

GENERAL INGREDIENTS

1 tbsp flour
½ tsp garlic powder
½ tsp onion powder
½ tsp salt (or to taste)
¼ tsp pepper (or to taste)
½ tsp baking powder
A few pinches of mixed herbs
1 set of fish wings (say approx. 300-500g/0.6-1.1lb)
Rice bran oil (or some other high heat oil, like canola oil)

BUFFALO SAUCE

2 tbsp unsalted butter
¼ cup Franks hot sauce (or any other you have around)
1 tbsp honey

METHOD

In a bowl, mix the flour, garlic powder, onion powder, salt, pepper, baking powder, and mixed herbs.

Coat the fish wings in the powder.

Prepare honey buffalo sauce: heat the unsalted butter, hot sauce and honey in a pot until fully melted and warmed, keep stirring this mix.

Heat a frying pan to a high heat and add oil.

Place wings on pan and sear each side on high heat (i.e. 1-2 mins each side). This stage is worth getting the camera out!

After the second side is seared, pour the buffalo sauce over the wings.

Drop heat to medium-high and cook the fish all the way through—how long depends on the thickness of the wings, but don't over cook your fish!! Keep it juicy.

Serve it with something that goes with buffalo wings, I know where my mind is going.

SPEARO CHEF

Harry Lindley
@harrylindleyy

ALTERNATIVE SPECIES

Most reef fish, mangrove jack

CHARCOAL GRILLED GOATFISH WITH KOMBU BUTTER

Cooking over coals adds a real depth of flavour to this dish. The goatfish was butterflied and put in the fridge uncovered for 8 hours to allow the skin to dry before cooking. This helps with keeping the skin intact when cooking.

COOK TIME 30 MIN | SERVES 2
Goatfish. Prior preparation required.

INGREDIENTS

250g (9 oz) butter, softened
2 tablespoons kombu, powdered or ground (nori or kelp work too)
100ml (3.5 fl oz) fish stock
Salt and pepper
1 lemon, ½ cut into wedges, ½ juiced
1 large goatfish, butterflied
Olive oil

ACTIONABLE TIP

Be sure the BBQ grill is clean and very hot before putting the seafood on to cook. This will prevent it from sticking.

- Yianni Barthelmess

METHOD

Get the coals ready for cooking. They should be glowing bright red.

Combine the butter with the kombu.

Add the fish stock to a saucepan and cook until it is reduced by half.

Add the butter to the stock, slowly over low heat while mixing.

Season it with salt, pepper and some lemon juice. Keep warm.

Rub the fish with some olive oil and place it skin side down on the grill.

Place a fish weight or a frying pan on the thickest part of the fish and cook for 2 - 3 minutes.

Move the weight to the skinnier part of the fish and cook for another minute.

Do not flip the fish on the grill. Once the fish is cooked through, place it on a warmed serving plate.

Drizzle the kombu butter over the fish and serve with some lemon wedges.

SPEARO CHEF

Yianni Barthelmess
@huntfishgrowcook

ALTERNATIVE SPECIES

Anything goes well with this butter

CAM'S BREAKY WRAP

During a 31 day stint of diving, I was eating a lot of fish, but having difficulty finding a solid way to get a mad fish feed that I felt like for breakfast. I had to trial different ingredients until I found, what I think is, the best way to make a breaky fish wrap! This breaky fish wrap tastes amazing, goes well with a coffee, and will keep your hunger sated all day long!

COOK TIME 15 MIN | SERVES 1
Any filleted fish

INGREDIENTS

1 wrap
1 smear of cream cheese
2 slices of hard cheese
½ a tomato
1 tbsp of capers
Few slices of onion
A squirt of aioli
Olive oil for the pan
1 fillet of fish (or 2 smaller ones)
2 eggs

METHOD

Decorate your wrap with all the ingredients other than the fish and egg, while heating up the frying pan.

Pop the wrap under the grill on a super-low heat to warm it up.

Put a bit of oil in your pan and turn the heat up, once the oil starts to smoke up, throw on the fish.

Crack in the eggs, and turn the heat down to about half (or however you like frying your fish and eggs). After a minute or so each side the fish should be done.

Put the fish and eggs on the wrap.

Top with some aioli, all the remaining ingredients, roll the wrap and enjoy!

SPEARO CHEF

Cameron Wayne Smith

ALTERNATIVE SPECIES

Any filleted fish

GRANDMA EIKO'S KARAAGE

Hiroko's and my friendship revolves around food, with a common love for seafood—I catch the fish, and together, we love making the most of it. Hiroko grew up in a small fishing village in Okayama, Japan. Her Grandmother Eiko passed this recipe on, and it was a staple in her home. We decided it should be the case in Melbourne too. Enjoy!

COOK TIME 30 MIN | SERVES 2
Flathead. Prior preparation req.

INGREDIENTS

500g (1lb) flathead fillets
½ cup cooking sake
½ cup soy sauce
Thumb sized chunk of ginger, finely grated
3-4 cups vegetable oil
1.5 cups potato starch
Kewpie mayonnaise
Lemon

ACTIONABLE TIP

Use a rack to drain fried seafood. Using paper towel will cause the food to sweat and it won't be as crispy

- Yianni Barthelmess

METHOD

Break down the flathead into 3cm (1 in) pieces. Remove pin bones with a tweezer if need be. Mix cooking sake, soy sauce and grated ginger together.

Marinate fish in sake, soy sauce and ginger for 30 minutes.

In the meantime, fill a heavy bottomed pot with oil to about 6cm (2 in) depth—just enough to cover the fish.

Heat oil to 170°C (340°F). Tip - use a wooden chopstick to test oil—when the bubbles form tightly around your chopstick the oil is ready.

Remove fish, piece by piece from the marinade with chopsticks (or other utensil) and dry on paper towel.

Lightly dust each piece with potato starch.

Drop fish pieces gently into hot oil.

Interfere as little as possible. Wait until the surface of the fish is crunchy. Turn only once and don't fiddle with it

Remove when golden brown and crispy and place on a draining rack.

Serve with Kewpie mayonnaise and lemon wedges.

Note: You can use the backbone and tail of the fish too if you want a great yield from your fish—just cook these parts longer until they're super brown and crispy.

SPEARO CHEF

Mark Cronje & Hiroko Ooka
@markcronje

ALTERNATIVE SPECIES

Any firm white flesh is suitable. Leather jacket is great too!

CRISPY SKIN FISH WITH SALSA VERDE

Crispy skin has always been something that has terrified me in the kitchen. More often than not the skin would end up charred and stuck to the pan. I'd be left scraping a broken fillet onto a plate muttering to myself "how do those restaurants do this properly"? In reality all you have to do is a little bit of preparation and leave it alone once it hits the pan to get that audibly crispy skin. You can either scale the fish using the traditional method of scraping them off or the more difficult cutting the scales off method. Both have worked well for me. Coupled with a punchy fresh salsa verde, this meal is sure to impress anyone.

COOK TIME 30 MIN | SERVES 2
European sea bass. Prior preparation req.

INGREDIENTS

1 fillet, skin on, scaled & deboned
Table salt
High heat oil (grapeseed or vegetable)

SALSA VERDE

1.5 cups parsley leaves
1 cup basil leaves
1 cup mint leaves
1 gherkin
1 clove of garlic
1 tbsp of capers
1 tbsp of dijon mustard
2 tbsp of red wine vinegar
⅓ cup of olive oil
Salt & pepper to taste

OPTIONAL EXTRAS

High starch potatoes for mash
Bunch of fresh asparagus for charring

METHOD

Pat dry your scaled fillet with some kitchen roll and place skin up onto a plate. Sprinkle table salt all over the skin and place the plate into a fridge for 30 minutes. The combination of the salt and the fridge will dehydrate the skin which will help make it crisp.

While the fish is in the fridge, prepare the salsa verde by chopping all the solid ingredients together on a board. You want them finely chopped but not mashed together like in a food processor.

Transfer to a bowl and add the dijon mustard, red wine vinegar and olive oil. It should form a lovely fresh smelling green sauce. Season to taste with kosher salt and cracked black pepper.

Remove the fish from the fridge. You will see the salt has absorbed a lot of the moisture. Using a knife, scrape the salt and moisture off in the direction of the scales (head to tail of the fish).

Wipe up any extra bits of salt and moisture with some kitchen roll.

Slice the skin every 1cm (⅓ in) along the fillet, pinching the fillet like a roll of skin. You will need a very sharp knife for this. Scoring the skin stops it curling as much when it hits the hot pan. Allow 15 minutes for the fillet to adjust to room temperature before cooking.

Heat a splash of oil in a pan. I've done this with a stainless pan but it's a lot less terrifying with a non-stick pan! You want it hot enough so that when you flick a drop of water in, the oil sizzles and cracks.

Lay the fillet skin side down and away from you to avoid splashing hot oil on yourself.

Keep pressure on the fillet for thirty seconds until it stops wanting to curl and shrink. The key here is to not move the fillet at all. Trying to make sure it doesn't stick will make it stick. Eventually, the fish skin will cook free from the pan.

Cook the fish nearly all the way through, skin side down. Take the pan off the heat and flip the fillet over letting the residual heat gently cook the other side.

Serve on a bed of potato mash, with charred asparagus and place the fillet on top. If done correctly you will hear the results when you run the tip of a knife over the skin. Crispy!

Dress with the salsa verde (all ingredients into a blender) and pour a glass of Provence rosé.

SPEARO CHEF

Daniel Mann
@Daniel___mann

ALTERNATIVE SPECIES

Fish with mid-sized scales - trumpeter, snapper, mangrove jack, moses perch, pearl perch, job fish, bream

A GUIDE TO HOT SMOKING FISH

Cornerstone Content Guide

Written by Michael Isbey,
@matakanasmokehouse_nz

Smoking is a great way of adding to the flavour of a fish and expanding the ways it can be used and stored. It's actually a relatively simple process, which can take you into a world of complexity. We have included a basic introduction from the Matakana Smokehouse who make some of the best smoked fish this side of wherever you are!

Fish can be either hot, or cold smoked. We have focused on hot smoking as it's accessible to most spearos. We have split the smoking process into three stages—smoker setup, preparing the fish, and smoking the fish.

STAGE 1: SMOKER SET UP

You can pretty much spend as much money as you like on a smoker, from a cheap tin box to a digitally controlled space-age gadget. The bottom line is that all you need is a box to catch and contain the smoke you create. So use your imagination: an old filing cabinet, clothes dryer or a clean 44-gallon drum will all do the trick. You ideally want a smoker big enough so the fish is far enough away from the heat source that it won't cook too quickly, and give it time to get the smoky flavour we want.

In the smoker you need a heat source: many guys use a gas cooker with a cast iron plate on top which holds the sawdust or wood chips. As the iron/steel plate heats up, your sawdust or chips will begin to smoulder, creating smoke.

It is important to keep the chips smouldering and avoid flames—you can keep these chips slightly damp to reduce flare-ups by soaking the wood chips in water, or even a cheap red wine if you want to add a nice flavour.

> **"IT'S ACTUALLY A RELATIVELY SIMPLE PROCESS, WHICH CAN TAKE YOU INTO A WORLD OF COMPLEXITY IF YOU LIKE."**

You can also use a steel smoke box like Shrek's one (pictured on right) and place it on the heat source (in this case, bbq briquettes).

The choice of wood chips is entirely your own. Some woods create sweeter smoke than others, cherry or apple for example. There may be a traditional wood for smoking in your area, so try starting out with that. The size of the chips also makes a difference—fine wood obviously burns faster, creating smoke quickly which is good for smaller batches of smoked fish.

STAGE 2: PREPARING THE FISH

Brining is the process of infusing fish with salt, sugar and flavour. Dry brine involves the application of dry ingredients and wet brine involves soaking the fish or seafood in a salt based solution.

Consider the portioning, size and placement of fillets to be used and located in the smoker. Keep the thickest, largest portions closest to the heat. If you are doing a short, fast smoke, then consider trimming your fillets into thinner portions to ensure they cook all the way through.

DRY SALTING

Sprinkle fish with non iodised salt, ensuring a liberal coating on all parts of the fillet. Repeat with brown sugar, or even better, use coconut sugar. Add any herbs, pepper, rum or whiskeys that you want to add flavour.

Most important step: let the fish cure and dry. Ideally, leave the fish in the fridge for a minimum of 5-6 hrs, though overnight is best. Salt will draw out the moisture of the fish, so allow it to run off the fish (use a wire rack, or hang the fish if you can).

Rinse and dry the fish. You want the fish to be dry before putting it into the smoker, as the smoke will not adhere to wet fish: it needs to be tacky and almost dry.

EASY GLAZE

Maple syrup makes a fantastic glaze to brush onto fish during the smoking process.
@benrennie_

STAGE 3: SMOKING

Time to fire up the smoker! Firstly, place your fillets in the smoker—make sure the air and smoke can fully circulate around the fish. Wire racks are best, never a baking tray. Start the heat under your wood chips. Temperature is the most important thing here.

Try to keep initial heat within the smoker to below 35°C (95°F) for the first hour or so. By doing this you are giving the smoke time to work its magic on the fish. You need to be able to adjust the temperature within the smoker, either by opening vents or dampening down the fire or gas.

The smoke will cure, colour and flavour the fish, so the longer you can expose your fish to the smoke the better. Try to keep some air and smoke flowing through the smoker. This allows for a drier environment. A smoker is one place you don't want too moist... Smoke your fish for a minimum of an hour, but ideally try to smoke for 3-4 hours—the longer the better.

When you're nearing the end of your smoke and you feel your fish might need a little more cooking, crank up the heat. As a gauge, aim for a finished internal temp of 60-65°C (140-150°F).

WET BRINING

Make a mix of 1 part salt to 6 parts water.

Add any additional flavours—herbs, spices or spirits to this mix. Submerge your fish fillets for at least 6 hours.

Remove the fillets and dry. Just like dry bring, you want the fillets to be dry and tacky so the smoke will adhere to the fish.

SMOKED FISH KEDGEREE WITH RAITA

COOK TIME 30 MIN | SERVES 3-4
500g of smoked fish

INGREDIENTS

SMOKED FISH KEDGEREE:
1 tbsp butter
2.5 cups basmati rice
6 eggs (or however many people want, fried or poached)
500g (1lb) smoked fish (our favourite is yellowtail kingfish and kahawai)
½ cup milk
½ cup of yoghurt
1 cup of cream
100g (4oz) butter
2 large onions, finely diced
1 tbsp minced garlic
1 tbsp minced ginger
1 tbsp minced fresh chilli (or to taste)
1 tbsp turmeric
½ tbsp cumin
½ tbsp garam masala
1 tsp mustard seeds
½ cup of finely chopped parsley
½ cup of finely chopped coriander/cilantro
Salt and freshly ground black pepper
4 lemons

RAITA (TO ACCOMPANY):
1 cup yoghurt
Half a cucumber cut into rough chunks
Juice of 1 lemon
Freshly ground black pepper and salt to taste

SPEARO CHEF

Michael Isbey
@matakanasmokehouse_nz

METHOD

RAITA

In a medium bowl, combine yoghurt, lemon juice, salt and pepper with the roughly cut cucumber. Stir well and keep in the fridge until serving.

KEDGEREE

Wash the rice under cold water.

In a large saucepan, place 6 cups of water plus the tablespoon of butter and bring to the boil.

Stir the rice into the boiling water.

Reduce to a simmer, cover and cook for 20-25mins until all the water is absorbed and the rice is soft to bite. Fluff up the rice with a fork and set aside.

Flake the smoked kingfish into a small saucepan, add the milk and cream, place on low heat and steep for 15 minutes just below simmering.

In a large saucepan, place the butter, onions, garlic, ginger, mustard seeds and fresh chilli. Saute over medium heat for a couple of minutes.

Add the turmeric, cumin and garam masala. Reduce the heat to low for 20 minutes, stirring occasionally.

Add the cooked rice and stir through to coat all the grains. Now add the steeped kingfish along with the milk, cream and yoghurt. Stir to combine.

Fold in the chopped parsley and coriander, then season with salt and pepper. Stir in the juice of one of the lemons and cut the other two into wedges.

In another large saucepan, poach or fry eggs to your liking, runny yolks are particularly nice on top of the kedgeree.

Divide the kedgeree into warm bowls, place poached or fried eggs on top, garnish with lemon wedge, coriander and a dollop of raita to the side.

Add extra chunks of smoked fish before serving for a more intense flavour. Sliced, hard boiled eggs are a great substitute for poached/fried eggs. Hard boiled eggs sliced up work in place of poached/fried if it's a big dish on the table.

SMOKED

Smoking is one of the most primitive methods of cooking fish, dating back thousands of years. It was originally used as an effective means of storing fish, however, novel techniques and equipment have elevated this practice into the modern day. This method is particularly effective at championing fish species that are typically overlooked or viewed as less desirable. While stronger tasting fish are often passed over in many recipes, smoking can often bring out the best in them.

The process of smoking fish can be broken into two categories. Hot smoking and cold smoking. Hot smoking uses direct heat, smoke and a short cook time while cold smoking involves lower temperature and an indirect smoke source.

In addition to your seafood of choice, all that is required for hot smoking, is a smoker/ BBQ, wood chips, fuel such as methylated spirits or gas, and brine. Brines can be both wet; mixture of water, salt and sugar) or dry; combination of spices and salt).

SMOKED SWEETLIPS

Sweetlips are often regarded as one of the worst-rated table fishes in Australia, but ironically they're one of the most commonly caught—especially when you're first starting out. These fish are quite large, and are generally pretty easy to catch. They're not the brightest of fish and are quite curious, so they're often the ones who find you—and, sometimes even swim right onto the end of your spear!

They cop quite a bad rap in the fishing community as an inferior table fish. I've seen Facebook posts in spearfishing groups that absolutely slam new guys for catching sweetlips and taking the piss out of them for not being able to catch anything that tastes better. However, the opprobrium is often served from those who probably can't tell the difference between salt and sugar—so take their words with a grain of salt...or sugar.

Sweetlip meat is very delicate and flaky, so consider this when choosing what to make with it. You can fry it in a pan, using plenty of butter and thyme, or add it to a curry at the last minute and simply turn off the heat—the residual heat of the sauce and pan will do the cooking for you (also, remember not to stir, otherwise you'll break up the delicate flesh).

My smoked sweetlip recipe is super simple. Serve with roasted potatoes and a salad—chilli sauce optional. Enjoy!

COOK TIME 30 MIN | SERVES 2
Gold-spotted sweetlip

INGREDIENTS

2 Sweetlips fillets
Your favourite spice rub
Salt
Fresh eucalyptus or melaleuca leaves, or use smoking chips if you prefer.

METHOD

CC

Heat your smoker and the add the smoking material - chips, leaves, bark etc.

Rub the fillets down with the spice and season with salt.

Place the fillets into the smoker and smoke on high for 10-15 minutes. Keep an eye on the temperature of your smoker as this will affect the cooking time. If it needs longer, then go longer.

Take the fillets out and let them rest. This is important!

SPEARO CHEF

Harry Foster
@hazfos

ALTERNATIVE SPECIES

Any firm white flesh is suitable

SMOKED MACKEREL CARBONARA

This recipe is one of our favourites using smoked fish, particularly using the last few fillets in the freezer. It is the ultimate comfort food and a great crowd pleaser! It is super easy to make and great for a quick midweek meal.

COOK TIME 30 MIN | SERVES 2
Spanish mackerel

INGREDIENTS

Smoked mackerel (can be prepared in the days before)
1 red onion
Mushrooms
3 cloves of garlic
3 pieces of bacon
3 spring onions
1 small container of light cream
Spaghetti or pasta of choice
2 eggs
Parmesan cheese

METHOD

Prepare your smoked fish. This can be done in advance.

Finely dice onion, mushrooms, garlic, bacon and spring onions (reserve some spring onion for garnish).

Fry these in olive oil until caramelised.

Add cream and reduce heat. Allow the sauce to thicken.

Boil water in a saucepan and cook pasta.

Crumble smoked fish through the sauce before removing from the heat.

Add cooked pasta and a little of the remaining pasta water to the sauce.

Whisk two eggs and parmesan cheese in a bowl before stirring through the combined pasta and sauce. Let the residual heat of the pan cook the eggs.

Top with spring onions, pepper and parmesan.

Serve immediately.

SPEARO CHEF

Ben Rennie
@benrennie_

ALTERNATIVE SPECIES

Most pelagic species are well suited to smoking (kingfish, wahoo, tuna etc.)

HOT SMOKED SPANISH MACKEREL

Hot smoking fish is easy once you get a few things nailed and should be embraced and not avoided. Brining greatly improves the texture and taste of any smoked fish. Keep it simple with an easy salt brine for just one hour. Serve the finished smoked spanish mackerel hot with vegetables, with salad or in a wrap. It's always great. When cooled and refrigerated smoked fish will keep for at least a week so can be used in a multitude of dishes until you can get out to dive again!

COOK TIME 90 MIN | SERVES 2
Spanish mackerel

INGREDIENTS

1 cup (300g/11 oz) salt
6 cups water
2kg (4.4lb) spanish mackerel fillet
2 tbsp brown sugar
1 handful hardwood sawdust

METHOD

Make a brine by mixing the salt and water, making sure all the salt is dissolved.

Cut fish into 20mm (1in) medallions, leaving the skin on.

Soak fish in brine for one hour, make sure it is fully submerged.

Remove the fish from the brine. Pat it dry and then sprinkle on brown sugar and rub it into the medallions.

Place the medallions in a hot smoker and cook for 18 minutes then turn off heat (Consult the how to hot smoke fish section for more details).

Leave fish in the smoker, without removing the lid, for another 8 minutes.

The smoked fish is then ready to serve, or remove and cool to use later.

CATCH, COOK & SHARE

Don't forget to share your cooking if you decide to recreate one of the recipes from our spearo chefs. Tag the spearo and use **#99spearorecipes**

SPEARO CHEF

James Sakker
Catch it Grow it Cook it

ALTERNATIVE SPECIES

Kingfish, trevally or any other oily fish

SMOKED FISH PIE

Smoked spanish mackerel or kingfish work perfectly for this dish. Great hearty meal in winter served with lots of vegetables. Very simple to make and will feed the whole family. When making this pie I use a blackbird, which is a hollow device to let the steam out of the pie as it cooks. If you don't have one, just make a couple of small slits through the pastry instead.

COOK TIME 45 MIN | SERVES 2
Spanish mackerel. Prior preparation req.

INGREDIENTS

WHITE SAUCE
2 tbsp butter
2 tbsp plain flour
750ml (25fl oz) milk
150g (5.3oz) tasty cheddar cheese

PIE
400 g (14 oz) smoked boneless, skinless fish
2 sheets frozen puff pastry
1 egg

METHOD

WHITE SAUCE

Melt the butter over a medium heat. Pour in the flour and stir continuously for 1-1½ minutes.

Gradually add milk and stir continuously to prevent sauce from sticking/burning.

Keep stirring until the sauce is thick enough to coat the back of a spoon.

Add the grated cheese. Remove from the heat, stir the cheese through until melted and combined, and set aside.

PIE

Preheat the oven to 220°C (428°F). Place bite size chunks of smoked fish in a pie dish.

Cover with white sauce.

Place pastry over the top and seal around the rim, making small incisions on top to let the steam out.

Brush with beaten egg and cook in the oven for 20-25 minutes until golden brown.

SPEARO CHEF

James Sakker
Catch it Grow it Cook it

ALTERNATIVE SPECIES

Any smoked fish

SMOKED FISH PASTA

Spanish mackerel is a fantastic fish to eat and great fun to hunt. The king mackerel in the US is almost identical to our southern hemisphere spanish mackerel and tastes just as great.

This recipe is very easy and uses up any leftover smoked fish you have, so you can maximise your enjoyment. It's very hearty and makes a great dinner. Serve with a lemon wedge.

COOK TIME 30 MIN | SERVES 2
Spanish mackerel

INGREDIENTS

250g (9oz) smoked fish—can be hot or cold smoked fish
100g (4oz) mushrooms
1 large spring onion or 2 small ones
1 large clove Russian garlic or 4 cloves Italian garlic
10 cherry tomatoes or 3 roma tomatoes
100ml (3fl oz/⅓ cup) cream
1 tbsp butter
1 lemon
1 small bunch continental parsley
350g (12oz) dried spaghetti
Ground black pepper
Salt

METHOD

Chop the mushrooms, garlic and spring onion and saute in butter in a large frying pan until tender.

Add cherry tomatoes and cook on medium heat for a few minutes until the tomatoes start collapsing.

Pour in the cream and grind in the black pepper and salt.

Break the smoked fish into bite size chunks and add it with the chopped parsley and juice of half a lemon. Reduce the heat to low.

Boil pasta in lightly salted water until al dente.

Drain the pasta, but save a little of the water. Add it to the pan with the sauce. Use some of the water to loosen the sauce if needed.

Serve with a lemon wedge and a little chopped parsley to garnish.

SPEARO CHEF

James Sakker
Catch it Cook it Grow it

ALTERNATIVE SPECIES

Kingfish, trevally or any other oily fish

SMOKED FISH PATE

Like most things, this recipe came about through proving that you can target all fish you just have to adapt your cooking to match. In the same way that using a 130cm inverted roller for spearing small reef fish in 1m of vis doesn't make it a terrible gun, just a terrible choice, the same applies for cooking fish. You can't use a one gun approach. The right fish may just require the right recipe. This pâté is dead easy and pretty quick to put together, perfect as an appetiser or when sitting around having a drink with your mates or family. Just put it into a bowl and put a plate of crackers next to it and watch it disappear!

COOK TIME 10 MIN | SERVES 4
Herring cale. Prior preparation req.

INGREDIENTS

1 plate sized fish (or fillet equivalent) that has already been smoked (see smoking CC)
2 tbsp of olive oil
Juice of 1 lemon
3 tbsp of crème fraiche
3-4 tbsp of ricotta cheese
Cracked black pepper for seasoning
Fresh chopped chives

METHOD

In a mixing bowl, carefully flake in all the smoked fish, being careful not to get any bones in the bowl.

Add in the olive oil and lemon juice and mix well while continuing to flake the meat with a fork.

Add in the crème fraiche, ricotta cheese, black pepper (to taste) and mix well.

Scoop the pâté into a smaller bowl and garnish with the fresh chopped chives.

Serve with crackers or nice bread.

SPEARO CHEF

Ben Hohnke
@hohnkeoutdoors

ALTERNATIVE SPECIES

Bonito, Australian salmon, tailor, mackerel

BAKED & ROASTED

Humans have been roasting food on fires for tens of thousands of years. Fire not only improves the taste of food, it aids digestion and prevents spoilage. In Australia there is archeological evidence of fish and shellfish being cooked on fires at the Mandu Mandu rock shelter in Western Australia at least 34,000 years ago. Imagine the first human sampling a freshly popped open steaming oyster straight from the fire. Baking has a long history with pit ovens used over 30,000 years ago at Lake Mungo in far western NSW. Many pacific countries still cook their meat, fish and vegetables this same way with a pit oven and hot rocks—what's better than the delicious smoky flavour of food cooked in an umu or a hangi!

This varied collection of recipes will help you get the most out of your seafood. Impress your friends and family with a whole fish cooked in a salt crust or knock up a decadent lobster mornay. The kids will go crazy for this simple pizza recipe and trout bombs are well...the bomb! Add some spice to your life with crispy skin tom kha pla or perhaps lebanese ling cod. So fire up the oven and enjoy these tasty recipes.

EASIEST PIZZA RECIPE EVER

First, NO PINEAPPLE. I've included a dough shortcut that makes this recipe pretty easy for all skill levels. I'll make a long story short. When I was in college we bought an Italian restaurant from my Uncle Dino. (What else would Walsh Irish folks do?) We served the same food there that my Mom made at home, some of the best Lasagne I ever ate—award winning even. Anyway, I was the pizza cook and the recipes for everything were generations old from the Italian side of our family.

COOK TIME 30 MIN | SERVES 2

Suits many species including lobster or squid.
Prior preparation req.

INGREDIENTS

DOUGH

3 tsp of active dry yeast (one small packet)
2 tsp of sugar
1lb (about 2 cups) of lukewarm water (110-115°F or 43-46°C)
1lb 13oz (825g) all-purpose flour
1 tbsp of salt
1 tbsp of olive oil

Note: If you are trying to make Napoli-style thin crust, try some double-0 ("00") flour, which is the "official" flour to use. We also used "Patent Flour" at the restaurant, but I doubt it's available in small quantities.

SAUCE

1 (8oz/approx 250g) can of tomato sauce for each pizza (this is real tomato sauce - more of a tomato puree, not ketchup!)
Adapt and experiment with the following to your preference:
1 tbsp of garlic powder (not garlic salt)
1 tbsp of oregano
1 tbsp of basil
Salt to taste
Pepper to taste
Grated cheese

Don't cook the sauce. It will cook on the pizzas, just mix it all together. The recipe above is for one pizza. Multiply ingredients depending on how many pizzas you are making. NEVER use bottled sauce premade from the store. These contain too much sugar and not enough spices. Note there is NO sugar in our recipe!!

TOPPINGS

Classic is pepperoni, but just get creative, except
NO PINEAPPLE!! Those are for Mai Tai drinks, not pizza.

I experimented with a bacon cheeseburger pizza and one called 'the works' with just about anything you can think of. My favorite is pepperoni, sausage, and fresh sliced baby portabella mushrooms.

METHOD

DOUGH

Whisk the warm water, yeast and sugar together and allow it to stand until bubbles form from the yeast (5 min).

Next mix the dough (I use a Kitchen aid stand mixer). Add salt to flour and whisk together.

Add about half the flour/salt to all of the liquid/yeast in the mixing bowl and place on low speed for about 8-10 min. Add the rest of the flour/salt when the mix has a good consistency (after a few minutes of mixing).

Cover the mixing bowl with a large flat plate or pan and let the dough rise in a warm place to double its size.

Remove the dough from the mixing bowl and punch it down, then cut and weigh into 16oz (450g) chunks and shape into balls (use extra flour as you are handling the dough if needed).

Let the balls rise for about 10 minutes to allow the balls to roll out easier. Flour the work area and then roll out to about a 13in (33cm) circle. I use a 13in greased deep-dish pizza pan. Push the dough out to the edges until the bottom of the pan is completely covered.

Use a larger pan if you want a thinner crust. If you make the dough a day in advance, this will enhance its flavour! Wait at least one hour or until the dough bases double in size.

Next put the sauce, cheese, and toppings on the crust, and bake in a preheated oven at 400°F (200°C) until golden brown on the bottom and edges.

TOPPINGS

Get creative! Prep in advance. Do not cook anything before putting it on the pizza, including sausage. You'll get a better flavour by cooking everything fresh.

The only issue you may have is moisture coming out of mushrooms; just blot the pizza with paper towels after it's cooked to remove any liquid that may form. Usually it's only veggies that lose liquids, so it's not a big deal.

SPEARO CHEF

Dan Walsh
@upfrontcomms

MEDITERRANEAN STYLE TUNA COLLAR

If you are planning a dinner, sometimes red meat doesn't quite cut it. You have been out for a dive and have plenty of tuna—so what do you do? I came up with this recipe to serve at parties as an appetizer, using traditional beef bone marrow serving and eating methods, but with a fishy twist. It will give your guests something to talk about on their way home.

COOK TIME 15 MIN | SERVES 2

2 tuna collars

INGREDIENTS

MEDITERRANEAN SPICES

½ tsp garlic powder
½ tsp onion powder
½ tsp oregano
½ tsp fresh dill
½ tsp parsley
½ tsp rosemary
½ tsp thyme
½ tsp of salt and pepper
2 tsp (or 2 cloves) fresh garlic, finely minced
1 tbsp olive oil or avocado oil, to coat
French bread baguette, cut into thin slices

METHOD

Clean the tuna collar (wings) of all dark blood and connective tissue. Butterfly it open.

Preheat the broiler (top down grill) to 550°F (290°C) and position the rack 8-10 in (20-25cm) from the heat.

Mix the herbs. Spread some fresh garlic on the fish collars and sprinkle on the herbs.

Place the fish skin side down on a baking tray and coat with a healthy amount of oil.

Place the tray of fish in the broiler for 8-10 minutes. This is for medium/medium rare—don't let the fish dry out too much.

Lightly toast slices of French baguette. Drizzle with olive oil and serve with the fish.

SPEARO CHEF

Christopher Lincoln
@christopherlincoln

ALTERNATIVE SPECIES

Yellowtail kingfish or other pelagic

CRISPY SKIN TOM KHA PLA

This meal is dedicated to my buddy Adam and his family. Adam is an exceptional example of a human. He has devoted the last 7 years to living in Southeast Asia to tend to families and children that are stuck in the crossfire on the frontlines of war zones. We love it when he and his family come to see us. On a recent visit, I got to take him spearfishing for his first time.

He dove to almost 10 metres, got his first fish on a pole spear and only puked a handful of times! Now he is hooked! In honour of this, I made a Thai meal from some of the fish we shot. This meal is easy, as there are no fancy techniques, but it does require some prep work. Prepping this with friends and family can be a great way to end a day of spearfishing.

COOK TIME 60 MIN | SERVES 4
California rockfish

INGREDIENTS

COCONUT SOUP
400g (14oz/1 can) full-fat coconut milk
750mls (25fl oz/3 cups) fish stock
1 tbsp red thai curry paste
1 bunch scallions, sliced thin
1 tbsp minced ginger
1 stalk lemongrass, remove upper and outer leaves then slice lengthwise)
2 chillis, minced
2 tbsp fish sauce
2 tbsp lime juice
60g (2oz/¼ cup) chopped coriander (cilantro)

GARLIC RICE
160ml (2/3 cup/5fl oz) jasmine rice
320ml (1.3 cup/11fl oz) water
3 cloves minced garlic
1 tbsp butter
Pinch of salt

ROCKFISH
1 whole rockfish, scaled, gutted and gilled
180ml (3/4 cup/6fl oz) fresh basil leaves
1 tsp fresh ginger, minced/grated on zester
1 tbsp peanut oil
1 tbsp sesame oil
2 tbsp fish sauce
1 tbsp brown sugar
3 cloves garlic, minced
1 chili, sliced or diced
Yellow capsicum, diced (remove seeds)
1 tbsp rice vinegar
1 tbsp water

SPEARO CHEF
Eric Keener
@finandforage

METHOD

COCONUT SOUP

In a large soup pan on medium-low heat, add the fish stock, lemon grass, chilli, onion, and ginger. Simmer for 15 minutes.

Add coconut milk, red curry paste, scallions, fish sauce, lime juice, and coriander (cilantro) and turn heat to low. Continue to cook until the fish and rice are done.

GARLIC RICE

In a medium pan, boil water and stir in rice, salt, butter, and garlic then cover and reduce heat to low.

Simmer until all water is absorbed—adding more as needed until rice is tender.

Once it's nearly cooked, increase heat to let all the water evaporate. Let a light brown crust develop on the bottom, then remove from heat.

FISH

Set your oven to 190°C (375°F) to preheat.

Prepare the fish by patting all surfaces dry with paper towels. Stuff the belly of your fish with the basil. Make 3 shallow, vertical slices in each side of the fish and sprinkle with salt.

To crisp the skin before baking, heat a frying pan to high heat. Add the peanut and sesame oils, wait 30 seconds and then add the fish to the pan.

After 45 seconds, flip the fish (ensure the pan is hot enough to have made the skin crispy and browned). Cook for 45 more seconds and remove from the pan. Retain the oil in the pan.

Place the fish on a baking tray lined with tin foil and roll the edges to create a shallow boat around the fish.

Drizzle the fish sauce over the fish and layer lemon slices on top.

Bake the fish in the oven for at least 25 minutes, or until flakey all the way through.

Reheat the frying pan over medium heat. Add the capsicum, ginger, and garlic.

Then add the tomatoes, rice vinegar, brown sugar, water and stir. Allow to simmer until it thickens to the desired consistency. For a thicker, more flavourful sauce, let it simmer longer.

The rice and soup can be started around the same time, followed by the fish once the others have begun cooking.

TO SERVE

This is served as a shared dish.

Strain the soup (or leave unstrained for additional texture and flavour).

Place a firmly packed mound of rice crust-side-up in the bottom of a large bowl.

Gently pour your soup around the edge of the rice, being careful to not displace it.

Place a few cherry tomatoes in the soup around the edges of the rice.

Add the fish on top of the rice mound.

Top the fish with the capsicum, chili and chopped basil. Finally, add slices or wedges of lemon.

"Than hai im, na khrap!" (Eat until you're full!)

ALTERNATIVE SPECIES

Grouper or cod

OMG YOU DID WHAT TO CRAYFISH?!

We all know small crayfish are sweet, but what do you do when you take home a big ol' crayfish that you couldn't resist grabbing, or just wanted to show off to guests with a large fish? I have adapted this from a Kiwi TV chef (Chelsea Winter), and her take on KFC. I had the pleasure of telling her via IG and getting her reply that she gave it a crack and had her mind blown.

I know cray is a bit of a delicacy to most people, but in Southland, NZ, they are a dime a dozen for a half decent spearo. So you can afford to experiment wildly with them there.

COOK TIME 30 MIN | SERVES 2

Crayfish/lobster

INGREDIENTS

1 medium or larger crayfish tail (meat filleted from the shell)
2.5 cups plain flour
¼ cup milk powder
2 tbsp salt
1 tbsp ground white pepper
1 tbsp ground black pepper
2 tsp ground ginger
2 tsp ground nutmeg
1 tsp ground allspice
2-3 cups of rice bran or grapeseed oil for frying

METHOD

Fillet the meat from the shell. The method I prefer, is to insert a long filleting blade into the underside of the shell all the way down to the end. Then, work it around the inside of the shell.

After a couple of shakes, the meat falls out onto the bench (or floor if you're drunk and your aim is poor).

Rinse the meat off, then dice up into mouthful, morsel-sized chunks.

Mix up all the dry ingredients into the flour mix (if you are camping do this before you leave home, it keeps for almost forever). A large bowl or big ziplock bag works as well.

Add fresh crayfish tail chunks to the flour mix. Shake it up while singing Taylor Swift (optional). Get a good coating of the flour mix onto the meat.

Heat the oil in a large saucepan over medium high heat—if you have fancy cooking tools you are aiming for 160°C (320°F).

When the oil is good to go, add the crayfish a few pieces at a time. Cook for 2 minutes or so until dark golden-brown all over.

Serve with whatever sauce you like, or none at all. Best paired with beer, or wine, or soda, or rum... Don't mix with tequila. In fact, never mix anything with tequila.

Photos recreated by Dan Walsh

SPEARO CHEF

Jeremy Arnold
@Hills_and_Gills

TROUT BOMBS

This recipe is the crew's go-to dinner when out camping or overnighting on the islands. It is super easy to make and most of the ingredients can be pre-prepared and kept in the Esky. It is a versatile recipe that works well with most fish, particularly firm white-fleshed demersal species (i.e. species that live on or near the seabed).

I learned this recipe from James, who was one of the crew on a trip to the ribbon reefs trip off far north Queensland. It was an absolute lifesaver that night as several of the boys were ruined with heat stroke and were revived back to life following this dinner. Good save James!

COOK TIME 15 MIN | SERVES 2

Coral trout

INGREDIENTS

2 coral trout fillets
1 handful of mushrooms
1 clump of ginger
1 large chilli
3 cloves of garlic
3-4 Spring onions (scallions)
1 bunch of coriander (cilantro)
1 lime
3 tbsp of sweet soy sauce
3 tbsp rice wine
Several drops of sesame oil
Drizzle of honey

METHOD

Fillet the coral trout (or other fish). Skin and debone the fillets. Slice in half to enable the fillets to fit in a bowl.

Thickly slice the mushrooms. Finely dice or grate the chilli, ginger and garlic. Roughly chop the spring onions and coriander.

To make assembly easier, line a bowl with two sheets of foil and one sheet of baking paper. This creates the lining of the parcel.

Place the mushrooms on the bottom, before layering the fish chunks on top.

Add the garlic, chilli, ginger and spring onions, as well as the sweet soy sauce, rice wine, sesame oil and honey.

Wrap the foil around the ingredients and seal.

Bake the parcel in the oven, grill on the barbecue or place on coals of a fire for approximately 10 minutes (depending on the heat source used) until the fish is steamed through and flakes away easily.

Best served over rice (we often use instant steamed rice) and topped with coriander and lime juice.

The BOMB!

SPEARO CHEF

Ben Rennie
@benrennie_

ALTERNATIVE SPECIES

Any fish can be used, however it works best with firm white reef fish that flakes away in large chunks

CRISPY SKIN BLACK DRUMMER

This recipe is a great way to test and improve your cooking skill, while also being really simple. It is a good way to practice and master simple but essential techniques—from getting the heat control right, to getting the butter brown without burning it and making a great tasting stock to cook the potatoes just right. It utilises most of the fish, by using the frames for stock and the fillets as the main star of the dish. Good execution of this dish will make it a real show stopper.

COOK TIME 30 MIN | SERVES 2
Black drummer (rock blackfish)

INGREDIENTS

DRUMMER STOCK

1 medium sized (30-40cm or 12-15 in) black drummer head and frame.
1.5l (50fl oz) water
1 carrot (peeled and cut into chunks)
1 onion (cut into chunks)
1 stick of celery (cut into chunks)

BOULANGÈRE POTATOES

4 medium desiree/red skin potatoes
Butter as required
1 sprig of thyme
1 sprig rosemary
3 Bay leaves
Olive oil
Salt and pepper
200ml (7fl oz) of drummer stock, see recipe

CRISPY SKIN FISH

2 black drummer fillets, skin on
30ml (1fl oz) of vegetable oil
150g (5oz) butter
1 tablespoon capers, rinsed and drained
1 bunch of parsley
Salt and pepper
1 lemon

METHOD

DRUMMER STOCK

Rinse the head and frame of the black drummer in cold water until all the blood is gone.

Remove the eyes and gills from the head.

Add head and frame to a pot with water, carrot, onion, and celery. Bring to a boil and simmer for 20-30 minutes.

Skim the fat and scum regularly.

Take off the heat and let it rest, then strain.

BOULANGÈRE POTATOES

Thinly slice potatoes (a mandolin or slicer helps).

Layer slices like fish scales in a baking dish.

Add a pinch of butter, a very small amount of salt and pepper and a few pieces of thyme, rosemary and bay leaf on each layer.

Repeat until all the potatoes have been used up.

Top the final layer with olive oil, salt, pepper and herbs.

Add 200ml (7fl oz) of drummer stock and wrap with foil.

Bake for 30 minutes, remove foil and bake again until slightly golden on top.

CRISPY SKIN FISH

Slice the fish fillets into manageable sized portions (2-3 portions per fillet). Score the skin on each portion.

Pat dry the fish thoroughly.

Preheat a heavy based or cast iron pan to a high heat, add the vegetable oil and heat until shimmering.

Sprinkle salt over the fish skin and gently place it skin side down in the pan.

Press down on the fish slightly and let it relax in the pan so the skin lies flat.

Reduce heat to medium and continue cooking until the skin is crisp and golden and the fish is about 70% cooked.

Add about a fifth of the butter to the pan.

Flip the fish over and spoon the foaming butter over the skin for about 20 seconds.

Remove the fish from the pan and place it onto the serving plates.

Quickly add the remaining butter to the pan with the capers and parsley.

Cook until crisp and the butter starts to brown.

Squeeze in some lemon juice and take off the heat.

Spoon the capers, parsley and brown butter over the fish. Serve with the boulangère potatoes and enjoy.

SPEARO CHEF

Jai Gibbons
@SpearoChef

ALTERNATIVE SPECIES

Morwong, bream, snapper, flathead, the meat has a firm, fatty white flake with a gelatinous layer under the skin

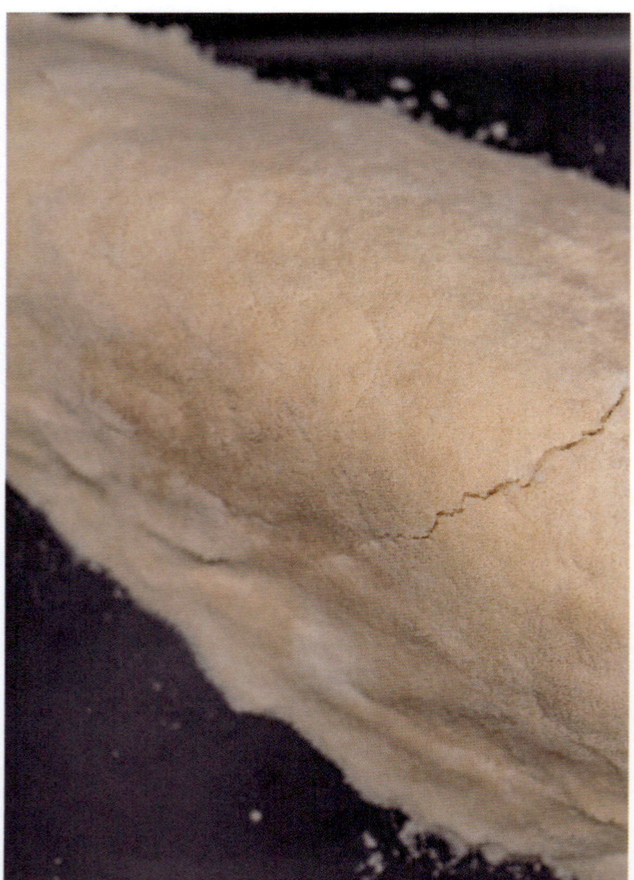

SALT BAKED SEA BASS

This recipe is the laziest way to make your guests think they are being treated to something truly special. I have never served it up without every phone in the room snapping away for the 'gram. Little do they know you couldn't put in less effort if you tried. You only have to take the guts and gills out of the fish for preparation and that is it. By completely covering the fish in salt and baking it, you form a seal around the fish which means it cooks inside the salt crush but remains incredibly delicate and moist.

The salt doesn't penetrate through the fish scales and despite using a few kilograms, this won't be in any way salty. I don't often put anything inside the gut cavity—this way you can really taste all the flavours of the fish and keep it clean. I tend to use sea bass (*Dicentrarchus labrax*) around 1.5kg because I don't have an oven or baking tray that can take much larger. Different shaped fish like red emperor (*Lutjanus saebe*) will allow you to get a heavier fish into the oven tray, should you need to feed more people.

COOK TIME 50 MIN | SERVES 4
Sea bass

INGREDIENTS

1.5kg (3.3lbs) sea bass, scales on
2-3kg (4.5-6.5lbs) table salt (depending on the size and shape of the fish)
2 eggs
Water as required
Optional stuffing—lemon and parsley

METHOD

It is critical that you don't scale the fish. Removing scales will allow the salt to be absorbed into the fish. This recipe relies on the flavour of the fish so you want to clear the gut cavity of blood, otherwise it can make the flesh bitter. I use a toothbrush to clear out the stubborn blood along the spine.

Preheat your oven to 200°C (390°F) on fan force (convection).

In a large bowl, add only the whites from the two eggs. Add in the salt and mix it in by hand (if you have any cuts on your hands, you will soon be aware of these). You are trying to get the consistency of snow or wet sand and will need to slowly add a splash of water at a time. The salt should hold its shape when compacted.

On a large baking tray, lay down a bed of the snowy salt in the shape of your fish. I keep the bottom layer around 15-20 mm (½-¾in) thick.

Place the sea bass down on the bed of salt. If you want to add some fresh parsley and lemon slices into the gut cavity, now is the time.

Now, completely cover the fish with the remaining salt and pat it down like you are making a sand castle. You want a nice layer at least 10mm (a little less than ½in) thick over the entire fish.

Bake the fish in the oven for 35-40 minutes. You can always err on the side of slightly longer cooking, because it is difficult to dry the fish out using this method.

When the fish is cooked, you will notice the salt has changed colour a bit, which is where the juices have exited the fish and formed a seal with the salt.

Using the back of a spoon, crack the crust with a few solid taps to the salt cocoon. Remove the crust of salt from the top of the fish and discard. The crust should stick together in large pieces. Gently remove the skin from the fish to reveal steaming hot, perfectly cooked sea bass.

Serve with a squeeze of lemon and a glass of Soave from Northern Italy.

SPEARO CHEF

Daniel Mann
@daniel___mann

ALTERNATIVE SPECIES

Small *Lutjanid* species, moses perch, small green job fish, snapper (*Pagrus auratus*)

WHITE FISH BAKE

One of the easiest ways to prepare a white fleshed fish, giving it heaps of flavour!

This is a lekker, quick and simple dish for when the pantry is almost empty. By using just a few simple ingredients the fish becomes the star of the show.

COOK TIME 60 MIN | SERVES 3-4
Soft white fleshed fish

INGREDIENTS

500g of fish, filleted, preferably with the skin on
Big bunch of fresh dill or parsley
250ml (1 cup) sour cream
Lemon
Salt and pepper

METHOD

Chop up all the dill and mix with the sour cream. Zest the lemon and add it to the mixture. Let it stand for about 30 min in the fridge.

Fillet your fish and place the fillets skin down on some baking paper.

Season the fish with salt and pepper and spread a generous layer of the sour cream mix over the fish, approximately 1cm (½in) thick.

Slice up the lemon and place on top of the fillets.

Let the fish stand for around 15 min while the oven is warming up to 180°C (350°F).

Bake your fish for around 15 min, depending on how thick the fillets are. Take the fish out at the stage right before it will separate easily with two forks.

At this point it's still slightly underdone, but the residual heat will cook it through while you are serving up. This prevents it from drying out.

Serve with whatever side dishes you want, from salads to potato wedges. To accompany it, have a good sized glass of rosé or white wine.

SPEARO CHEF

Eckart
@salt_sessions_freediving

ALTERNATIVE SPECIES

Snapper, flathead, bream. You could also use a firmer fish like kingfish or Spanish mackerel

BAKED KINGFISH

One of the things about shooting a big fish, like a yellowtail kingfish, is you are suddenly faced with a lot of meat to eat. This recipe can use a big lump of fish all in one go as a centerpiece for a meal to serve a group of people—which is a real treat. The soy marinade compliments the richness of the kingfish without overpowering the fish flavour, resulting in the best of both worlds. The great thing about this recipe is that it's not an exact science and you can find your own balance of soy and lemon juice. Embrace experimentation! This marinade will work well with a firmer fish such as most species of game fish. You can cook it in the oven but it tastes even better over some coals with a medium heat. I personally wouldn't recommend using a gas BBQ or frying pan to cook this dish as it will tend to overcook the outside of the fish.

COOK TIME 30 MIN | SERVES 2+
Kingfish. Prior preparation req.

INGREDIENTS

1 kingfish, filleted, scaled, skin on
½-1 cup soy sauce
3 lemons
1-2 tbsp olive oil

METHOD

Fillet your kingfish and place the pieces into a tray with the skin side up.

Squeeze the juice of the lemon onto the fish, add the soy and let the fillets marinade for 40-60 minutes. You want the ratio of approximately 2 units of soy to 1 unit of lemon juice.

After that, place the pieces of kingfish skin down onto some baking paper on a baking tray.

Lightly coat with olive oil and bake at 180°C (350°F) for approximately 20 min, depending on the size of the pieces.

You want to slightly undercook the fish. The residual heat will continue cooking the fish while it's out of the oven and resting before serving.

BONUS LEFTOVERS RECIPE

Any fish that you don't eat on the night can be used over the following days:

Simply flake the left-over fish into a bowl and mix in some kewpie mayonnaise and chopped pickles (can also add chopped dill or parsley) and have it on sandwiches or crackers.

SPEARO CHEF

Eckart
@salt_sessions_freediving

ALTERNATIVE SPECIES

This recipe works well with any firmer fleshed fish like kingfish such as Spanish mackerel

LOBSTER SPANAKOPITA

A spanakopita is a Greek spinach pie which is usually shared between family or friends. If you only get one cray, this is a great way to stretch it out so you can feed a few people. It's an easy, quick recipe and the mix of cray, cheese and greens tastes unreal!

COOK TIME 45 MIN | SERVES 3-4
Lobster

INGREDIENTS

1 lobster medium-large (roughly 1.5-3kg/2-6lb)
1 bunch of silverbeet leaves (spinach or beetroot tops will work as well)
150g (5oz) ricotta cheese
50g (2oz) parmesan cheese
1 egg
1 tsp nutmeg
1 lemon
Filo pastry (a packet)
Butter
Salt and pepper

METHOD

Poach the whole lobster for 8 minutes in boiling salted water. Remove and pop it in an ice bath to stop the cooking process.

Remove the stems from the silverbeet leaves. Cook until soft. Roughly chop and push out excess water through a sieve.

Remove the lobster flesh from the shell and roughly chop it.

In a bowl, mix the lobster, silverbeet, ricotta, parmesan, egg, nutmeg and lemon zest. Combine everything well and season with salt and pepper.

Melt some butter and brush the inside of a baking dish.

Layer two pieces of filo on the inside of the dish.

Add the filling on top of the filo pastry.

Cover with scrunched pieces of filo pastry.

Brush with melted butter.

Bake at 180°C (360°F) in a fan forced oven until the top is golden brown.

Serve with a fresh side salad and enjoy.

SPEARO CHEF

Yianni Barthelmess
@huntfishgrowcook

ALTERNATIVE SPECIES

Goatfish, bug, snapper

LOBSTER MORNAY

My favourite lobster to use for this recipe is *Sagmariasus verreauxi* (eastern rock lobster) although you can use any other lobster species from around the world for this recipe. They live in cracks and caves in the reef and most of the diving to catch them is done in less than 10 metres (30 ft) of water. One small lobster per person or half a big one is perfect. I like to serve with mashed potatoes and steamed vegetables in winter or with potato salad and green salad in warmer months.

Scallops are easy to catch once your eye is in, they are a tasty treat and provide good diving exercise. This dish is just as great with scallops and pairs well with mash and veggies. You should allow 6-10 scallops per person for a good portion.

COOK TIME 40 MIN | SERVES 2
Lobster

INGREDIENTS

Two small lobster or one big lobster (two serves) or
6-10 scallop meats and roe per person + shells to serve
3 tbsp plain flour
3 tbsp butter
500 ml (17fl oz) milk
1 tbsp dry white wine
100g (3.5oz) aged cheddar cheese
50g (1.75oz) parmesan cheese
Pinch of freshly ground black pepper
1 tbsp dijon mustard to make lobster thermidor (Optional)

METHOD

LOBSTER

Kill your lobster humanely.

Cut the lobster in half lengthwise and wash the yellow gut material out.

Remove the meat and cut into bite size chunks. If you semi-freeze or par boil (3-4 minutes) the lobster before cutting it, the meat will come away from the shell very easily.

You can also make this recipe with fully cooked (boiled) lobsters.

Return the meat to the shell evenly and set aside.

WHITE SAUCE

Melt butter and add plain flour at a 1:1 ratio.

Stir the mixture over low heat to cook out the flour (do not brown it) for about 8-10 minutes.

Add milk slowly and stir until the sauce becomes very thick.

Add more milk to adjust thickness. Keep the sauce on the thick side for scallop mornay or for lobsters not so thick.

Add a splash of dry white wine.

Grate parmesan (or other cheese such as a well aged cheddar) into sauce to taste.

Add a pinch of freshly ground black pepper.

COOK LOBSTER

Pour 2 tbsp of white sauce over each lobster half.

Grate some aged cheddar over the top.

Cook in a very hot oven 250°C (482°F) until cheese browns and the lobsters are bubbling, usually 8-10 minutes.

Serve with mashed potato, steamed carrots and steamed greens.

SCALLOPS

Shuck your scallops. Remove the gut and return the meat and roe to the shell. Put an extra scallop in your biggest shells.

Allow 3 to 4 shells per person as a main course, less as a starter.

Preheat oven to very hot (250°C or 480°F)

Make a white sauce by melting butter and adding plain flour in a 1:1 ratio. Stirring the whole time.

Gently cook out the flour (do not brown it) for about 8 to 10 minutes.

Add milk slowly and stir until the sauce becomes very thick.

Add a little more milk and a splash of dry white wine. Stir again.

Grate in the cheeses but reserve some aged cheddar.

Add a pinch of black pepper. Keep stirring the mixture.

Put a tablespoon of sauce over the scallops in each shell. Grate the remaining aged cheddar over the top.

Cook in the oven until the cheese browns and the sauce in the shells is bubbling—usually 8 to 10 minutes.

Serve with mashed potato, steamed carrots and steamed greens—Enjoy!

SPEARO CHEF

James Sakker
Catch It Grow It Cook It

ALTERNATIVE SPECIES

Scallop

LOBSTER WITH MISO BUTTER

Lobsters are easy to catch for some but are challenging for others—myself included. I've had great luck at night catching them as they are much more active and tend to be on walkabout. The way I prepare this delicious little bug dish is easy to eat and presents very well for whoever you serve it to. We all know, however, when we catch a good lobster when we catch a good lobster, it's usually only for yourself, and close friends and family only!

COOK TIME 30 MIN | SERVES 2
Eastern rock lobster

INGREDIENTS

1 eastern rock lobster
1 tbsp white miso paste
3 tbsp unsalted butter
Fresh lemon juice
Sea salt flakes

METHOD

Dispatch lobster humanely. A quick knife to the head is usually my go to.

In a large pot of boiling water, blanch the lobster for 1 minute then immediately place into iced water to cover. This will stop the cooking process and make for easy handling.

Cut and split the lobster in half lengthwise. Gently pull the tail meat out and remove the poop vein. I prefer to keep the head juice (yellow roe looking part) in but some people do not.

Remove the brains and any small shell fragments and the top of the head.

Cut the tail into bite sized pieces. Around 4-5. Place the tail meat back into the shell in the opposite way you took them out. This will ensure the thinner tip of the tail does not over cook and the thicker parts of the tail are all cooked at the same time.

In a small saucepan, melt the butter before adding the miso, and whisk together.

Once prepped and ready to go, pour the butter over the two halves and broil in the oven (180°C/360°F) until the meat is tender and cooked. About 3-6 minutes depending on the size of your lobster.

Serve with a salad and garlic bread on the side to soak up all the lobster juices and leftover sauce.

SPEARO CHEF

Eli Ravines
@Aquaholic173

ALTERNATIVE SPECIES

Any lobster or bug

SAMPHIRE FISH

Samphire is a coastal sea vegetable and it has a salty flavour reminiscent of asparagus, broccoli or beans. It can be eaten raw but the flavour is more palatable and complimentary to fish when sauteed. If you're not lucky enough to find it in a store, samphire can be found in coastal areas and around many estuaries on Australia's southern coasts. Often older and bigger shoots will have a woody centre so when selecting samphire go for newer, greener shoots during the summer months.

COOK TIME 30 MIN | SERVES 2
Whole white fleshed fish

INGREDIENTS

1 whole white fleshed fish
2 knobs of butter (approx 4 tbsp)
7 garlic cloves
1 lemon sliced into wheels
Samphire
Preferred cooking oil
Salt

METHOD

Scale and wipe down the excess moisture from the fish.

Stuff the fish with lemon wheels, 4 crushed garlic cloves and a knob of butter.

Make 3 slices on each side of the fish, to allow it to cook evenly and for the seasoning to penetrate. It also makes portioning easier when serving.

Oil and salt the exterior (both sides) and bake the whole fish at 180°C (350°F) for 25 mins.

Check the fish is flaky with a fork, or even try a piece.

You can always flip the fish over and hide this later when serving. Bigger fish may need longer.

While you wait for the fish to cook, heat a frying pan and add a splash of cooking oil.

Mince 3 cloves of garlic.

Toss the samphire through the oil for a couple of minutes.

Add a knob of butter and your minced garlic (don't be afraid to be generous as this will make up a sauce to pour over the fish as well).

Toss the samphire through the butter and garlic on a low heat.

You want the garlic to become fragrant but not quite cooked.

Remove the fish from the oven and place on a serving plate or dish (hiding any of your snacks along the way).

Pour the contents of the frying pan over the fish stacking the samphire on top.

SPEARO CHEF

Josh Bollen
@bosh.jollen

ALTERNATIVE SPECIES

Any suitable species for baking

LEBANESE STYLE LING COD

Lebanese flavours may be new to many spearo cooks, but don't let that put you off—use the opportunity to try something new! Here we use za'atar, a lebanese spice mix most often composed of dried thyme, oregano, marjoram, sesame seeds, salt and sumac. As a spice mix it is extremely versatile, used on breads, "pizzas" (man'ousheh), meats, fish, or vegetables—you can explore and experiment with it, as you like. We'll be making our own za'atar but it can be found in most Middle Eastern stores, or online, as can the ingredient sumac.

Ophiodon elongatus or ling cod, are typically solitary fish that can be found in holes. They are found along the west coast of North America from Alaska to Baja. Don't worry if you haven't got access to a ling cod, this is an easy recipe that goes with most fish. Serve with a side of hummus, olives or fattoush (levantine salad).

COOK TIME 40 MIN | SERVES 2
Ling cod

INGREDIENTS

ZA'ATAR SPICE MIX

2 tbsp of dried thyme
2 tbsp of dried oregano
1 tbsp of dried marjoram (skip if unavailable)
2 tbsp of ground sumac
2 tbsp of toasted sesame seeds
1 tsp of salt

FATTOUSH SALAD

1 large cos/romaine lettuce (purslane is used traditionally, but many find it a bit odd)
1 large tomato
1 large lebanese cucumber (or a sweet, local variety)
½ of a red onion
3-5 red radishes
½ cup fresh flat leaf parsley
½ cup fresh mint
2 loaves of lebanese bread or pita bread
1/2 cup olive oil
Salt and pepper
2 tbsp pomegranate molasses
2 lemons
1 tsp sumac

FISH

4 lingcod fillets
2 tbsp extra virgin olive oil
4 tbsp za'atar spice
Salt and pepper to taste

SPEARO CHEF

Omar Aljundi
@spearoms

METHOD

ZA'ATAR SPICE MIX

Heat in a heavy-based frying pan to a medium heat. Do not use oil or butter, but simply add your sesame seeds to the preheated pan.

Gently toast the sesame seeds, stirring constantly with a wooden spoon to ensure they do not burn. Once golden, remove from the heat and pour onto a plate lined with paper/kitchen towel.

While your sesame seeds cool, use a mortar and pestle to finely crush the dried spices (alternatively, finely chop them).

Transfer your spices to a bowl and add the remaining ingredients (if you can only find whole sumac, simply crush/chop it very finely. All sumac substitutes leave something to be desired however a tbsp of finely diced lemon zest mixed with a tsp of salt and a pinch of citric acid can come close).

Note: any leftover za'atar can be eaten on lebanese bread as a dip, or tossed over potatoes before baking.

LINGCOD

Preheat your oven to 180°C/350°F.

If using a whole fish, scale, gut and clean it before removing the fillets and skin them (save any remaining fish such as collars, heads and frames for other great recipes in this book).

Mix the olive oil and your za'atar in a large bowl. Play with the quantities of oil, you want it more wet than a paste, but predominantly composed of the spices.

Rub the fillets generously with the spice mix, ensuring they are well coated.

Wrap each fillet securely in aluminium foil (place the fillet on a sizable rectangle of foil, raise the long sides together and fold each of the shorter sides in 1cm (1/2 in) toward the centre repeatedly to seal both ends.

Once the sides are sealed, repeatedly fold the top down over itself to seal the "boat") and place on a baking tray.

Bake for 30 minutes (be careful of steam when opening the parcels).

FATTOUSH SALAD

In the oven, toast the bread until crispy and golden. Remove, and allow it to cool before breaking it into bite sized pieces.

Wash, dry and chop the lettuce into 5cm (2in) pieces (if using purslane wash thoroughly and remove any damaged leaves or stems).

Dice the tomato, halve the cucumber lengthwise and thickly slice (1cm/0.4in thick). Peel, halve and finely slice the red onion.

Wash the radishes, remove the stems and ends, halve lengthwise and very finely slice.

Wash, dry, and roughly tear the mint and parsley.

Assemble all the ingredients, excluding the toasted bread, in a large salad bowl.

To assemble the dressing: juice the lemons and mix the juice, oil, pomegranate molasses and sumac until it has formed an emulsion. Season it with salt and cracked black pepper to taste.

Pour the dressing over the salad and toss to coat.

Add the toasted bread just before serving.

TO SERVE

Unwrap the ling cod from the parcels, being careful of steam and arrange two fillets per plate.

Add a generous serving of salad.

Left over, untoasted lebanese/pita bread can bring the meal together—try using it as a means of picking up the food instead of cutlery, pinching fish and salad between some bread.

Add hummus/baba ganoush and lebanese pickles for a more authentic feel.

"Sahtayn!" (Lit. "double health"—enjoy your food before and after eating—the lebanese "*bon appétit*).

VERMILLION ROCKFISH PROVENÇAL

This is classic fish preparation from France. It is simple and adaptable using just about anything caught from the sea and is always totally delicious. Cooking can be done in the oven or on the BBQ, simply wrap the ingredients in foil and place on the grill. I like to serve this with rice, roasted potatoes, or with crusty grilled bread. It can be accompanied by a fresh salad or sautéed greens like mustard or bok choy, making it one of the most versatile dishes I know!

COOK TIME 30 MIN | SERVES 2
Vermillion rockfish

INGREDIENTS

One whole fish, about 5lb or 2.3kg, gilled, gutted and scaled. It is perfectly fine to use fillets or steaks too.
5 large ripe tomatoes, sliced
1 head of garlic, peeled and sliced
1 small white onion, diced
1 rib of celery, sliced
1 sweet bell pepper, diced
½ cup (180g/6oz) whole pitted black olives like nicoise or kalamata
½ cup (180g/6oz) capers
1 medium lemon
½ cup each of fresh basil, parsley, and tarragon, stems removed
2 tbps fresh thyme, leaves only
½ bottle of dry white wine
4 tbps stick butter, sliced into ¼in (6mm) thick pats
¼ cup extra virgin olive oil
Salt and pepper

METHOD

Preheat your oven to 425°F (220°C)

Pat the fish dry and score both sides, almost to the back bone, several times. Liberally salt and pepper the fish.

Place 75% of the vegetables, olives, capers, and herbs in the bottom of an ovenproof pan. Salt and pepper them liberally.

Slice and layer half of the lemon on top of the vegetables. Drizzle with olive oil.

Stuff the remaining 25% of the ingredients into the cavity of the fish, with a few more lemon slices.

Add pats of butter around the pan. Lay the fish on top of the vegetables and butter. Place extra pats of butter on the fish.

Top the fish with a few thin lemon slices.

Pour the wine into the pan and on top of the fish. Drizzle the fish with olive oil.

Place it in the oven. A 5lb/2.3kg fish should take about 45 minutes to finish (about 10 minutes a pound/0.45kg).

Check it after about 20 minutes of cooking and baste it.

You want to make sure the meat is slightly underdone near the centre. Remove from the oven and allow it to sit for 10 minutes, at room temp, before serving.

Serve with your choice of accompaniments—rice, potatoes or crusty bread are all good choices.

SPEARO CHEF

Matt Bond
@cutprofessor

ALTERNATIVE SPECIES

Just about any fish or shellfish will work well

BAKED ORANGE AND YELLOWTAIL

This recipe is super easy to make and you can add and take away ingredients as you wish, just keep the fruit rings on! Experiment with other types of fruit and find your favourite combination! The big danger with this, as with many other recipes, is overcooking. You want to cook it hot and fast! I stumbled upon this recipe when trying to make a more interesting roast chicken dish. I tried it on fish and have never looked back!

The citrus flavours of the orange and lemon give off a lovely aroma and season the fish wonderfully while keeping it juicy and tender. Turn the oven up for the last few minutes to get some lovely colour grilled into your dish. I make it with *seriola ialandi* (yellowtail kingfish) but any firm flesh will work well.

COOK TIME 30 MIN | SERVES 4
Yellowtail kingfish

INGREDIENTS

2 fresh yellowtail fillets
150g (5.3oz) unsalted butter
Small bunch leeks
Small bunch spring onions (scallions)
2 oranges
2 lemons
4-6 potatoes (or a cup of rice)
1 egg yolk
1 clove of garlic
½ tsp brown sugar
Salt
Black pepper
Coriander
Cumin
Paprika

METHOD

Preheat the oven to 200°C (400°F).

Slice onions and leeks keeping the whites separate from the green leaves.

LEMON BUTTER SAUCE:

In a medium heated pan, place butter, a half tsp of brown sugar and cook until the smell becomes nutty. Take off the heat and don't let it burn.

Add the egg yolk with a pinch of salt, black pepper and a clove of garlic with a squeeze of lemon.

In the hot pan, stir for 30 seconds-1 minute until everything is well mixed and hot.

Pour the lemon butter sauce out of the hot pan to stop it cooking.

COOKING THE FISH:

Place fish fillets into a suitable size oven dish, skin down.

Sprinkle coriander, cumin and paprika onto the fillets.

Cut the lemons and oranges into rings and place them in an alternating pattern on top of the fish.

Crack black pepper and sprinkle salt over the fish with a bit extra on the lemons and oranges.

Sprinkle the spring onion and leek whites all over and in between the fish. I like the leaves too so I sprinkled some of those on as well.

Pour the lemon butter sauce over the fish and fruit. Cook in the oven for 20 minutes.

Serve with potatoes, rice, chips, etc.

EXTRA STEP

After 10 minutes, turn the oven up or switch to grill for the last 10 minutes to give some nice roasted colour to the fish and fruit.

SPEARO CHEF

Brandon Swanepoel
@CapeTown_Spearos

ALTERNATIVE SPECIES

Any white flesh fish or any fish you would oven roast

TAILOR PIE

I enjoy tailor in this dish as it has a nice balance of oily texture and light white flesh, its frame also makes a particularly good broth. If you have the time and means to do so, smoking the frame before making the broth adds a great layer to the dish and will satisfy the cries of the old sea-dogs that think it isn't a fish pie unless it has something smoked in it! This recipe make a great template for any type of seafood pie! Works great with any combination of your favourite seafood and vegetables.

COOK TIME 40 MIN | SERVES 4
Tailor

INGREDIENTS

1-2 tailor approx (1.2-1.5kg/2.6-3.3lb before processing),
Gut, fillet, debone and keep the frames.
3l (¾ gallon) water
3 sheets puff pastry
1 egg

SAUCE
300ml (1.25 cup) thick cream
1 leek
60g (2oz)butter
100g (3.5oz) shallots
3.75 tbsp (30g/1oz) all purpose flour
300ml (1.25 cup) fish stock
Salt

SEASONING
20ml (3/4fl oz/1 tbsp) olive oil
½ cup of chopped parsley
Zest of 1 lemon
Juice of 1 lemon
Salt
4-6 rainbow (swiss) chard stalks (stem on) cut into 1cm (½ in) strips across

METHOD

THE SAUCE

Place the fish frame(s) in a pot with the water, bring to a boil, and then reduce to a very gentle simmer. Skim off any scum that bubbles up, using a ladle. After 30 minutes, strain the stock.

Return to a medium heat and reduce to approx 1l.

In a clean pan, over very low heat melt half of the butter, add the leek, shallots and a generous pinch of salt. Fry until very soft but not browned.

Transfer to a blender, or using a stick blender, blend with the thick cream until smooth.

In a pan, add the other half of the butter, melt it over low heat, add the flour and whisk until smooth.

Slowly add the fish stock, bit by bit, whisking the whole time.

Finally, add the cream mix and let it simmer over very, very low heat and stir frequently. It should be thick like custard, if it gets too thick, whisk in a splash more stock.

THE FILLING

Put olive oil in a pan on high heat until you see a whisper of smoke, add rainbow chard and sauté until wilted and soft.

Add the juice of half a lemon and a pinch of salt. Once the liquid has mostly evaporated, remove from the heat and set aside.

Slice the tailor fillet into 1.5cm (⅔in) strips. Combine with lemon zest, parsley, chard and a generous pinch of salt. Let sit for 10-20 minutes.

TO ASSEMBLE THE PIE

Preheat the oven the oven to 200°C (390°F)

Oil a pie dish approximately 3cm (1.2 in) deep and 30cm (12 in) in diameter. Line with pastry leaving a small overhang.

Mix the sauce and seasoned fish, and pour into the pastry lined pie dish.

Cut a lid in the shape and size of the dish, out of another sheet of pastry and use it to seal the pie.

Poke 2 holes for steam to get out and use the remaining pastry to make a cute picture to decorate the pie lid, like a fish.

Whisk the egg in a bowl and brush over the top of the pastry.

Bake for 20 minutes.

SPEARO CHEF

Ric & Bee Divola
@bar_que_sera

ALTERNATIVE SPECIES

Combination of prawns, mussels, lobster and reef fish. Smoked is ideal

ROASTED KINGFISH BELLY WITH EGGPLANT KASUNDI ON TOAST

This is a nice versatile chutney recipe that goes well with a lot of different fish sides/bellies. This recipe makes quite a large quantity too, which means you can stash it away for another day for when you're feeling peckish. It will also last for a couple of months as it is a preserve. The recipe is quite easy to make and takes only a couple of hours to prepare/cook.

When you're ready to have a feed of kingie belly again, it's already prepared for you, so you can slap it on and you're away laughing. Generally, a kingfish belly will feed 2-4 people. It goes down a treat when you have a few mates around while sinking some brews. The dish acts as a good conversation starter as well, as the fish you're eating has a story behind it that you can share with your mates.

COOK TIME 120 MIN | SERVES 4
Kingfish

INGREDIENTS

500g-1kg (1-2lb) fresh kingfish belly (either the collar end or the tail end)

KASUNDI

(Asian variety of mustard sauce or relish) spice mix:
10g (.35oz) fenugreek seeds
15g (.5oz) cumin seeds
20g (.7oz) mustard seeds
50g (1.75oz) fresh ginger
75g (2.65oz) garlic
12g (.4oz) turmeric
15g (.5oz) cumin seeds
65ml (¼ cup) malt vinegar
300ml (1.25 cup) canola oil
500g (1lb) white onion, diced
50g (1.75oz) garlic, finely chopped or crushed
50g (1.75oz) fresh ginger, finely grated
250ml (9fl oz/1 cup) malt vinegar
300g (10.5oz) white sugar
45g (1.5oz) salt
125g (4.4oz) fresh red chilli
1.25kg (1.5lb) eggplant (aubergine), diced

METHOD

KASUNDI

In a bowl: toast off the kasundi spice mix until fragrant.

Grind into a powder with a mortar and pestle.

Gather all of the ingredients for the wet paste and blend them together.

In a large pot or pan: Sweat off the onions in oil for approximately 10 minutes, then add the ginger and garlic. Cook until the onions, garlic and ginger start to get colour.

Add the kasundi spice mix and wet paste. Make sure you stir it continuously to prevent sticking.

Add the malt vinegar, red chilli, sugar, salt and diced eggplant. Cook down until all flavours have infused and it has become a jam-like consistency.

Set aside to cool down. Once cooled, store in pre-sterilised clean sealable jars.

KINGFISH

Marinate the kingfish belly or collar with a good basting of kasundi for at least an hour in the fridge. Apply kasundi liberally.

Heat a large cast iron skillet or pan until it's really hot on the BBQ and lay the marinated kingie belly/collar skin side down and close the lid to let it roast.

Try to get a nice colour on the marinade as well, as colour equals flavour and it will form a nice crust.

Cook the fish through to your liking (remember to always undercook just a little as it will continue to cook through after you remove it from the heat).

Serve the belly with half a lime or lemon, cracked black pepper and a sprinkle of chopped coriander or micro coriander.

Serve this with a side of charred broccoli for ultimate satisfaction.

SPEARO CHEF

Anthony Thodey
@anthonythodey

ALTERNATIVE SPECIES

Kahawai side or hapuka belly

SCALLOP BAKE

This is the best and simplest way to prepare scallops for the greatest flavour! One of the best tips to maximise your ability to collect scallops is to use a cray/catch bag attached to your waist. This way you have the bag with you all the time instead of having to swim off to one attached to your float.

Once you have a good number of scallops in your catch bag you can then fill your catch bag on your float. This will save you a lot of time and conserve energy during your dive. They freeze well if you use a vacuum sealer and can last months in the freezer. However, they are best fresh and enjoyed with friends and a beverage of your choice.

COOK TIME 35 MIN | SERVES 1-2
Scallop

INGREDIENTS

15-24 scallops (per person)
5-8 scallop shells (per person)
100g (3.5 oz) butter (just enough to coat the scallops)
Handful of parsley
3-4 garlic cloves
Panko breadcrumbs (approximately half a packet)
Hard cheese—parmesan or something similar (equal ratio to panko breadcrumbs)
Kewpie Mayonnaise (enough to lightly coat the scallops)
1 tbsp Curry powder

METHOD

Shuck and clean scallops and place in a bowl. You want enough scallops to place at least 3 (depending on the size of the scallops) per shell. If you don't have enough scallops you can skin a fillet of fish and cut the fillet into "scallop" sized pieces and add to your scallops.

Scrub clean 5-8 shells per person (can even run them through the dishwasher afterwards). Divide the scallops in half.

Crush the garlic and chop the parsley and place in a small bowl. Add butter to garlic and parsley mix and heat in the microwave until the butter has melted.

Mix through half the scallops and set aside for 20 minutes.

Add some kewpie mayo to the remaining scallops. Just enough to very lightly coat the scallops.

Mix through two teaspoons of curry powder and marinade for 20 minutes. Grate the hard cheese and mix with the panko breadcrumbs (50:50 ratio).

Place empty shells on a baking tray and place approximately 3-4 scallops per shell.

Generously cover with the breadcrumb/cheese mixture. Bake at 200°C (390°F) for approximately 7 minutes.

Take it out to serve!

SPEARO CHEF

Eckart
@salt_sessions_freediving

ALTERNATIVE SPECIES

Cubes of fish fillets (preferably soft white fleshed fish)

THAI INSPIRED FISH SAUSAGE ROLLS

A super easy recipe that everyone will love. This recipe came about from a "what's in the fridge?" moment. These sausage rolls are made with some leftover fish (black drummer and luderick), pastry, a few vegetables and curry paste from the pantry. Off to the oven—easy as!

These were so delicious my three boys inhaled them like there was no tomorrow. Surprisingly, they didn't even think they were fish, so it might be a good recipe for reluctant fish eaters out there!

COOK TIME 30 MIN | SERVES 2
Luderick and black drummer

INGREDIENTS

500g (1lb) fish fillets
1 large carrot
¼ white onion
2 spring onions (shallots)
1 handful of spinach /rocket mix
2 sheets puff pastry
2 eggs
Massaman curry paste (pod or similar)
Sesame seeds
Salt and pepper to season

METHOD

Dice or mince the fish fillets. Put in a large bowl.

Finely dice carrot, white onion, spring onion (shallot) and spinach/rocket mix. Put it in the bowl.

Add the massaman curry paste and one egg, mix to combine. Add salt and pepper to taste.

Lay out the puff pastry and spoon on rows of the mixture approximately 2cm (0.75 in) across.

Roll the pastry. Cut into desired size.

Repeat until all the mixture is used.

Coat the pastries with egg wash.

Sprinkle with sesame seeds.

Cook in the oven at 180°C (350°F) for 20 minutes or until golden.

SPEARO CHEF

Aaron Kiggins
@aaron_kiggins_

ALTERNATIVE SPECIES

Leftover odd fillets or slightly undesirable species

CRAB MAC N CHEESE

Dungeness Crab (*Metacarcinus magister*) is a Pacific Northwest staple. The locals affectionately refer to them as "Dungees". Every season opener, my dive buddy and I break out the ceremonial crab axe and we clean our crab on the beach. This recipe is not difficult to make, and it's good enough to impress the in-laws! We dive early in the morning and then cook and prepare the dish for dinner.

Throw on a movie or a podcast to pass the time while cracking the shells. There is always left over crab meat, so feel free to eat some meat as you go on cracking! In my opinion the most important part is the crumb topping, make sure it's golden brown so you have a good crunch. I serve the dish as is, but a side of spinach salad never hurts. This'll feed about 8 people.

COOK TIME 60 MIN | SERVES 8
Dungeness crab

INGREDIENTS

CRUMB TOPPING

1 tbsp butter
1 tbsp olive oil
1 cup panko bread crumbs
¼ cup grated parmesan cheese

MAC N CHEESE

1lb (450g) elbow macaroni
½ cup of butter
3 tbsp of flour
2 cups milk
⅓ cup heavy whipping cream
3 cups mild yellow cheddar cheese
1 cup extra sharp white cheddar
¼ cup grated parmesan cheese
1 tsp sea salt
½ tsp mustard powder
1.25 cups of crab meat. With extra meat to sprinkle on top of the casserole

METHOD

CRAB

After the dungees are cleaned, put them in boiling fresh water with salt and old bay seasoning. I prefer the old bay cajun seasoning. Fully submerge them in the pot of boiling water for 15-20 minutes until they're bright orange.

Let them cool and then start cracking. If crab cracking is new to you, I'd recommend using a nutcracker-like tool. Otherwise your hands are sufficient—just beware of spikes.

Preheat the oven to 375°F (190°C).

In a medium frying pan, heat the butter and oil. Add panko and cook, stirring until light brown.

Remove from heat and stir in parmesan cheese. Then set aside for later.

Cook the pasta in boiling water until al dente. Drain well.

In a medium saucepan, melt the butter and whisk in flour. Cook and stir for several minutes until bubbling.

Whisk in milk and cream and cook, stirring constantly, until thickened and smooth.

Remove from heat and add the cheeses, salt, and mustard powder.

Stir in most of the crab meat and all the pasta, mixing well.

Lightly butter a casserole dish and spoon in the mixture.

Place the last of the crab meat on top and sprinkle the crumb topping all over.

Bake for 25-30 minutes until the sauce is bubbling and the crumb topping looks golden.

SPEARO CHEF

Cameron Jutila
@Jutilathehun

ALTERNATIVE SPECIES

Red rock cod is also a good substitute but you need to get more of them because they have less meat

FRIDAY FISH PIE

Pip and I have developed a great relationship—I'd catch the fish and Pip uses her vast knowledge to turn my average catch into culinary masterpieces! Fish pie on Friday's has become a bit of a tradition at my apartment and this recipe is the outcome of wine fueled experimentation and represents what we believe to be the perfect Friday fish pie!

Best enjoyed with friends and a crisp white wine! P.S: This also doubles as a great way to use offcuts/parts of your fillet that are not as presentable for other dishes. Works well with frozen fish too!

COOK TIME 60 MIN | SERVES 4
Flathead or ling cod and scallops

INGREDIENTS

2 leeks, white part only
100g (3-5oz) tiny button mushrooms
1 fennel
1kg (2lb) white firm fish
200g (7oz) scallops (no roe) or alternatively fresh green prawns
1 bunch dill, chopped
Lemon juice
3 large "floury" potatoes like desiree or dutch creams, peeled and cut into 3cm-ish cubes. Put in a pan of cold salted water.
200ml (7fl oz/1 cup) milk
250g (9oz) butter
500ml (2-2.5 cups) good fish stock
200ml (7fl oz/1 cup) milk
100ml (3.5fl oz/½ cup) crème fraîche
80g (3oz) butter
80g (3oz) plain flour

METHOD

Preheat oven to 180°C (350°F)

Peel and roughly chop the potatoes. Put the potatoes on medium heat in a pot of water. Peel and finely slice the white part of the leek, dice the mushrooms and finely chop the fennel

In a wide based pan, sweat the leeks in olive oil without colouring until soft.

Add fennel and mushrooms and continue to cook for 5-10 minutes until tender. Slice the flathead and scallops into 1-2.5cm (½-1in) pieces.

Add fish and scallops or prawns while the vegetables are still hot, then set aside.

Bring fish stock and milk to the boil then turn off.

Melt butter in a medium saucepan then add butter and stir with a wooden spoon for 5 minutes to make a "roux".

Swap to a whisk and start adding the fish stock/milk liquid a little at a time while whisking constantly until all incorporated. The sauce should be a thick sauce consistency.

Pour the sauce over the veg/fish mixture, gently fold through with the chopped dill, crème fraiche and some lemon juice. Season with salt and white pepper.

Taste and adjust the seasoning as needed. At this stage the heat of the sauce will only cook the fish slightly.

Transfer the mixture to a serving pie dish.

When the potatoes are well cooked, drain and put through a potato ricer or mouli mill (alternatively mash).

Add the butter bit by bit mixing with a spatula adding a little milk to achieve a smooth but still pipeable consistency. Season with salt only.

Pipe or spoon the potato over the fish mixture.

Bake in a preheated oven (180°C/350°F) for 20-25 minutes or until the top is golden and the sides are bubbling.

Serve with green salad.

SPEARO CHEF

Mark Cronje & Philippa Sibley
@markcronje & @philippasibley

ALTERNATIVE SPECIES

White firm fish and prawns can work in place of scallops

A GUIDE TO LOBSTER DIVING

Cornerstone Content Guide

Written by James Sakker
Other Contributors: @ethanyeo1, Sam Rowbotham, Jason Wing, Chloe Skilling, Captain Dan Walsh, Ben Rennie, Oliver Wady, Rhys Clay

A beginner's guide to catching, cleaning, and preparing lobster. By James Sakker and the spearfishing community.

Eastern rock lobsters (packhorse crayfish in New Zealand) were the only thing I chased when I started diving in the 1990's. This species is the biggest spiny lobster in the world and can grow to 15kg or over 30lbs.

I lived next to the ocean in Port Stephens which is a fantastic spot to learn to dive for lobsters. There were so many lobsters there and you could make lots of mistakes which helps to rapidly improve your technique.

WHEN & WHERE TO GO

For divers, lobsters are normally found in oceanic rocky or coral reef at depths of 1-16 metres (3-50 feet) with 3-6 metres (10-20 feet) the prime depth.

The great thing about lobsters is that you can go any-time of the day and a nice calm sunny day is best when starting off.

In New South Wales (NSW), winter and spring are the best seasons but you can catch them year round in Port Stephens and the South Coast.

"This is similar in Queensland as we also get our best visibility across these times of year. Generally for inshore diving, visibility is the limiting factor. Crayfish can also be found out on the Barrier Reef all year round."
- Rhys Clay

"For east coast spearos in NSW you will find lobster numbers start to dwindle coming into summer as they head offshore, this is when it's time to test the breath hold techniques you've been working on and try getting into the 10-12m+ depths and hunt the white boulder areas."
- Sam Rowbotham

"Here in California, lobsters lay in the eelgrass quite often (you can't see them) so if you crawl through it, they will shoot out making for easy pickings at times."
- Jason Wing

"In Southern California and Baja Mexico, night time is best for lobster as the spiny lobster here leave their caves/ledges/homes to forage, primarily in shallow water (<20 feet)."
- Captain Dan Walsh

"In the tropics, lobster can be found along fringing reef, inshore islands or reef lagoons offshore. Look for large plate coral where they can shelter, or isolated rocks/coral heads in shallow sandy lagoons. Unlike the southern species, their white antenna will often protrude from their hiding place making them easier to locate."
- Ben Rennie

SPECIES

In Australia, lobsters are found all the way around the coast and the species change depending on where you are. From North Queensland to the mid-north coast of NSW you have 4 species of tropical lobsters to hunt. In NSW we have the eastern rock lobster and slipper lobsters along the whole coast with Yamba to Eden the best places. Tropical lobster species are common from Port Macquarie, NSW to the Queensland border. Southern NSW, Victoria, Tasmania and South Australia have the mighty Southern rock lobster and Western Australia has a huge industry and recreational fishery around the western rock lobster.

"In NSW the eastern rock lobster stocks have rebounded significantly since the 70's and 80's when a total stock collapse was imminent (stock believed to down to less than 10% biomass). This fishery, due to a combination of research, compliance, management and cooperation between commercial and recreational fishers, has now established itself as a sustainable fishery with a biomass well above 30%. It is a credit to all parties on the way to work collaboratively to develop and sustain a fishery that is showing increased biomass every year"
- Oly

"In the USA, California spiny lobster range from 3-15lb and are commonly taken at night. In the Sea of Cortez/Baja, the spiny lobster are more tropical with blue/green bodies, still with no claws. They taste the same as west coast bugs." - Captain Dan Walsh

GEAR

Your basic diving setup is all that is required plus a lobster measurer (free from Fisheries in NSW and most dive stores) and a mesh keeper bag (you can buy these in the tackle shop, they call them scaler bags). Don't get a huge one as it's too much trouble. I weight myself to be neutral at 5 metres so as not to float up too much while I'm trying to grab a lobster.

Always have a float and I like to take my gun to mark lobster cracks and shoot the odd snapper attracted by your cray diving. For gloves, I use $5 impregnated cloth ones from the reject shop.

They give you a much better feel and grip on the lobsters with the downside being the urchins can get through them.

"Check that things like cray snares or hooks which can be legal in some states/countries but may not be legal where you are. Check with your local fisheries department about what is legal."
- Marty

"A lot of guys and gals wear Kevlar gloves in South Australia (especially for grabbing southern rock lobsters as they have the sharpest spikes)."
- Ethan Yeo

"As you get more advanced and are diving deeper water or hunting in deeper ledges, a quality dive torch is your best friend, it will really improve your find rate and allows you to better plan your attack by pinpointing where in the cave a lobster is sitting and what escape routes he has, it can however lead to some frustrations as you will undoubtedly find more lobsters that you cannot, no matter how hard you try, reach."
- Sam Rowbotham

"For us a torch is a must, it's very rare to find a cray you can see without a good torch. That's generally for those that are on a mission down south, for the noobs that have spotted one and want to have a crack - this guide will still work. When we cray dive properly, a torch takes priority over a gun. It might be worth mentioning (for southern rock lobster at least) that if you beam Lobster directly with your torch, they will scare and back up. When positioning a torch in preparation for a grab, you are better off shining it off to one side so it lights up the cray but does not spook them. If you have the room to play, you can even shine your torch at their tails to get them to shuffle forwards a little bit as they can get spooked by the light behind them (they need to be comfortable/ moving around still). This obviously works by tickling their tail with snares too!

I messed up most of my crays at the start by moving slightly while their antennae were on my hand (probably had a lot to do with being comfortable/breath hold). If you make contact with their antennae, it's worth pausing and striking once they have moved their antennae away from your hand or reattempt the grab on the next drop (again, this is for southern rock lobster which can be flighty little pricks). SA fisheries have free measuring tools too!"
- Chloe Skilling

"In California, every diver must have their own measuring device. It's a very good idea to compare your device to one as used by our Fish and Wildlife Wardens. If on a boat with others, everyone has to have a fishing license, and is limited to 10 hoops per person."
- Captain Dan Walsh

"Be mindful of carrying or wearing too much excess gear when diving for lobsters. Items such as belt reels, weight vests, catch bags worn on the waist, GoPros etc, can all get caught in tight caves and be both a hindrance and potential safety risk. If carrying a loaded gun, be mindful where this is placed on the bottom and what direction it is facing.

A float boat style float, combined with a drop weight is an effective piece of equipment. Large lobsters can create significant drag if stored on a float, whereas a boat style float stores them out of the water and is easier to swim with. They can also be useful on long swims similar to a boogie board. A drop weight on a rig line is an effective way to mark holes or caves in deep water and do repeated dives."
- Ben Rennie

TECHNIQUE

Catching lobster is fairly similar wherever you are but the rules change quite a bit between states so check with your local Fisheries department to stay out of trouble. In NSW you can only use a gloved hand (or your bare hand if you want some serious lacerations!).

Lobsters have two long antennae that they use to sense what is going on around them as well as two eyes. Often the first thing you see is the antennae—look out for straight brown lines. Not too much is straight in nature and once you get used to seeing this pattern, the lobsters are a lot easier to see. Lobsters tend to live in long horizontal or vertical cracks with marine vegetation around and over them. There can be anywhere from 1-50 lobsters in a crack especially if a lot of them are undersized. Eastern rock lobsters will usually back up into the crack/ledge/cave or under rocks they are living in once they have detected you.

If you have a speargun, place the gun next to the crack making sure it is not aimed at you. It is very easy to lose track of just which hole the lobsters are in and marking the spot really helps, especially if you are going to be able to get more than one lobster out of it. If there are lots of just undersized ones you might have to pull out a few and measure them before you get a legal sized one.

Don't rush straight into the hole trying to snatch one. Have a good look and see then go back to the surface and think. Can the lobster back up out of reach? Which one looks legal size? Can I use two hands? Is there a back entrance? What I'm getting at is that it's good to plan before you rush in.

Lobsters will drop their antennae and legs if you grab them so you need to get to the base of the antennae known as the "horns" or else grab them around the head or tail (lobsters have sharp spines under the

tail and will give you a touch up if your hand ends up underneath them). Once you decide to grab one, go hard and fast and try to pin the lobster against the rock and get a really good grip on it before you try and pull it out. Lobsters will play possum and then suddenly kick hard in your hand so don't relax your grip!

Once you start grabbing lobsters from a crack the other ones are going to want to leave so get your mate to go down and grab one, this is the best way to maximise your catch. If there is a back door to the crack, get your mate ready to grab any lobsters trying to escape out the back. Diving together and working the spot is great fun and very productive.

"If you'll be going deep in a cave/ledge to get a cray and might get stuck and won't be able to communicate with your dive buddy, tell your dive buddy that if you cross your fins that means to dive down and pull you out." - Ethan Yeo

"Don't be put off if you don't catch a cray soon after starting out, I always say to people that you will take months to find your first one, then it could be months before you find the next, after a while you will start putting 2 and 2 together and be able to identify the 'types' of cracks/holes/ledges that lobsters haunt and will save yourself a lot of fruitless trips to the bottom but it just takes time and lots of dives." - Sam Rowbotham

"An old 'Bottom Scratchers' dive club member explained it this way: 'Imagine you have a 20 dollar bill in your hand and the wind rips it from your hand. You reach to grasp your money as quickly as possible. This was his explanation of the best lobster grabbing method!" - Captain Dan Walsh

"A useful trick for wary southern rock lobster in tricky spots can be to hold a small piece of fish flesh between the fingers of your grabbing hand. Alternatively, rub fish or abalone over your gloves to transfer the scent. Often, the lobster will walk forward and come within grabbing range. If using a torch, avoid directly shining it on the lobster as they will quickly retreat. Using your fingertips, you can filter the torch beam so there is only enough light to see by.

In southern waters, keep a close eye out for empty abalone shells on the seafloor. This is often a great sign that a large lobster is residing in a cave nearby. In Queensland, Australia, it is legal to use a speargun to catch crayfish. Where possible, I encourage divers to collect them by hand as it is difficult to determine if the lobster has eggs stored under the tail or a tar spot.

Collection by hand allows these lobster to be returned unharmed and continue to reproduce. Keep a detailed log of your holes or caves, this allows you to find your way back easily and rotate spots regularly.

Screenshots from google earth with basic drawings and notes etc can be invaluable for future dives." - Ben Rennie

"One other trick for lobsters in deep holes is to put an octopus (tako) into the hole as lobsters will make a quick exit to get away from them. Just be prepared to chase them down as they can really move when they want to." - Oly

HAZARDS

In addition to the normal spearfishing hazards of boat traffic, sea conditions and shallow water blackout (struggling to get a lobster out of a crack uses a lot of energy), there are a few other critters to take care with. Sea urchins are very common and can puncture through your gloves. Wobbegong (carpet) sharks can and occasionally will bite you, I've been bitten three times in the last two years by small ones. A big wobbegong can latch on and drown you so use your eyes and don't reach into really dark big places that are large enough to hold a big one. Moray eels will move into lobster cracks, especially if there are a few broken legs and antennae.

They love to bite you! I can't count how many times I got bitten in Port Stephens. Red rock cod have poisonous spines and live in the same area and are hard to see. Even the occasional numb ray will be encountered.

Don't let this put you off though. I have done literally thousands of lobster dives and still love it! The other main risk is getting stuck in a crack or having your gear get tangled on the bottom. Don't stick your arm right into deep cracks in very surgy conditions and minimise things hanging off your weight belt. I tuck my lobster bag through my weight belt so if it gets tangled it just pulls out and doesn't trap me on the bottom.

"In Southern California and Baja Mexico, I have found that larger lobsters over 10 pounds have much stronger wills to survive and protect themselves, which is probably why they get so big. With my hands on a 12 pound lobster at Cortez Banks off of Southern California, I grabbed for the big boy and it charged me so fast and hard that it hit my mask and broke the faceplate, but I did manage to hang on and get him in my bull bag." - Captain Dan Walsh

"If shore diving, be mindful of swell and changing conditions. Often they are found in shallow water which can have breaking surf. Have a

TRANSPORTING AND PREPARING YOUR CATCH

Lobsters can live out of water for a few hours in a cool dark place like in your dive tub with your wet wetsuit over the top, so keep them alive until you want to prepare them. Before cooking, submerge your lobsters in fresh water or an ice slurry for 15 to 20 minutes to kill them.

If you are going to cut the tails from the head use a long sharp knife and insert it where the tail joins the head. Push all the way to the top of the head, parallel to the body and cut around until the tail comes out.

Break off a section of antennae and insert the broken end about 1.5cm (0.5 in) into the anus of the lobster (under the tail fan) and rotate it about 5 times in one direction and pull it out. This will remove the intestine of the lobster. Rinse the tail under freshwater and then wrap in glad wrap to freeze or cut lengthways if you want to grill or BBQ.

If you are going to boil your lobster, leave it whole and bring a large pot of heavily salted water to the boil. Drop in your dead lobster. Cooking a lobster alive is not only inhumane it will cause the legs to drop off so make sure you kill your lobster before cooking or tailing. The smallest legal size lobster in NSW is about 450 g or a pound and it needs 10 minutes of boiling from when the water comes back to the boil.

For every 250 g (0.5 lbs) heavier, I add about 2½ minutes. Once your lobster has finished boiling take it out and run cold tap water over it or place it in an ice slurry to cool it. This will ensure the meat pulls away from the shell cleanly and stops it overcooking.

Lobsters will keep for a week in the fridge and actually taste better after two to three days. If you are going to do a lobster mornay you can use either an uncooked or cooked one. Just cut it lengthwise, rinse the yellow guts out and add your sauce. The meat will come out of a boiled one easily but not for a green one unless it has been frozen.

Check out my Youtube channel Catch it Grow it Cook it for lobster diving action and great recipes.

"The care for your catch piece I hold very close to my heart. We have a lot of people that freeze them whole and don't even rinse them.

So a few points: Glad plastic food wrap is a must to stop freezer burn you can wrap multiple tails together, but make sure you use a few layers of glad wrap.

If you freeze a whole cray, the tail can still deteriorate, the underside is only thin. It also will wilt and soften if not wrapped. Freezing the tails (and legs if it's big enough) separately will reduce the chance of spoiled meat. It will also save space.

Freezing and defrosting lobster with the guts in is risky and the meat can go chalky and soft (if not just totally spoiled).

Any time spent cleaning and preparing your catch before freezing or refrigerating is a must to ensure the meat does not deteriorate (and your hours in the water are not wasted!)

Note on boiling: If you have pulled all the limbs off just be aware the lobster may become a bit watery inside so drain a bit before serving.

Note on braining: "I would seriously recommend putting it to sleep on ice first, it can be very unpleasant otherwise! I am sure there is a way to do it so it kills them quickly but if it's your first cray chances are you won't be so lucky and it can be pretty unsettling."
- Chloe Skilling

QUICK GUIDE TO BOILING LOBSTER

INGREDIENTS

- 1 cup salt
- 1 or 2 lobsters 450g (1lb) each
- 3 litres (101 fl oz) water

METHOD

Humanely dispatch your lobsters.

In a large pot, add the salt to 3l (101 fl oz) of water and bring to the boil.

When boiling, add lobster/s.

Once the lobsters come back to the boil, cook for 10 minutes.

Remove from water and run under a cold tap, or place in an ice slurry, until cool.

Refrigerate to store for up to 1 week—though they are best after 2-3 days.

Note: This is for 450g lobsters—add 2.5 minutes cooking time for every extra 250g (1/2 lb) so a 750g (1.5lb) lobster takes about 13 minutes boiling.

STEAMED & POACHED

Steaming and poaching are fantastic ways to cook delicate and mild flavoured seafoods. Whether it be a whole steamed coral trout, dressed with ginger and a bouquet of South East Asian herbs, or even a whole lobster tail, slowly poached in a bath of aromatic butter.

These cooking methods are incredibly versatile and can be used in a whole manner of ways while also being suitable for many different types of seafood.

STAUB

STEAMED & POACHED

One of my personal favourite steamed seafood dishes is the classic Cantonese whole steamed fish. Shrouded in generous handfuls of fresh ginger and stupid amounts of finely chopped spring onions and finished with a dousing of hot peanut oil to release the herbs' aromatics.

The best part about the dish is being able to get into all the nooks and crannies of the head, cheeks and especially the wings. Leave nothing behind but bones!

Steaming and poaching can sometimes be quite unforgiving, so consideration must be taken when cooking different species and with different methods. The key to poaching and steaming is keeping the temperature gentle and steady. Seafoods are typically delicate proteins so we generally want to avoid the shock of putting a soft fleshed fish fillet in a screaming hot steamer. A gentle rolling simmer is often more than enough and as a general rule, when poaching seafoods, never bring anything to a full boil.

This same rule applies to making stocks as well. Having a steady and consistent temperature is also going to ensure that we aren't going to overcook our meat.

Using a wooden skewer is a great way to determine if your fish is cooked—a gentle poke through the thickest part of the meat allows us to feel for resistance. If you feel resistance and push, your fish isn't quite cooked yet. If your skewer goes through the flesh with ease, you're probably bang on cooked.

Remember also that your fish will keep cooking even after you've taken it off the heat. Take this into consideration when determining your cook times.

When building flavour profiles there are a few things to consider; type of fish, freshness of your fish and the type of herbs you want to use to flavour the fish. Let's explore this in more detail.

When steaming fish avoid species that are considered "fishy" and steaming can often highlight those characteristics. Stay away from species like tuna, Australian salmon, small mackerels and some trevallies to name a few. It's best to choose white fleshed fish with a mild flavour.

The freshness of your catch is also going to make a lot of difference when steaming or poaching. When your fish starts to break down after a few days, you're going to get more of a fishy flavour than a fish that is caught and cooked the same day.

Remember to gut, gill and scale your fish before cooking.

Finally, fragrant herbs will always make a welcome addition to any poached or steamed dish. Think ginger, fresh coriander, kaffir lime leaves and lemongrass. For a European styled cuisine try dill, tarragon, lemon and garlic.

Happy steaming!

SPEARO CHEF

Harry Foster

@hazfos

"THE KEY TO POACHING AND STEAMING IS KEEPING THE TEMPERATURE GENTLE AND STEADY."

Harry Foster

LUXURY LOBSTER ROLLS

Lobsters (aka crayfish) aren't something that many people have access to. Sure, you can pop down to your fishmonger any day of the week and pick some up, but they're bloody expensive. When you happen to find a lobster in your possession, you want to make sure you're getting the absolute most out of it. This recipe highlights the lobster, without too much fuss, or too many ingredients.

COOK TIME 20 MIN | SERVES 2
Lobster or crayfish

INGREDIENTS

1 fresh lobster/crayfish
1 tbsp chilli sauce—I use Korean chilli paste
Juice of ½ a lemon
Bunch of spring onions (aka scallions or green onions)
2 tbsp kewpie mayo
2 pane di casa rolls (aka vienna rolls)—Make sure they are fresh
Butter
Toasted sesame seeds

METHOD

Boil the lobster tail for 8-12 minutes in salty water—sea water is best.

Once cooked, plunge the lobster straight into an ice bath to prevent over cooking.

Mix a tablespoon of chilli sauce, juice of half a lemon, diced spring onions and a generous squirt of Kewpie mayo in a large bowl.

Once cooled, dice the meat from the lobster tail into 2cm (1 in) chunks. Toss the lobster chunks through your bowl of mayo mix and chill in the fridge.

Warm (not too hot) the bread rolls in an oven.

Slice the bread rolls down the middle and scoop out the soft bread inside. This is to have more room for the lobster.

Butter the rolls generously and fill with the mayo lobster mix.

Garnish with more spring onions and toasted sesame seeds. Extra chilli sauce is optional.

SPEARO CHEF

Harry Foster
@hazfos

GREEK OCTOPUS SALAD

This is my Greek octopus salad recipe. I learned this recipe after watching a TV show as a kid but I've slightly changed it over time. I'm not Greek so perhaps these changes have just made it a Wet Mammal octopus salad. Who knows? What matters though is that it's absolutely delicious!

COOK TIME 45 MIN | SERVES 2
Octopus

INGREDIENTS

1 whole fresh octopus
Sea salt
1 cup (240ml) white wine, ideally sauvignon blanc
2-3 tbsp olive oil
2 limes
2 garlic cloves
Fresh parsley
1 lettuce
2 tomatoes
1 red pepper (capsicum)
200g (7oz) kalamata olives
200g (7oz) Greek feta
Black pepper

METHOD

Clean the octopus. Remove as much of the skin as you can.

Boil enough water to accommodate the octopus in a big pot. Add a pinch of salt.

Holding the octopus hood, dip the tentacles into the boiling water. This causes them to curl up, so repeat this until you are happy with the presentation.

Put the octopus into the boiling water.

Add the wine to the water, then reduce the heat and let the pot simmer for about 45 minutes to an hour or until the octopus is tender.

Remove the octopus from the pot and allow it to cool.

In a separate bowl, mix the olive oil, lime juice, chopped garlic and parsley.

Cut the cooled octopus into bite-sized pieces and add it to the bowl. Mix thoroughly with the dressing.

In a large bowl prepare a salad with the lettuce, chopped tomatoes, chopped capsicum, kalamata olives and feta.

Top the salad with the dressed octopus, season with salt and pepper to taste.

SPEARO CHEF

Sam Clothier
@wetmammal

ALTERNATIVE SPECIES

Squid or cuttlefish

GARLIC THYME BAMBOO STEAMED KUMU

I prepared this recipe with a kumu (goatfish) found all around the Hawaiian islands. This is a very simple recipe to make. I created the recipe myself with my background in Chinese cooking. This recipe is a great one for a family of 2-4. It is an awesome showcase dinner or entree and is such a fun process to watch. Great for dinner parties. I like to serve it with steamed bok choy and brown rice.

COOK TIME 20 MIN | SERVES 2-4
Kumu (goatfish)

INGREDIENTS

1 white onion
1 lemon
Fresh rosemary
1 kumu (goatfish)
Hawaiian NOH seasoning (a local favorite)
Salt
Pepper
5 garlic cloves
Fresh thyme
1 head of garlic
Green onions (scallions)
Cilantro (coriander)

The Hawaiian NOH seasoning used in this recipe is the best. There are all kinds of spices with the NOH brand I use but for this recipe I used the All Purpose Garlic, Vinegar and Chili Pepper.

METHOD

Prepare bamboo steamer by lining it with parchment paper on each layer.

Lay slices of the white onion, lemon and a few sprigs of rosemary on parchment paper.

Make several diagonal cuts along the body of the fish on each side. Coat fish with Hawaiian seasoning and salt and pepper.

Cut fish in half. Place head in one tray and tail in the other (as pictured).

Stuff the diagonal cuts with onion, garlic cloves, rosemary and thyme.

Top with chopped cilantro and green onion. Lay slices of lemon on top.

Fill wok with an inch and a half (4cm) of water. Stack steamer into wok.

Bring water to a gentle boil and allow to steam into fish until water is completely evaporated.

While the fish is cooking, cut the top off a head of garlic and bake at 350°F (175°C) for 10 minutes.

Remove the fish from the steamer, chop roughly and add the baked garlic on top of the fish. Arrange head with tail on a gorgeous plate along with sides and serve!!

SPEARO CHEF

Amanda Bratton
@underwaterbrat

STEAMED SEA BASS WITH GREEN SAUCE

In Portugal, robalo or sea bass is often grilled over coals, which is the best way to taste this fatty fish. However, this method can get repetitive, and there are a myriad of other ways to cook this fish. This recipe has an Asian-inspired twist. This should take you 30 minutes to prepare, although the fish itself is only cooked for 4 minutes. You can go crazy on the veggies you pair it up with. The world is your oyster!

COOK TIME 30 MIN | SERVES 2
Robalo aka sea bass

INGREDIENTS

2 sea bass fillets (save the head and frames for a fish soup!)

GREEN SAUCE
1 green chilli
2 cloves of garlic
Coriander (cilantro) stems
Juice of 1 lime
2 tbsp of fish sauce
1 pinch of white sugar
1 pinch of salt
1 cup (230ml/8fl oz) of water

VEGETABLES
3 carrots, sliced
1 head of cauliflower
1 tbsp olive oil
3 cloves of chopped garlic
Chilli to taste
1 zucchini (courgette), sliced
1 handful of bean sprouts
2 tbsp soy sauce
Fresh coriander (cilantro) to taste

METHOD

Blend all the green sauce ingredients with a little water. Divide the sauce into two equal parts.

Coat the sea bass fillets in half the sauce. Season with a little salt and pepper.

Marinate for 15 minutes. Meanwhile, boil the carrots and cauliflower.

Heat a pan and add a little oil, garlic and chilli pepper. When the oil starts to crackle and get that beautiful smell, add all the vegetables and stir fry for 3 minutes.

Add soy sauce to the stir fried vegetables, taste and season further to taste.

Place the fish in a steamer with some of the green sauce on top and steam for 4 minutes, or until the fish turns translucent.

(If you don't have a steamer, add 2cm (1 in) of water to a normal pan and place some spare dishes inside the pan.

Place the sea bass dish on top, so it doesn't touch the water. Bring water to the boil and cover the pan).

Place the vegetables on a plate and cover them with the steamed fish. Pour the reserved green sauce over the fish.

SPEARO CHEF

António Cardeal
@antoniocardeal

ALTERNATIVE SPECIES

Any white fish

PARCEL STEAMED FISH

For this recipe I have used red morwong as it is a pretty common fish for a noob spearo to come across in Australian waters. This recipe is as easy as it comes, and is my go-to after a long day in the water. It takes about 10 minutes to prepare, and about 10 mins to cook. I would recommend 1 fillet per person as a good portion size. I like to serve this fish with rice on a cold day, or with a nice salad in the summer.

COOK TIME 20 MIN | SERVES 2
Red morwong

INGREDIENTS

2 red morwong fillets
Drizzle of oil
8 cherry tomatoes, cut in half
2 shallots (scallions or spring onions) roughly chopped
2 wedges of lemon
20g (1.5 tbsp or 0.7oz) of butter
Salt and pepper

STEAMING TIPS

When steaming a fish in a bamboo steamer, lay down some herbs and bok choy underneath the fish. It will soak up extra juices and breathe delicious herbs into the body.

@underwaterbrat

METHOD

Preheat oven to 200°C (390°F)

For each fillet, cut a piece of aluminium foil to be approximately 5cm (2 in) longer than the fillet on each end.

With the foil shiny side up, drizzle a small amount of oil on the foil, then place the fish on the foil.

Place cherry tomato halves, shallots and a lemon wedge on each fillet.

Add the butter on the fillets.

Add salt and pepper to taste.

Pull the two long sides together and roll them together to create a seal. Repeat for the two remaining sides.

Bake in the oven for 12 minutes (add a couple of minutes for thicker fish).

Enjoy!

SPEARO CHEF

Adam Mori
@Mozzz04

ALTERNATIVE SPECIES

Any white flaky fish

WHOLE STEAMED CORAL TROUT WITH GINGER AND SHALLOTS

A whole steamed coral trout can usually be found in a top-end Chinese seafood restaurant selling for hundreds of dollars, but don't let that scare you off! It's very easy to make, with few ingredients needed. This dish is a crowd favorite in a bigger dinner setting with family and friends, but is also great on date nights when spearfishing brownie points are needed. When served, the whole steamed trout will always be the most impressive dish on the table. Serving over a bowl of steamed rice is a must, allowing all the sauces and flavours to soak in. A fish steamer is the perfect tool for this recipe, but a roasting pan with a wire rack on top large enough to fit the fish will work as well.

COOK TIME 20 MIN | SERVES 2
Coral trout

INGREDIENTS

Plate sized coral trout, about 800g-1.5kg (1.75-3.5 lbs), whole, scaled and cleaned
100ml (3.5floz) rice wine vinegar
1 tbsp sesame oil
200ml (7floz) soy sauce
4 garlic cloves
100g (3.5oz) ginger
5 scallions (spring/green onions)
One bunch (or 3) bok choy

METHOD

MARINATE THE FISH

Make 5-6 deep cuts along each side of the fish using a sharp knife (cut on the same angle you'd use on the first cut behind the head if you were taking the fillet off). If the fish doesn't fit in the steamer or pan, cut the head off, but make sure to steam it as well.

Combine the rice wine vinegar, sesame oil, and roughly 150 ml (5.25fl oz) of soy sauce in a large bowl and mix together.

Marinate the fish in the bowl for 15 minutes or so while you prep the veggies.

Keep turning the fish over and spoon sauce over the fish to make sure it soaks it up.

PREPPING THE VEGGIES

Cut ginger and garlic into long skinny pieces. Cut the scallions into thin strips, roughly 3cm (1.2 in).

Cut the bok choy in larger bits as it will wilt when cooking.

COOKING THE FISH

Add a little bit of water to the fish steamer and turn the heat to high. Lay the fish in the steamer and reserve the marinade.

Stuff all the cuts along the fish with ginger and garlic, filling it up.

Pour a little bit of marinade over the fish and shut the lid of the steamer. Repeat every few minutes for about 15 minutes or until the fish is nearly cooked.

When the fish is nearly done, throw in the bok choy and two thirds of the scallions slices and pour some more marinate over it all.

Cover and steam for about 5 more minutes or until the fish has cooked and veggies are ready.

Transfer the fish onto a large serving platter and surround with the steamed veggies.

Add the rest of the soy sauce and pour a bit of the marinade from the bottom of the steamer over the fish.

Place the remainder of the scallions on top of the fish.

Heat peanut oil in a small saucepan on high heat until it's very hot.

Carefully pour the hot peanut oil over the fish (be careful of splattering).

Serve immediately with steamed rice. Coriander can be used to garnish to taste!

SPEARO CHEF

Zac Kenway
@zackenway

ALTERNATIVE SPECIES

Cod/grouper or smaller tusk fish

DRUNKEN SCALLOPS IN MUSTARD CREAM

This is an extremely easy recipe guaranteed to impress! It's also really versatile and can be adapted for anyone. This dish makes an impressive entree. You can also add chunks of white fleshed fish to make it a main course for two or three people.

COOK TIME 15 MIN | SERVES 2
Scallops

INGREDIENTS

250ml (/9fl oz1 cup) fresh cream
500 ml (17.5fl oz/2 cup) white wine
3 tbsp of seeded mustard
Two dozen scallops (additional white fish fillets, cut into large chunks for the group version)

METHOD

Put cream and white wine into a pan and heat until nearly boiling.

Add seeded mustard and lightly stir.

Carefully add the scallops. If using fish, add this first, as it may take longer to cook than the scallops.

Poach for around 5 minutes until scallops are just cooked through.

Garnish with parsley and serve.

SPEARO CHEF

Max and Ben MacDonald Spearokids NZ
Spearokidsnz

ALTERNATIVE SPECIES

Any white fleshed fish

GREEN LIPPED ABALONE IN A TERIYAKI SAUCE

This is the perfect entree for 2-4 people depending on the size of the abalone. Other species of abalone could be substituted. Abalone can become tough if not prepared properly, but the 'boil and then cold-shock technique' works well. Prior to boiling, you can put them to sleep first by placing them in a tub of seawater in the refrigerator overnight.

COOK TIME 20 MIN | SERVES 2-4
Green lipped abalone

INGREDIENTS

1 large abalone
1 tbsp vegetable oil
1 tbsp butter
4 cloves of garlic, chopped
4 tbsp light soy sauce
4 tbsp mirin
1.5 tbsp sugar
Salt
Pepper
Sliced chilli
Coriander (cilantro)
Spring onions (scallions)

METHOD

Boil the abalone whole in a pot of boiling water for one minute.

Remove from boiling water and plunge into cold water immediately.

Shuck the abalone. Trim frills off and cut into bite sized pieces.

Cube the rest of the abalone.

Heat a pan and add the vegetable oil and butter. Once butter is melted, add the garlic.

When garlic turns golden, add soy sauce, mirin and sugar.

Turn the heat right down and add abalone.

Stir well to coat abalone in sauce and to heat the abalone for about one minute.

Remove from heat.

Add salt and pepper.

Garnish with chilli, coriander and spring onions.

SPEARO CHEF

Deryck Tan
@deryck.gyotaku

ALTERNATIVE SPECIES

Brown lipped abalone

SOY SAUCE STEAMED SNAPPER FILLET

Steaming fish can help retain vitamins and minerals that you partially lose when frying or searing. Fish is packed with omega 3 fatty acids which improves cardiovascular health so that you can feel good about making your family healthy while eating in style. Steamed fish also has fewer calories and and less fat than fish cooked in butter or oil.

COOK TIME 20 MIN | SERVES 2
Pink snapper

INGREDIENTS

One snapper fillet
Salt and pepper
Ginger, sliced and julienned
Peanut oil
Spring onions (scallions), sliced thinly
Fresh chillies, sliced
Coriander (cilantro)
2 cups steamed rice

SOY SAUCE MIX

2 tbsp light soy sauce
2 tsp dark soy sauce
1 tbsp shaoxing wine (substitute dry sherry, or mirin)
1/2 tsp sesame oil
3 tsp sugar
4 tbsp hot water

METHOD

Heat up a pot and add the ingredients for the soy sauce mix, stirring to combine.

Season snapper fillet with salt and pepper.

Place julienned ginger on plate and lay fillet over the ginger.

Steam on low to medium heat until cooked (roughly 8 min).

Discard the juice.

Heat 4 tablespoons of peanut oil until smoking, then pour over fish being careful not to splash yourself.

Pour soy sauce mix over fish.

Garnish with spring onions, chilli and coriander.

Serve immediately with steamed rice.

SPEARO CHEF

Deryck Tan
@deryck.gyotaku

ALTERNATIVE SPECIES

Most reef fish fillets will work with this recipe.
Small fish can be steamed whole

EIKO'S SIMMERED SNAPPER

This is the ultimate quick snapper feast. A 10-minute meal with maximum oriental flavour. Best served with rice and pickles. Okra, also known as gumbo or ladies' fingers, is a vegetable utilised in this recipe. If you can't find okra, zucchini, green beans, or eggplant have a similar flavour and could be used as replacements. Cooking is all about getting out of your comfort zone and trying something new so enjoy!

COOK TIME 10 MIN | SERVES 2
Whole snapper

INGREDIENTS

4-5 pieces okra, for garnish
½ cup sake
½ cup soy sauce
½ cup mirin
1 ½ cup water
1 thumb sized piece of ginger, finely sliced
1 whole snapper (pan sized)
Tsukemono (pickles)
Salt
Japanese short grain rice

METHOD

Roll the okra gently in salt to remove the husk.

Blanch it in boiling hot water for 2 minutes.

Cool in ice water. Drain and set aside.

Place the sake, soy, mirin, water and ginger into the pan.

Bring to a boil to remove the alcohol.

Score the whole fish on one side only.

Reduce the liquid to a gentle simmer and place the fish in the liquid, scored side up.

Place a drop lid (otoshibuta) or a light lid on the fish to gently hold the fish down. Baking paper will do if you don't have something suitable.

Cook for 5-10 minutes, gently spooning sauce over the fish to cook the top side.

Remove from heat just before the fish is ready. Rest for 5 minutes.

Garnish with the cooked okra and tsukemono.
Serve with rice.

SPEARO CHEF

Mark Cronje & Hiroko Ooka
@markcronje

ALTERNATIVE SPECIES

Any whole white flesh fish with delicate edible skin

TURBAN TACO AKA SNAIL CHOY BAO

The military turban *(Turbo militaris)*, a species of sea snail, is a marine gastropod mollusk. The military turban is a marine gastropod mollusk. They can be found in shallow, oxygen rich coastal waters around mossy rocks. Shells can be used ornamentally in the dish or as jewelry.

COOK TIME 30 MIN | SERVES 2
Military turban snail

INGREDIENTS

5 large turban snails
2 tbsp yuzu sauce
2 tbsp hoisin sauce
1 tsp minced garlic
1 tsp rice wine vinegar
½ tsp sesame oil
1 cup of rice (feel free to use packet rice)
8 cos lettuce leaves
1 packet of fried shallots
Wasabi (optional)

METHOD

Fill a pot with water and bring to the boil.

Place the snails in and boil for 5 minutes (7 minutes if snails were refrigerated).

Mix the yuzu, hoisin, minced garlic, rice wine vinegar and sesame oil in a bowl to create the marinade.

Remove snails from the pot and rinse under cold water for a minute or two to cool and prevent overcooking.

Tap the snails on a cutting board to loosen them from the shell, then use your finger and/or a knife tip or skewer to twist the meat out from the shell.

Remove the curled gonads and innards then slice the meat of each snail. Remove the small circle of gritty innards from each piece and rinse meat in water or under tap.

Note: you can eat the entire content however the innards will give your taco a sandy texture.

Mix cleaned snail meat into the bowl of marinade and place in the fridge.

Cook rice: Peel and wash cos lettuce leaves and place on a plate.

Once rice is cooked, mix in the marinade and snail meat and let rest for 2 minutes until meat is heated through.

Scoop into lettuce leaves. Finish by drizzling some yuzu or hoisin and sprinkle with fried shallots.

SPEARO CHEF

Rhys Gotje
@rhysiedundee

ALTERNATIVE SPECIES

Abalone or other turban snails

FILIPINO GRANDPA'S STEAMED FISH & BEANS

My grandpa was a cook in the US Navy. It's what brought him from a fishing village in the Philippines to America. He traveled the world cooking for various admirals and I loved cooking with him growing up. Recently, I asked him what his favorite fish recipe was. He said it was steamed fish with beans, and then he pulled out the recipe on a beat-up index card. Fish and beans is not my first choice, but I had to try it. It's a solid, hearty meal, one that'll keep you full while not wrecking your macros. It's super easy to make, so if you're in a hurry, give it a try.

COOK TIME 30 MIN | SERVES 2
California yellowtail

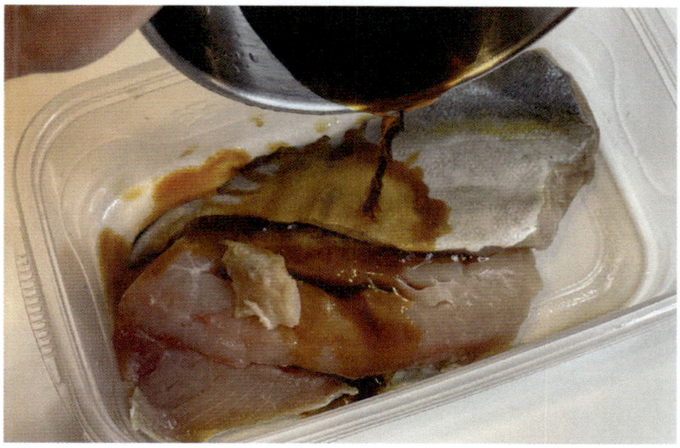

INGREDIENTS

1lb (500g) fish
1 tsp sugar
1 tsp salt
2 tbsp sherry
2 tbsp soy sauce
1 tbsp oil
1 onion, sliced
1 tbsp ginger, chopped
1 cup black beans
1 clove of garlic, crushed

METHOD

Mix sauce ingredients including sugar, salt, sherry, and soy sauce.

Next, clean fish and rub the sauce onto it If you have time for it, allow to marinate for several hours.

Place on a deep plate or baking dish and cover fish with oil, onion, ginger, black beans, and garlic.

Cover and steam for 20 minutes.

SPEARO CHEF

Jon Stenstrom
@castandspear

ALTERNATIVE SPECIES

Perch, white sea bass, grouper, and freshwater fish like tilapia

SHEEP CRAB CALIFORNIA ROLLS

This is a super simple recipe that takes just a few ingredients and a little prep work. It's a great one to do with friends or family, as you can divide the preparation of ingredients into teams. It uses an often overlooked California crab variety, the sheep or spider crab, *Loxorhynchus grandis*. One large crab made into these California rolls will feed quite a few people. So there's a reward for everyone who gets involved.

COOK TIME 40 MIN | SERVES 6-8
Sheep crab. Prior preparation req.

INGREDIENTS

3lb (1.4kg) of meat from a large crab, steamed, picked, and chilled
6-8 cups of cooked sushi rice
Sushi vinegar for the rice
2 cucumbers, peeled, seeded, and cut into strips lengthwise
3 avocados, peeled, seed removed, and sliced
½ cup (125ml/4lf oz) (or more) kewpie mayonnaise (other brands can be substituted)
¼ cup (60ml/2fl oz) grated lemon rind
1 tbsp sesame oil
Black pepper to taste
1 tsp salt
8 sheets of toasted nori (seaweed) for rolling sushi
Toasted sesame seeds for garnish
Soy sauce, wasabi, and pickled ginger to serve

METHOD

PREPARE THE CRAB

Dispatch the crab in the brain, or put it in ice/a freezer to kill it. Note: That killing any crustacean by braining them, particularly crabs, will make meat removal post cooking easier.

Clean the crab's shell, by scrubbing or spraying it if it is dirty (like sheep crabs often are).

Pull its shell off. It helps to run a small knife around the circumference of the thorax and where the shells meet.

Remove all the guts and gills and get rid of any residual gunk with a spray of water.

Snap the thorax (main body/chest section) vertically in two, leaving you with two sides of legs and claws and the connected body meat.

Steam these for 15-20 minutes.

Let the crab cool. Crack the shell, pick the meat out and place in the refrigerator.

PREPARE THE OTHER INGREDIENTS

Cook the rice. Add prepared sushi vinegar to your taste. Let the rice cool to room temp or below.

PREPARE THE ROLLS

In a large bowl add crab, mayonnaise, lemon zest, sesame oil, pepper, and salt. Mix until combined.

Cover a sushi mat or a magazine with plastic wrap.

With wet hands, spread enough rice across the plastic coated roller to entirely cover it at a depth of about half an inch (1.25cm).

Place a sheet of nori on top of the rice.

Spread a generous amount of crab filling across the centre of the nori (starting and stopping a half inch, or 1.25cm, before the edges) in line with the direction you will make the roll.

Put a line of cucumber sticks and avocado slices next to the crab.

Carefully roll so both ends of the nori now touch and this seam is on the bottom of the roll.

Firmly, but carefully, squeeze and press the roller to compact the roll. You want the roll to stay together without all the fillings squirting out. It might take a couple tries to figure out the correct amount of rice, filling and pressure but perfection takes time!

Unroll and sprinkle sesame seeds to cover the rice outside of the finished roll.

Using a wet knife to stop it from sticking, slice the roll into ¾-1in (2-2.5cm) thick rounds.

Serve with soy sauce, wasabi, and pickled ginger.

SPEARO CHEF

Matt Bond
@cutprofessor

ALTERNATIVE SPECIES

Any other crab, lobster, cray, shrimp, prawns

SOUPS, STEWS & CURRIES

Soups and stews have been a part of culinary history for well over 22,000 years since the first person heated water and added ingredients. This preparation method is a great way to extract flavour and use as much of the fish as possible. Keeping heads, bones, and fins to use in stock will result in a great broth you can continue enjoying long after the fillets have been consumed.

I also enjoy using thick, hearty chunks of fish for soups and stews. Those full, flaky bits of meat give great flavour when paired with seasonal vegetables. I often look for edible wild plants and mushrooms while returning from spearing or fishing to add to my soups.

Using ingredients from the same area I've harvested in creates a great flavour profile because all those elements interact naturally on a day to day basis.

BOTTOM SCRATCHERS CIOPPINO

Cioppino is an Italian-American fish stew originating in San Francisco, California. This dish often makes an appearance at the infamous Bottom Scratchers Diving Club parties, using their passengers' fresh catch of the day. It was also served on the "Bottom Scratcher" and "Spirit of Adventure" dive boats that I was the captain of for many years. The recipe sounds difficult, but is really easy if you follow the steps. You can substitute or add many different types of seafood—but avoid tuna, as we've found it becomes very chewy or rubbery.

COOK TIME 60 MIN | SERVES 6
White flesh fish

INGREDIENTS

1 finely sliced brown onion
½ cup (60g/2oz) of chopped celery
¼ cup (30g/1oz) of chopped parsley
2 cloves minced fresh garlic
½ cup (120ml/4fl oz) olive oil
1 (28-ounce/800g) can of diced tomatoes (I use "San Marzano" Italian ones, they're great!)
1 (8-ounce/250g) can of tomato sauce
1 teaspoon (6g/.2oz) salt
½ teaspoon (3g/.1oz) pepper (add more to make it spicier)
½ teaspoon (3g/.1oz) dry basil leaves
½ teaspoon (3g/.1oz) paprika
1 cup (230ml/8fl oz) red wine
4lb (1.8kg) of mixed seafood (Suggested seafoods: squid, abalone, assorted white flesh fish, clams, shrimp, crab legs, mussels.)

METHOD

Chop the garlic and ginger. Saute the onions, celery, parsley, and garlic in hot olive oil.

Add the tomatoes, tomato sauce, seasonings, and wine.

Simmer for about an hour.

Chop up all your seafood into evenly sized pieces. If you are adding abalone, use small trimmings and tenderize them with either a mallet (but not too much), by boiling, or by pressure-cooking them.

Add the seafood, except for the clams and mussels. Cook for around 10 minutes until the seafood is done.

Add clams and/or mussels—the shells will open to indicate they're done.

Time to serve your world famous Bottom Scratchers Cioppino to your guests with some crusty garlic bread!

As an alternative, if your guests are very hungry, you can use pasta as the base for this dish.

SPEARO CHEF

Dan Walsh
@upfrontcomms

ALTERNATIVE SPECIES

Abalone, lobster, shrimp, calamari, clams, crab legs, mussels all add to the flavour & appearance of the dish

DISTRICT 6 CURRY FISH

This was the most popular fish dish at the District 6 Restaurant in Cape Town, that I owned in the mid 1990s. Traditionally in Cape Town there weren't modern chilling facilities, so this was one way to extend the shelf life of fish. "Kerrievis" or curry fish is a South African favourite. The origins of this recipe can be traced back to the Cape Malay cooking style developed by early Indonesian slaves of the colonial Dutch.

COOK TIME 30 MIN | SERVES 2
Kingfish

INGREDIENTS

5 medium cloves of garlic (or teaspoon of garlic flakes)
1kg (2lbs) kingfish (or any firm fish–butterfish or moki), scaled and filleted, skin left on
Coarse salt, as required
Oil for frying
1 tsp chopped ginger
3 large onions
1 cup grape vinegar
½ cup water
½ cup brown sugar
8 peppercorns
4 cloves
4 whole allspice
2 bay leaves
1 tbsp mild curry powder
1 tsp ground cumin
1 tsp turmeric
1 tsp ground coriander (cilantro)

METHOD

Chop the garlic. Peel and slice the onions into rings.

Firm up the flesh of the fish by sprinkling coarse salt on both sides of the fillet and letting it stand in a glass bowl for maximum 20 minutes (longer than this will result in the fish being too salty).

Thoroughly rinse the fillets under running water. Pat dry with a paper towel. Cut the fish into bite sized cubes, leaving the skin attached.

Heat oil in a heavy based frying pan and fry the fish until just cooked through.

Place the rest of the ingredients in a large heavy based pot. Bring to the boil, then reduce heat, stirring to ensure the brown sugar dissolves and does not burn.

Simmer for approximately 7-10 minutes until the onions are cooked but still firm.

Layer the pieces of fish with the sauce and onions alternately in a ceramic or glass serving dish or in sterilised jars, ensuring that the last layer of fish is covered with sauce.

Leave to cool and then refrigerate. Will keep for at least a few weeks in the fridge.

Serve fish and onions with sprinkled fresh coriander (cilantro) on cold basmati rice or with a nice green salad and crispy rolls.

SPEARO CHEF

Philip van Zijl
Philip van Zijl Senior

ALTERNATIVE SPECIES

Any firm fish. In NZ butterfish (aka greenbone) works well

GOATFISH RAMEN

This goatfish ramen packs huge amounts of flavour while getting the most out of your fish. Minimal effort and ingredients are required for this recipe, which is surprising when you taste it. To really get the most out of it, you can make more stock than you need and simply freeze it to use later down the track.

COOK TIME 45 MIN | SERVES 2
Black spotted goatfish

INGREDIENTS

1 large goatfish about 500-600g (17-21oz), scales removed, filleted and bones saved for stock
1.5 tbsp rice bran oil
4 cups of cold water
1 small knob of ginger sliced thick
1 green spring onion (scallion) whole
5g (1 heaped tsp) of bonito flakes
Salt and pepper
Soy sauce to taste (I prefer yamasa soy)
Asian greens of choice (bok choy, choy sum, etc)
2 bundles (180g/6oz) of dry ramen noodles
1 green shallot thinly sliced
Bamboo shoots cut into matchsticks

METHOD

PREPARE THE FISH

Remove the fillets from the goatfish and set the main bones aside.

Remove the pin bones from the fillet with tweezers and cut the rib cage off.

Portion the fillets into 3 manageable pieces.

Take your goatfish bones and break them into manageable pieces. Remove the eyes, gills and any residual blood and soak everything in cold, lightly salted water for approximately 20 minutes.

PREPARE THE STOCK

Drain the bones and pat dry. In a small pot, combine the bones with the rice bran oil.

Toast the bones while stirring on a medium heat until golden and just starting to stick to the bottom of the pot.

Deglaze with a litre of water and scrape the bottom to get all of the flavour. Cook for approximately 10 minutes on a very gentle simmer.

Add the ginger and the spring onion and cook for another 10-15 minutes.

Once a red/orange oil forms on top, and the liquid underneath looks rich and creamy, bring the stock to a gentle boil.

Add the bonito flakes and remove the pan from the heat. Let it steep for 2 minutes.

Strain the stock through a fine metal strainer.

Add a very small amount of soy (approx. 2 tbsp) and salt until the seasoning is right for you.

PREPARE THE RAMEN

Bring a pot of water to the boil for your noodles and lightly season it with salt.

Put a steamer on the stove for the fish and put your stock back onto the stove to bring it up to a simmer.

Place the vegetables into the steamer to lightly steam them.

Lightly oil some pieces of baking paper that match the size of the fish you are going to steam. Season the goatfish with salt and pepper and place them onto the paper and into the steamer. Cook for between 4-7 minutes, depending on the thickness of the fish.

Put your noodles into the boiling water. Once cooked, strain them off and put them into your bowls for serving.

Once the fish is ready, pour the hot goatfish stock over the noodles - just enough to cover. Top with steamed greens, shallots, bamboo shoots and lastly the goatfish.

For an extra treat, blowtorch the skin of the steamed goatfish if you want crispy skin and even more flavour.

SPEARO CHEF

Jai Gibbons
@SpearoChef

ALTERNATIVE SPECIES

Red mullet, any other goatfish species

MOQUECA (BRAZILIAN FISH STEW)

Moqueca is an awesome dish which hails from Bahia in the north-east of Brazil. It takes inspiration from African flavours and is great when you have a variety of smaller fish. Leatherjackets and goatfish are perfect for this recipe, though any smaller white fleshed fish are brilliant substitutes. There are a host of variations of this dish, but this one is easy and quick. It will impress even the fussiest eaters!

COOK TIME 30 MIN | SERVES 4
Leather jacket and goatfish

INGREDIENTS

2 white fish (filleted and skinned)
2 limes
½ onion, diced
2 cloves garlic, crushed
1 carrot, diced
1 red capsicum, diced
1 cayenne chilli (optional), chopped
2 roma tomatoes, chopped
150 ml (⅔ cup/5fl oz) fish or chicken stock
1 can tomato paste
1 tbsp paprika
½ tbsp cumin
300ml (1.25 cups/10fl oz) coconut milk (liquid and solids)
½ cup coriander (cilantro), chopped
Olive oil
Salt and pepper

METHOD

Cut the fish into big chunks and place in a glass or china bowl.

Add a large pinch of salt and the juice and zest of 1 lime to the fish. Mix and set aside for 15 minutes.

Sauté the onion in a large pot with some oil until soft.

Add the garlic and the carrot. Cook for a further 2-3 minutes.

Add the capsicum, chilli and tomato. Cook for a further 2 minutes.

Add the stock, tomato paste, paprika, cumin and coconut milk.

Nestle the fish into the stew and ensure the fish is covered in the sauce.

Cook for a further 3-4 minutes or until the fish is beginning to flake.

Garnish with a sprinkle of coriander and a squeeze of lime. Serve with coconut rice.

SPEARO CHEF

Yianni Barthelmess
@huntfishgrowcook

ALTERNATIVE SPECIES

Leatherjackets, goatfish and any mixed seafood works with this stew

SEAFOOD CHOWDER

Variety is the key with a chowder. The more types of seafood the better it will be. Shellfish, lobsters, prawns, smoked fish and any fish fillets are all great in this dish. This tastes great after a big dive when you're cold, and it keeps really well in the fridge for a quick hearty meal after you have been out for a dive all weekend. Best served with crusty bread and butter.

COOK TIME 20 MIN | SERVES 2-4
Shellfish, lobster & fish

INGREDIENTS

2kg (4.4lbs) of mixed seafood
- white fleshed fish fillets
- lobster/crayfish
- shellfish—mussels, scallops, tua tua, pipis, paua, abalone
- peeled green prawns

1 tbsp olive oil
2 red onions
1-2 chillies
6 cloves garlic
300ml (10fl oz) dry white wine
3 spring onions
500g (1lb) smoked fish
Cracked black pepper
500ml (18floz) cream or half cream half milk
100g (4oz) butter
3 potatoes
3 carrots
Crusty bread and butter to serve

METHOD

Clean and debeard mussels. Discard any which are open. Clean the remaining shellfish using the appropriate method.

Heat olive oil in a large pot. Add the chopped red onions and chilli to the pot. Crush the garlic directly into the pot and saute.

Add your shellfish and cover. Steam for a couple of minutes until the shells start opening.

Add the dry white wine and three chopped spring onions. Cover and cook until all the shells are open.

Remove the shellfish from the stock, reserve the stock. Allow to cool slightly for handling.

Reheat the pot with the stock. Add the smoked fish and season with pepper. Add the cream and a generous knob of butter. Bring to a simmer.

Remove the meat from the shellfish and set aside. Discard any which have not opened.

Chop the potatoes & carrots into approximately 1cm (½ in) cubes and cook gently until the vegetables are tender. Season with freshly cracked black pepper to taste.

Top up your chowder with the remainder of the seafood ingredients—add a mix of white fish fillet pieces, shelled lobster meat, scallops, paua/abalone or peeled green prawns.

Simmer until it is all cooked and serve with crusty bread and butter.

SPEARO CHEF

James Sakker
▷ **Catch it Grow it Cook it**

ALTERNATIVE SPECIES

Prawns, crab

THE SERGEANTS RAMEN

Ramen is an awesome dish to make the most of your catch. Heads, bones and flesh scraps all add to produce a tasty broth. Fish such as sergeant baker (dragon snapper) are perfect for this dish. These fish are often looked down upon and considered too bony to be edible. They actually have beautiful white flesh with no overly strong flavours.

To avoid the bones, it is easiest to cut them out of the fillets which leaves you with a fair amount of wasted flesh. This flesh is perfect for your broth. Any clean-fleshed fish can be used but be wary of anything overly bloody or smelly as these things can taint your broth. Keep your fish wings to add to your ramen.

COOK TIME 30 MIN | SERVES 2
Sergeant baker

INGREDIENTS

COOKWARE
Stock pot
Frying pan
Strainer (additionally a muslin cloth/rinsed chux cloth can help filter out small pieces)
Aluminium foil

RAMEN
1 head of garlic
1 brown onion
Cooking oil (rice bran, canola, vegetable)
Salt
Fish frames/scraps
Dried shiitake mushrooms
1.5l (50oz) water per serving
1 spring onion
1 soft boiled egg per serve
Katsuobushi (dried bonito flakes)
Ramen wheat noodles

METHOD

BROTH

Slice off the top of the garlic and place in a dish covered with oil and wrap with tinfoil. Roast in the oven at 180°C (350°F) for roughly 30 min.

While the garlic roasts, halve the brown onion and fry flat side down on a low-medium heat to caramelise. As the onion becomes golden, forms a crust and starts to soften, place it in the stock pot.

Split fish head in half to flatten then shallow fry with any bones and meat you wish to use. Once these have a golden crust add them to the stock pot. Take garlic out of the oven, it should be a golden-brown colour and be soft to the touch.

Add the garlic to the pot along with a handful of dried shiitake mushrooms. Pour in water and simmer for between 1-1.5 hours. Taste along the way to see how your flavour is developing. Salt to taste.

Slice white and light green portions of spring onion into thin strips lengthways. Place these strips into water and put them in the fridge to curl. Roughly chop the leftover darker ends of the spring onion. Now is the time to cook your egg.

Once the broth has reduced to around a third, turn the heat off and add roughly chopped spring onion with a small handful of bonito flakes (katsuobushi). You don't want to apply excessive heat to these ingredients as they can drastically affect the flavour of the broth. Let it sit to steep these ingredients.

Now is the time to cook your noodles to the packet directions and shallow fry your fish wing(s) or other ingredients to add to your bowl. Shallow frying skin side down on a medium-high heat will produce an awesome crust and crisp the skin even with scales on (smaller scales when fried in oil can be eaten and make for a satisfying crunch).

Frying skin side down also protects the meat inside the wing from being easily overcooked.

Strain broth and pour in over noodles.

Garnish with fish wing, egg, spring onions and katsuobushi (optional additional ingredients include: mushrooms, seaweeds—both dry and fresh, sesame seeds, octopus, squid, abalone etc).

SPEARO CHEF

Josh Bollen
@bosh.jollen

ALTERNATIVE SPECIES

Kingfish, flathead, bream, snapper (Any non-weed-eating, clean fleshed fish)

MILLIONAIRE'S MISO SOUP

Miso is a delicious staple in many areas of the world, and anyone could argue that lobster goes well with anything! Millionaire's miso soup is a prime example of why it is so much fun to play. Not only is it a meal fit for a millionaire, it's straightforward to make and beautiful to serve! I am super fortunate to be a part of a community of spearfishing foodies that love to gift and share specialty and exotic ingredients.

This miso soup was the first course of a fine dining experience we created to highlight the group effort of foraging and hunting. It speaks to just how wonderful our dive community is.

COOK TIME 30 MIN | SERVES 2
Crayfish or lobster. Prior preparation req.

INGREDIENTS

SOUP

Kombu kelp, 6x6in (15x15cm) or more
600ml (21fl oz) water
500ml (17fl oz) fish stock
Shelled crayfish or lobster tail
30g (1.5oz) dried bonito flakes
Foraged sea lettuce, sliced in strips (can substitute other edible seaweed)
4 tbsp white or yellow miso paste

OPTIONAL GARNISHES

Lavash bread, toasted
Edible flowers and leaves—such as nasturtium, borage, beefsteak (shiso)
Squid ink lace tuile (see Sauces and Accompaniments)
Ikura (salmon roe)

METHOD

Rehydrate the kombu kelp overnight.

Add kombu, water and fish stock to a large pot.

Heat the mixture on a medium heat, but do not let it boil—this is vital! Let sit for about 5 minutes.

When the liquid is close to boiling, add the lobster. If you want clearer miso, poach the lobster separately and add it once cooked (see Guide to Lobster Diving).

Add the bonito flakes and after a minute reduce the temperature to minimum.

Leave this to steep for 10 minutes.

Strain the broth using a fine sieve. Save the lobster to be added at the end.

Add the sea lettuce and miso paste to the broth.

Roll a piece of lobster tail in shiso leaves (optional) and place in a serving bowl, cover with the broth and then garnish.

GARNISH

Using a sharp knife and a stencil, cut out an interesting shape from the lavash bread.

Lightly coat it in oil and broil (grill) it until just golden brown.

Place bread on the lobster, decorate with flowers, leaves or salmon roe.

SPEARO CHEF

Eric Keener
@finandforage

CORAL TROUT LAKSA

This laksa uses coral trout, however a variety of firm white fleshed fish can be substituted. We regularly use spangled emperor, spanish mackerel, and mangrove jack. This recipe is super easy to make and ideal for a fast mid-week dinner. In addition to being a healthy and filling seafood recipe, it's ideal for warming up on a cold evening.

COOK TIME 30 MIN | SERVES 2
Coral trout

INGREDIENTS

2 brown onions (yellow onion)
3 cloves of garlic
1 large red chilli
Several mushrooms
4 spring onions (scallions)
1 tbsp olive oil (alternatives ok)
4 tsp (20ml or 0.5fl oz) of laksa paste
1 can (400ml or 13.5 fl oz) can of coconut cream
500g (1lbs or 17oz) coral trout fillets and skins per person
Half a packet of thick rice noodles
2 cups (500ml or 17fl oz) beef stock
2 limes
1 bunch of coriander (cilantro)

METHOD

Thinly slice brown onions, garlic, chilli, mushrooms, and pale ends of the spring onions. Reserve some chilli and spring onion for garnish.

Heat oil in a wok or sauté pan. Brown the onion mixture.

Add laksa paste and fry until fragrant.

Add the coconut cream to the wok and simmer until thickened.

Cube the flesh into large chunks and slice the skin into small strips.

Place rice noodles into a bowl with boiling water and leave to soften for 5 minutes.

Add beef stock to wok and simmer before adding the fish chunks.

Cook until the fish has turned opaque.

Add the cooked rice noodles.

In a separate pan, flash fry the strips of trout skin until golden and crispy.

Serve the laksa over the cooked noodles in a large bowl Top with remaining chilli, spring onions, and coriander (cilantro).

Add a generous squeeze of lime juice and top with crispy trout skins.

Enjoy!

SPEARO CHEF

Ben Rennie
@benrennie

ALTERNATIVE SPECIES

Any firm white fleshed fish is well suited. It is a suitable recipe for stronger flavoured fish

OCTOPUS TOM YUM

Tom yum soup usually uses prawns as the main protein, but octopus works a treat as an addition or as an alternative. Octopus can turn tough if overcooked. Freezing them for a week helps tenderise them. The soup is easily made but if Tom yum paste is readily available, use it.

COOK TIME 30 MIN | SERVES 2
Octopus

INGREDIENTS

350g (12oz) whole prawns
750ml (3 cups) water
125ml (½ cup) chicken stock
3 lemongrass stalks, crushed
3 slices galangal*
5 kaffir lime leaves, crushed
2 chillies, preferably birds eye
3 cloves of garlic, minced
120g (4oz) mushrooms, preferably oyster
1 tomato, diced
½ onion, sliced
1 octopus, cleaned and if desired, cut into bite sized pieces
3 tbsp lime juice
1 tsp sugar
3 tbsp fish sauce
Coriander (cilantro)

*The best substitute for galangal is to use 1 tbsp fresh ginger root with ¼ tsp fresh lemon juice

METHOD

Shell the prawns.

Place water and chicken stock in a pot.

Add prawn heads and shells, lemongrass, galangal, kaffir lime leaves, chilies and garlic.

Simmer for 10 minutes.

Strain the broth.

Add mushrooms, tomato and onions to the broth and simmer for 4 minutes.

Add prawns and octopus and simmer for 1 minute.

Add lime juice and adjust the taste to suit.

Garnish with coriander.

If tom yum paste is readily available, make the soup with it according to instructions and then add the mushrooms, tomato, onion and octopus.

SPEARO CHEF

Deryck Tan
@deryck.gyotaku

ALTERNATIVE SPECIES

Squid, cuttlefish

CAMPFIRE MUSSELS

This is a classic recipe and has got to be one of my favourite—so quick and easy! It is something you can even do over a campfire. You could spice it up by trying to forage some wild parsley or samphire found growing near the mussels. This buttery sauce combined with the mussels' own brine goes perfectly with some crusty bread after a big day out.

COOK TIME 30 MIN | SERVES 2
Mussels

INGREDIENTS

Mussels
Oil for frying
4 shallots or 1 brown onion
250g (9 oz) butter
1 full head of garlic
½ bottle of oaky chardonnay (white wine)
Continental parsley or wild foraged parsley
Baguette or other crusty bread to serve

METHOD

Clean your mussels—scrape and debeard with an old knife. Discard any which will not stay closed.

Heat some oil in a large saucepan. Fry the diced onion.

When the onion starts to brown, add butter and move the pot to a part of the fire with just a few coals until the onion and garlic turn translucent.

Add minced garlic. Cook until fragrant.

Pour in half a bottle of Chardonnay and move pot back over the hotter coals. Reduce wine for a couple of minutes.

Add mussels to the saucepan.

Pull the saucepan to the edge of the fire and continue to simmer. Roughly chop parsley.

Once the mussels have opened, stir in the parsley.

Discard any mussels which have not opened.

Serve with the crusty bread.

CATCH, COOK & SHARE

Don't forget to share your cooking if you decide to recreate one of the recipes from our spearo chefs. Tag the spearo and use #99spearorecipes

SPEARO CHEF

Josh Bollen
@bosh.jollen

CEPHALOPOD BOLO

Spaghetti bolognese (bolo) is an Aussie favourite. It is not always made from scratch or with seafood but it's extremely easy to make, damn delicious and can bulk up the freezer for an easy meal after a long day. When I was cooking in New York, we had a similar way of processing octopus for one of our pasta dishes. I thought it would make a perfect substitute for the traditional meat used in a bolo.

This is pretty much the same technique you would use for a regular bolo but with octopus, squid or cuttlefish. I've used all three together and each individually as well.

COOK TIME 60 MIN | SERVES 2-4
One or a mix of octopus/squid/cuttlefish

INGREDIENTS

1.5kg (3.3lb) minced cephalopods—octopus, cuttlefish and/or squid
2 tbsp olive oil
2 large brown onions, diced
1 large carrot, diced
1 stalk of celery, diced
6 large garlic cloves, crushed
2 tbsp chopped parsley
350ml red wine (12fl oz/1.5 cups or roughly a half bottle)—get something that's not too shit so you can have a couple glasses while you wait
2 tins of crushed tomato
1 tbsp tomato paste
2 bay leaves
Salt and pepper to taste (add each little by little, tasting each time, so you don't stuff it up)
Finely grated hard cheese eg. parmesan (optional)

METHOD

Clean the fresh octopus, squid or cuttlefish well.

Chop up into small pieces and then, with a table top meat mincer, mince the meat (alternatively use a food processor or dice extremely finely).

In a large pot, add a little oil to coat the bottom. Fry off the cephalopods until most of the liquid has evaporated.

Remove mixture and set aside. In the same pot add a bit more oil and brown off the diced veggies.

Once the veggies are soft and evenly browned, turn up the heat and deglaze with red wine.

Cook off the wine, until it is almost dry on the base of the pan.

Add tins of tomato and tomato paste, bay leaves, salt and pepper and the cephalopod meat (add stock or water if the consistency is not runny enough).

Bring to a simmer and let ride for 2 hours.

When almost ready, boil some salted water and cook your preferred pasta until al-dente. Drain the pasta.

Use the sauce as you would a regular bolo, topping the pasta with as much as you'd like, and serve with grated hard cheese if you please (I love pecorino pepato—a pure sheep's milk cheese from Sicily that is flavoured with whole black peppercorns).

SPEARO CHEF

Eli Ravines
@Aquaholic173

ALTERNATIVE SPECIES

Octopus, squid, cuttlefish

ARIKI BOAT CURRY

I'm a self-confessed sub-par spearo, but a self-professed above-par cook, and I try my best to make the most of my catch. This curry can be cooked with any fish but for me it was actually best with an ocellated rock cod (whitespotted grouper - *Epinephelus coeruleopunctatus*) I shot at St. Bees Island just out from Mackay.

As someone who spends a lot of time out at sea, my recipes usually start with fresh or raw ingredients and as time goes on the curries come out. This one gets used when my vegetables are starting to wilt and we are trying to make the best of them as we look forward to our next sight of land.

COOK TIME 30 MIN | SERVES 2
Grey mackerel

INGREDIENTS

500g (1lbs) grey mackerel or ocellated rockcod
1 red onion
3 cloves of garlic
3 thumb sized pieces of ginger
Desiccated coconut and a sachet of powdered coconut milk
4 hot chillies
2 limes
300g (10.5oz) okra (or not if you can't find it)
1 carrot
1 red capsicum
Palm sugar
2 tbsp fish sauce
Turmeric, cumin, more chilli, fennel seeds
1 cup of rice (220g/7.5oz)

METHOD

Fillet and turn into 1in (2cm) cubes. Chop onions, garlic and ginger. Make sure you chop roughly as it's a boat curry, nothing should be perfect!

More ginger and garlic than appropriate should be used, as there's nothing subtle about boat curry. Chillies too! Take a dollop of coconut oil from the tin and chuck it all in a pot for a bit.

Add whatever spices you can find on the boat. Make a mental note to buy more next time. Then forget!

Add coconut milk. I have sachets of powdered coconut milk to save on space and rubbish, so I just add that and top-up later. Also, add dessicated coconut.

Then whatever fruit and veg is going off next. I found okra in the shops once in London and had the best curry ever. Roughly chopped okra with red capsicum is used here.

Add the coconut, palm sugar and fish sauce.

Quarter the lime and squeeze it in. Also add the limes too as I like people finding lime quarters in their curry. Cook till the veg is hot.

Add fish and pay as much attention to the fish as you would if the sharks were circling. Actually, once it's half cooked it's cooked. Take the pan out somewhere else with the lid on. It'll cook through with the residual heat.

Cook rice. Flatbreads in the pan are better. Serve with even more lime wedges. Cold beers first then warm beers.

SPEARO CHEF

Henry Hunter
@henbomb86

ALTERNATIVE SPECIES

Mackerel, cod, grouper

MID-SPEAR, 2 MIN FISH RAMEN

Winters in Sydney really aren't too bad, but after three hours in 16°C (60°F) water with a stiff southerly, I need a mid-dive hot meal recharge to keep me going for another three. Looking for the simplest way to have hot food on my spearo jetski led me to this dependable 2-minute noodles/ramen adaptation. Boil up some water, drop in some fish bits and you're good to go. With a few minor extras, this meal becomes a go-to feast!

COOK TIME 5 MIN | SERVES 1
Yellowfin bream

INGREDIENTS

THE BASICS

150g (5oz) fresh caught fish (anything will do)
250ml (9fl oz/1 cup) fresh water to boil
2-minute noodles, cup pack

MAKE IT BETTER

100g (3.5oz) broccolini (or whatever veg you're into)
Lemon wedges
Soy sauce
Wasabi

EQUIPMENT

Jetboil/camp stove to boil water
Fork, or noodles with a fork packed in them
Dive knife/fillet knife

METHOD

FISH AND BITS

Cut your fish into strips about the size of your little finger.

Squeeze a little lemon juice over the strips (pre-cooks it a bit).

Mix up a bit of soy and wasabi and have one of the strips as a little sashimi starter before the main event.

Chop the broccolini (pre-chop if you're clever).

Put your water on to boil.

NOODLES

This is good with any 2-minute noodles, they're all the same noodles, just the flavour sachets are different. Tom yum style is a winner for me.

Open up your 2-minute noodles, with the lid only half off.

Don't forget to feel bitter shame and guilt as you unveil the plastic packaging nightmare of convenience within.

Take out the sachets and add your broccolini on top of the noodles. Layering is everything.

Get ready to add the flavour. Rather than faffing around trying to open the little plastic sachets, just roll them together and cut them all open with a knife in one hit.

Pour all your flavour sachets in, on top of the broccolini (you're right—this is going to be freakin awesome!).

THE POUR

Pretty easy stuff really, just make sure your water is properly boiling so that it's as hot as it can be to the end.

If you've put some lemon juice on earlier, then the fish will have already started cooking. If not, make sure your bits are thin enough to cook through.

For some extra flavour, throw a wedge of lemon into the cup. The hot water will bring out the oil in the rind, giving it that amazing sour flavour you're always surprised you like.

Leave it to sit with the lid on for 2-3 minutes to cook through.

This is the time you'll realise you've forgotten a fork—it's all cool, just swish around with your dive knife to break it up, then chug it down straight from the cup!

If you're doing this at home, put it in a bowl and gram it on to Insty so all your mates know how clever you are.

SPEARO CHEF

David McGowan
@davidjamesmcgowan

ALTERNATIVE SPECIES

Silver trevally, anything that holds itself well in a soup

JETBOIL
Instant Cup Noodles
わさび

Instant Cup Noodles
Mi goreng
Fried Noodles
NET WEIGHT 75g

A GUIDE TO SEA URCHINS

Cornerstone Content Guide

Written by Spencer Allen
@el_spencerino

Considered by some to be an adventurous, texturally dubious culinary choice, sea urchin (uni) roe (technically the reproductive organs themselves, but roe just sounds nicer) is widely seen as a delicacy of the highest order worldwide.

Where one might pay market price for a single order of sushi, you can simply walk into the water and have yours in a single dive.

GUIDE TO SEA URCHIN

Spearfishing is a downright difficult sport. It can take a lot of effort, especially in the beginning, to find any gratification. This is why it can be important to celebrate the small wins where you can find them. For me, there's no bigger small win than the red and purple sea urchin of Southern California, also known globally as sea biscuits, uni, kina or sea hedgehogs.

Depending on where you live, it's good to know when the spawn occurs, as the yield is often better leading up to the event (March-April in Southern California, or late June/July to August in Eastern Australia) and diminished afterward.

Keeping the sea urchin out of the water is pretty easy. First of all, don't put them directly on ice as freshwater and extreme cold will kill them pretty quickly. So long as they're kept damp, they can survive in the cooler overnight, and then in the refrigerator in a bowl for a couple of days.

You'll want to keep them alive until right before you crack and serve them, as the shelf life of the roe is pretty short.

Sea urchin roe can be served in a number of ways, but the first focus here is on the actual preperation from shell to serving.

PREPARATION

I like to set up my work station with the following:
- Clean cutting board
- Kitchen shears
- 2 soup spoons
- 1 teaspoon
- Large bowl for waste while cleaning
- 2 small bowls for rinsing the roe.
- Salt

First, fill two small bowls with ice water, one with a solution of saltwater and the other freshwater.

On the underside of a sea urchin, you'll find a soft place in the middle with a 5 pointed beak. Cut around the outer edge of the soft spot with your kitchen shears, then remove the beak and the bone structure, known as Aristotle's lantern.

Drain the shell of any excess liquid, and with the shears make cuts on either side of the opening directly across from one another (eg. at the 12 and 6 o'clock position), about halfway to the outer edge of the shell. This should make just enough room that you can insert two soup spoons facing away from each other as pictured. Squeeze the handles together and that should break the shell in half.

Spaced equally apart, you'll find five sets of golden colored roe inside the shell. Very carefully, using a spoon small enough to fit the contour of the shell, scrape away the roe. Then very delicately, you will pull away the viscera from the roe. Starting out, it's pretty normal to accidentally rupture some.

It's about as delicate a process as separating egg whites, only on a much smaller scale and even more tedious.

Place roe in the salty ice water as you finish cleaning away the viscera. It doesn't have to be 100% clean for this part, as the ice water bath will firm up the roe and make it easier when you transfer it to the freshwater for the final rinse.

Once fully cleaned in the final freshwater rinse and place on a paper towel to dry.

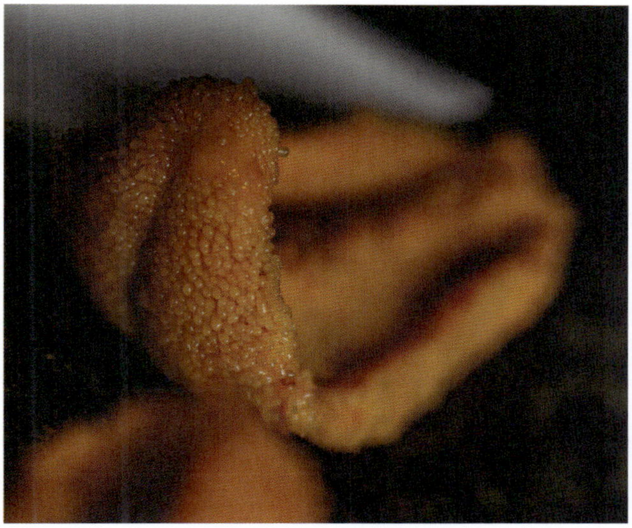

SEA URCHIN RECIPES

Uni is pretty amazing by itself. Southern California sea urchin is remarkably sweet, with a subtle, oceanic umami flavour.

The majority of the time I don't gild the lily at all, and just eat it on its own. It's also great on toasted nori or sushi style.

Sea urchin also makes a great complement to just about any fish crudo, and I'll often use it as a final garnish to a ceviche or sashimi. To this day, the best I've ever had was on top of a piece of fatty toro.

UNI BUTTER

If you want to go all-in, there are few better ways to eat urchin than as uni butter, especially on pasta. This is a remarkably simple recipe.

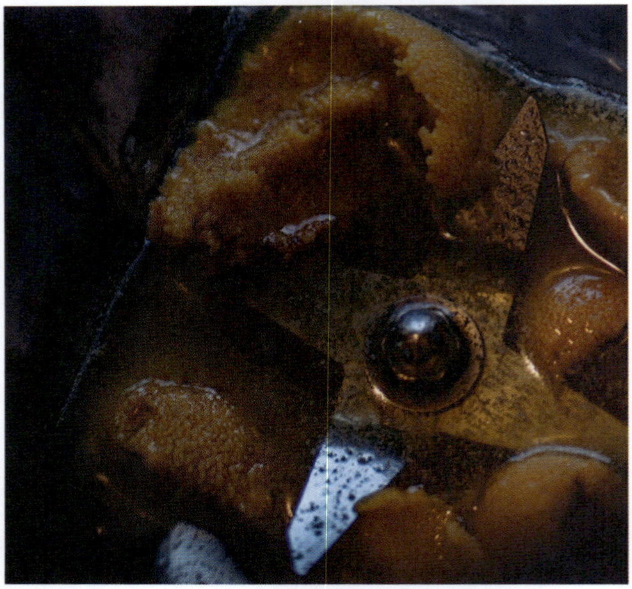

INGREDIENTS

- Half a stick of salted butter (¼ cup/2oz/56g)
- 5-7 pieces of urchin roe
- Squeeze of lemon (optional)

METHOD

First up, melt the butter in a saucepan until just liquified.

Pour the butter into your chosen receptacle, add the roe, and vigorously whisk. Alternatively, put the ingredients in a food processor, or do like me and toss it in the blender on high until fully emulsified.

I find the blender really gets it nice and smooth, and this stuff to me is like oceanic hollandaise. In fact, I've been meaning to try it on a crab/fish cakes benedict or risotto? Just add uni butter.

For uni pasta, just boil up your choice of pasta (in this case I went with thin angel hair pasta) and toss with as much uni butter sauce as you like, then plate. I like to serve mine with a piece or two of uni roe as a topper, and a couple of turns of black pepper. I dare you to find a better pasta dish.

IT DOESN'T MATTER WHAT FISH I FIND OR CATCH AFTER A DAY OUT ON OR IN THE WATER, MY WIFE'S QUESTION WILL ALWAYS BE "DID YOU BRING ME UNI?" AND WITH GOOD REASON.

PASTA & RISOTTO

When you have a scarcity of ingredients I turn to pasta & risotto.

I have been fortunate enough to travel to Italy spearfishing and have experienced the wonder that is simple pasta. Often overcomplicated in western countries, bolognese doesn't even exist in Italy—the closest thing being ragù. As with most seafood dishes, simple can often lead us to fantastic results.

Only caught one crab or lobster? A stunning linguine will turn a small portion of crab meat into an entire main. Remember to keep the shells and frames of the fish you are cooking with the pasta. Simply boiling them down with some salt, peppercorns, onion, fennel and celery will give you a girthy stock.

Cook your pasta or rice in the stock to add turbo flavour to your dish. Remember, you can't really ruin a pasta dish—adapt to your local ingredients and taste buds!

SIX SPINE RAVIOLI

Pasta is an awesome way to use up any trimmings or lower quality pieces left over from the filleting process. Six spine is an awesome eating leatherjacket and the best I have come across on the coast of New South Wales (Australia). The quickest way to dispatch and clean leatherjackets is to cut down behind the "horn" until you break through the spine, avoiding the gut cavity. From here you can rip the head off with the offal attached, allowing you to remove the gut without puncturing anything and potentially tainting the meat. For this recipe, I prefer a regular filleting method as the head and frame make a great base for the sauce.

COOK TIME 20 MIN | SERVES 2
Six spine leatherjacket. Prior preparation req.

INGREDIENTS

PASTA DOUGH

200g (8oz) high protein flour
2 eggs

FILLING

Leatherjacket fillets, skinned and deboned
2 shallots or 1 brown onion
4 cloves of garlic
4 rashers of bacon
1 bunch of sage
Salt
Freshly granted parmesan (to taste)
Olive oil

SAUCE

50-100g (1.7-3.7oz) butter
2 cloves of garlic
2 leaves of sage
Leatherjacket head and frame
⅓ cup dry white wine

METHOD

PASTA DOUGH

Put the flour in a mixing bowl and make a well in it. Beat the eggs and pour them into the well. Slowly start incorporating the two, until they are fully combined into a dough.

Knead the dough for at least 20 mins, until it has a smooth and silky feel.

Cover your dough in cling wrap, and rest it in the fridge for a minimum of 30 mins.

FILLING

Cut the fillets into 1cm (½in) cubes. Slice your shallots (or onions) finely and roughly chop the garlic.

Heat a pan to medium heat. Cut the bacon into small strips and start to fry it.

When the bacon starts to render, add onions and garlic.

Once the garlic gets fragrant, throw the fish in the pan. Rip up the sage leaves and chuck them in. Add a pinch of salt.

Fry the fish until there is some colour on the outside, but don't cook it completely as it will cook further in the ravioli.

Take ingredients out of the pan and allow them to cool.

RAVIOLI

Roll the dough out to about 2mm (.05in) thick or 2nd setting from thinnest if you have a machine. You want to keep the sheets wide and long.

Using a teaspoon, place filling along the pasta sheet at even spacings of around 2cm (¾in) apart.

Sprinkle some freshly grated parmesan on top of each filling.

Fold your pasta sheet over onto itself and seal around each filling by pressing the sheets together, working from the folded edge and squeezing out any trapped air.

Slice ravioli along the seams. Boil a pot of water adding a pinch of salt and a splash of olive oil.

Add your ravioli to the boiling water and cook for 6-8 mins.

Test the ravioli—it's always worth sacrificing a few to make sure the rest are properly cooked.

SAUCE

In a pot, heat some butter. Add a couple of crushed garlic cloves and a pinch of sage.

Fry the leatherjacket bones and head until they begin to turn a golden colour. Deglaze the pan with the white wine and briefly let it simmer with the bones.

As the wine begins to reduce, add another tablespoon of butter to enrich the sauce. Once everything has reduced, take the pan off the heat.

SERVE

Drain the pasta and place back into its pot. Strain the sauce into the pasta pot and mix gently to coat.

Serve ravioli in bowls, topped with some fresh parmesan and enjoy!

SPEARO CHEF

Josh Bollen
@bosh.jollen

ALTERNATIVE SPECIES

Sergeant baker, red rock cod

CREAMY GARLIC AND CHILLI PIPI FETTUCCINE

Plebidonax deltoides, are a marine bivalve mollusc with a smooth wedge-shaped, cream to pale brown shell (sometimes slightly yellow or green and with pinky-purple bands) containing dark (often bluey-purple) meat.

They are found all around the Australian coast and are hand-harvested from the sand on low tide from beaches with good surf (from about 10cm or 4 in below the surface). A PVC pipe commonly used as a fishing rod holder makes the job a lot easier than digging with your hands! Commonly called 'pipis'—other names include beach pip, clam, coorong cockle, eugarie, goolwa cockle, pippie, ugari.

COOK TIME 30 MIN | SERVES 2-4
Pipis'

INGREDIENTS

1kg (2.2lbs) live pipis (purged)
½ packet fettuccine (an alternative is to replace with crusty bread)
1 tbsp olive oil
1 tbsp butter
4 spring onions (scallions), finally chopped
4 garlic cloves (crushed)
1-2 tsp freshly chopped chilli (to taste)
175ml (¾ cup/6fl oz) sauvignon blanc
½ cup continental parsley, finely chopped
60ml (¼ cup/2fl oz) thickened cream

SPEARO CHEF

Tim Hall
@walkerhilsdale

ALTERNATIVE SPECIES

Crayfish, prawn, scallops, bugs

METHOD

After harvesting the pipis, sit them in a bucket of cool, clean seawater for 24 hours (preferably refreshed every 12 hours) to allow the pipis to purge any sand. This step is critical to the success of the recipe and there is no shortcut. There is nothing worse than biting into sand!

In a large pot, bring water to the boil and add fettuccine. Cook until al-dente. Drain the water, stir through a splash of olive oil, and set aside.

In a large heavy-based saucepan, heat olive oil and butter over low heat.

Add spring onions and sauté for a couple of minutes. Add garlic and chilli and continue to cook until spring onions are translucent and soft.

Add wine and bring to a simmer. Reduce by about a third.

Add pipis, stir and cover with a lid. Cook for a couple of minutes until the pipis start to open.

Remove the lid and stir in parsley and cream. Continue to cook until all pipi shells have opened. As the pipi shells open, set them aside in a large bowl using a slotted spoon and cover with foil to keep warm. Discard any pipis that do not open.

Add pipis and sauce to the fettuccini and stir through on low heat.

Serve, garnished with freshly sliced spring onion, freshly cracked pepper and flakes of parmesan cheese.

UNI LINGUINE

Sea urchins can seem a daunting beast to try to eat, with sharp spines and hard shells. They are actually really easy to break into and collect the sea urchin roes—which are the part we eat. There are a number of methods of doing this, using a knife or pair of scissors, right up to specialist tools if you really love them!

The sea urchin roes can change flavour over the season, so it is always worth trying a few raw to make sure they are up to standard.

COOK TIME 20 MIN | SERVES 2
Sea urchins

INGREDIENTS

20 sea urchin roes (5 roe per urchin)
300g (10oz) dried linguine
2 tbsp vegetable oil
3 cloves of garlic, crushed or minced
80ml (⅓ cup/3fl oz) heavy cream
Salt and pepper
Chilli
Spring onions (scallions)

METHOD

Prepare linguine al-dente following the instructions on the packet.

Heat up a pan and add the oil and garlic, stirring until golden.

Pour in the cream and thicken for 2-3 minutes.

Carefully place in the sea urchin roes. Do your best to keep them whole.

Add the drained linguine and gently toss to mix all the ingredients.

Season with salt and pepper.

Transfer into a bowl and garnish with more sea urchin roes, cut chilli and spring onions.

STOCK TIPS

Fish or seafood stock make great additions to pasta or risotto. Large batches are simple to make and can be frozen for use as required.

SPEARO CHEF

Deryck Tan
@deryck.gyotaku

KINA CRAYBONARA

Before I knew how to grab lobsters, I used to grab sea urchins, or kina as they say in New Zealand. I think they're delicious. Then I learned to grab lobsters, and voilà, a culinary match made in heaven. The subtle ocean taste of the kina against the sweet, beautiful, buttery lobster flesh is one of my all time favourites.

COOK TIME 30 MIN | SERVES 2
Rock lobster, sea urchin (kina/uni)

INGREDIENTS

3 kina (sea urchin/uni)
1 rock lobster (600g/1.5lbs)
Linguine pasta
More butter than you think you need (start with at least 2 tbsp)
1 garlic clove, minced

METHOD

Cut your kina in half with a sharp knife or scissors and remove the 5 orange gonads/roe (15 in total). Place these in a bowl to the side.

Cook the whole lobster in a pot with boiling water (6-8 minutes for this size).

Remove the lobster and add your pasta to the boiling water.

Pull every last piece of lobster from the frame, especially the yellow meat in the head. Shred the flesh into bite sized portions.

In a frying pan over medium heat, melt a lot of butter and add the minced garlic, slowly stir for 2 minutes.

Mix the kina into the butter.

Once the pasta is al-dente, drain the water from the pan.

Stir the pasta in with the kina butter and lobster chunks.

Serve with the best view you can find.

LOBSTER TIPS

For tips on how to catch, prepare and cook lobster, make sure to check out pg. 168, How to Catch Lobster cornerstone content guide by James Sakker .

SPEARO CHEF

Henry Hunter
@henbomb86

ALTERNATIVE SPECIES

Other lobster species

LOBSTER FETTUCCINE

My wife finds garlic butter lobster too rich so this is a good way to make a meal out of it or can be used when you've eaten too many garlic butter lobsters and need some variety. Speaking of variety, I have made this recipe with blue swimmer crabs, mud crab, prawns, abalone and various types of lobster/crayfish, so it is seriously flexible and I find that I use whatever is in season—so crabs in summer and lobster/crays in winter and spring. Serve with a glass of chilled white wine, I prefer a semillon sauvignon blanc or pinot gris.

COOK TIME 30 MIN | SERVES 2
Eastern rock lobster

INGREDIENTS

3-4 shallots or small onions
2-3 garlic cloves
1 long red chilli
1 tin anchovies
1 punnet cherry tomatoes
1 bunch coriander aka cilantro (coriander stalks in the sauce and coriander leaves to garnish)
1-2 eastern rock lobsters depending on size (average size we get is 700g-1kg/1.5-2lbs)
1 tbsp olive oil
2 cups vegetable or chicken stock
½ cup white wine
Salt and pepper to taste
500g (1lbs) packet fettuccine or linguine pasta (fresh is better)
Parmesan cheese

METHOD

Get a big pot and start to boil the salted water for the crays.

Whilst waiting for that to boil, prepare all the other ingredients.

Finely chop all the shallots, garlic, and chilli and place in a bowl. In another bowl, repeat with the anchovies and the tomatoes.

Take off coriander stalks, finely slice and add to pasta sauce.

Once the water is boiling, put the crays in for 7 mins to cook.

Once they are cooked, pull them out and place in a slurry of ice and cold water to stop them from overcooking.

Clean all the meat out, it should be slightly underdone and opaque in the middle—this is so once it gets tossed through the pasta sauce it will cook to perfection and not be overdone.

Put this to one side.

In a large pan, put a good slug of olive oil in and once hot, add the shallots/onions, garlic and chilli for 1-2 mins.

Then add the anchovies, tomatoes and coriander stalks.

After another 1-2 mins add the stock and white wine. Simmer until the liquid is reduced by about half. Usually about 10 mins on low. Season to taste.

Whilst you are doing this, boil some salted water for the pasta. The benefit of using fresh pasta is it only takes 4-5 mins to cook, and results in a better texture.

Once the pasta is almost done and the sauce is reduced, add the cray meat for a couple of minutes and stir through.

Drain the pasta and then place in a serving bowl, pour over the cray and pasta sauce and stir through with the roughly chopped fresh coriander.

Season to taste, add some parmesan cheese and serve.

SPEARO CHEF

Alex Hamilton
@alex.hamilton1979

ALTERNATIVE SPECIES

Abalone, blue swimmer crab, mud crab or any other type of crayfish or prawns

SPEARO CRAYFISH PASTA

This is an awesome recipe that will make you look and feel like a way better chef than you actually are. Trust me, it's a great Sunday night special or if you don't do the cray head broth, you can slap this together after a long spearfishing day at the reef within 20 mins. So why not be the star of your own catch and cook show within your own household and put the kids to bed early, if you know what I mean.

COOK TIME 20 MIN | SERVES 4
Rock lobster

INGREDIENTS

1 Rock lobster
Olive oil
Garlic cloves
1 birds eye chilli
Salt and pepper
1 cup chives
1 cup white wine
1 cup chicken stock
1 cup trident chilli sauce
1 tbsp cornflour
Egg pasta (enough for 4 people)
Parsley

METHOD

Start by separating the tail from the head of the world's most unluckiest crayfish you speared (or caught, this is dependent on your local regulations) the day before.

I like to semi-freeze or semi-thaw the crayfish as it helps with the shelling and cubing process of the tail.

Separate the guts and anything non-white from the head of the crayfish and chop off the feelers and simmer for a couple of hours in a pot to make cray stock.

Break up cray feelers and legs for entree.

Start the fry pan about the size of a groupers head on medium heat with a dash of outboard oil (olive oil) to lube the finely burley size pieces of crayfish as they quick sear in the pan, but just remember the crayfish's dive buddies, the finely chopped garlic clove and birds eye chilli, only add a couple of bird eyes as he's a newcomer to the dive crew and less experienced, add salt and pepper and only sear for a minute or so and set aside whilst throwing in the chives and stirring through.

In the saucepan add the following, one cup of white wine.

One cup of chicken stock and two cups of the cray stock that you strained from the earlier simmering.

A couple of yacht club sized nips of trident sauce. Another dash of outboard oil.

Chopped clove of garlic. Salt and pepper.

Simmer for at least an hour to make the crew become closer dive buddies and be at one with each other.

Thicken a touch with some cornflour to give the brew a saucy texture.

Ask your neighbour to borrow his boat (spaghetti pot) and let the lobster boil on the surface then chuck in the sea worms (egg pasta).

Once cooked throw in a touch of outboard oil, finely chopped parsley and chives and stir through the sieved and strained pasta.

Serve up your bowl of sea worms by adding the seared crayfish to the top and pouring the burleigh sauce over the top.

SPEARO CHEF

Tony 'Taz' Alcock
@tazyarns

ALTERNATIVE SPECIES

Crab or other lobster

GARLIC BUTTER PASTA IN A HURRY

This is a great dish to eat on the beach or on the boat as most of the work is done before the trip. It is an awesome way to fill up the crew quickly and it's super delicious as well.

COOK TIME 15 MIN | SERVES 2
Squid and red morwong. Prior preparation req.

INGREDIENTS

250g (9oz) pasta
1 tbsp olive oil
150g (5oz) butter
2 garlic cloves, minced
1 lemon, zested
½ cup chopped parsley
Salt and pepper to taste
1 squid
1 red morwong

METHOD

PREPARATION AT HOME

Cook the pasta as per the directions on the pack.

When it is cooked, run the pasta under cold water to stop the cooking process.

Drizzle 1 tbsp olive oil over the pasta and mix it through.

Store the pasta in a container.

Soften the butter and add the garlic, lemon zest, parsley and salt and pepper.

Store mixture in a separate container.

Pop these 2 containers into the esky ready for later.

ON THE BEACH OR BOAT

Chop the squid and fish into bite sized pieces.

Add a tablespoon of the garlic butter to a hot pan and cook the fish for 1 minute.

Add the squid and the rest of the butter and cook for another minute.

Add the pasta and cook until it's warmed through.

Serve and eat with a huge grin!

SPEARO CHEF

Yianni Barthelmess
@huntfishgrowcook

ALTERNATIVE SPECIES

Any seafood at all. That's the beauty of this dish

SPIDER CRAB LINGUINE

Spider crabs (UK) head to the shallows of Europe during the springtime. They can be found in massive breeding congregations in very shallow water. This makes them ideal for divers of all skill levels to target the males with large claws. In the UK they are regularly found in excess of 2 kg. You can use any crab for this recipe but I find the spiders to be particularly sweet and flavourful. However, it's a tedious task to pick out the meat.

COOK TIME 30 MIN | SERVES 2-4
Spider crab

INGREDIENTS

Picked meat from 1 large crab
50ml (1.7fl oz) olive oil
50g (1.7oz) ghee
8 garlic cloves
1 hot red chilli
4 spring onions or 1 echalion shallot
250g (9oz) dried linguine pasta (half a packet usually)
½ cup finely chopped parsley
2 lemons (one for juicing and the other for wedges)

METHOD

PICK THE CRAB MEAT

Boil the crab in a large pot of heavily salted water (as salty as the sea, 35g/L or 4.7oz/gal). For a 1.5kg (3lbs) crab, 8 minutes is usually enough to allow the meat to be easily picked. Start the timer once the water has reached a rolling boil again after the crab has been added.

Remove the crab from the boiling water and plunge into an ice bath to stop the cooking process. Pick all the meat from the legs, claws and body. You can use the brown meat as well for that turbo-crab flavour.

LINGUINE

Start by cooking the linguine according to the packet instructions.

Meanwhile, in a large saucepan or wok, add the olive oil, ghee, roughly chopped garlic, finely chopped chilli (seeds included if you like it spicy) and finely chopped spring onions.

Bring to a low to medium heat until the ingredients soften and the flavours permeate through the oil and ghee mix.

Once the pasta is al-dente, drain and keep the pasta cooking water.

Add the linguine to the frying pan and thoroughly mix to coat all the linguine.

Increase the heat and fold in the crab meat, parsley and the juice of one lemon until it is all mixed through. Add a few tablespoons of the pasta water to the mix to keep it from drying out and becoming sticky.

Garnish with more parsley and a lemon wedge.

Serve with a glass of bubbles and candles on the table.

SPEARO CHEF

Daniel Mann
@daniel___mann

ALTERNATIVE SPECIES

Any crab

SOUTHERN CRAY SPAGHETTI IN BACON & TOMATO CREAM

Everyone needs a quick and easy pasta that will work with any seafood. This is mine. The king of seafood—crayfish or lobster can be easily replaced with whatever you have, but the traditional flavours and rich cream are always a winner. And everything's better with bacon...

COOK TIME 30 MIN | SERVES 2
Lobster

INGREDIENTS

1 southern crayfish (southern rock lobster)
2 tbsp olive oil
150g (5oz) butter
½ chopped onion
2 chopped garlic cloves
200g (7oz) smoked bacon diced
300ml (10fl oz/1 ¼ cups) cream
400g (14oz) tinned cherry tomato
300g (10oz) spaghetti
¼ cup chopped parsley
Salt and pepper

METHOD

Lightly poach the crayfish in salted boiling water for 5 minutes then pop it in cold water. It should be firm enough to remove the meat from the shell, but not fully cooked.

Remove the crayfish meat from the shell and chop it into pieces.

Heat a pan to a high temperature. Add some olive oil and fry the lobster meat until it gets some colour.

Remove from the pan. Keep this to one side.

Allow the pan to cool a touch and add a little more olive oil.

Fry the onion and garlic until the onion softens.

Add the bacon and cook for 5 minutes.

Add the butter. Once melted, stir in the tomatoes.

Pour in the cream, season with salt and pepper. Allow the sauce to thicken.

Cook the spaghetti according to the instructions on the packet.

Drain and add the spaghetti to the pan and toss it through the sauce.

Return the cooked crayfish and stir through the mixture.

Top with the parsley and serve.

SPEARO CHEF

Yianni Barthelmess
@huntfishgrowcook

CRAYFISH RISOTTO

In this recipe we used two eastern rock lobster (*Sagmariasus verreauxi*) and one slipper lobster (*Scyllaridae*), which were all caught on a trip out to one of the NSW Central Coast's headlands. The eastern rock lobster seems to prefer shallower, weedy bottoms. Whereas slipper lobster tends to be found in vertical cracks on deeper ledges. This dish requires a little bit of focus and patience, as you stir in the stock and poach your lobster tails. To help the time pass, we recommend doing so with a beer in hand; which will also be the perfect pairing with your meal. This dish is best to serve when you really want to impress your friends.

COOK TIME 30 MIN | SERVES 2-4
Crayfish

INGREDIENTS

CRAYFISH STOCK
Crayfish shells
3l (12 ½ cups) water
3 tsp chicken stock powder
2 tsp paprika (we like smoked)
2 cloves of garlic, finely chopped

POACHED CRAYFISH TAILS
½ cup water
4 cloves of garlic, finely chopped
3 sprigs of thyme
240g (10oz) butter, chilled and cubed
3 crayfish (lobster) tails

RISOTTO
3 French shallots, finely chopped
3 cups arborio rice
1 cup white wine
½ cup freshly grated parmesan
Salt and pepper to taste
Spring onions (scallions)/chives to serve

METHOD

Boil the water in a large stock pot and submerge each crayfish separately for approximately 2 minutes (until the shell turns red), then cool each crayfish under cold tap water. Leave the water boiling, as this will be used for the stock.

Remove the tail from the crayfish by running a knife around the joint between the tail and carapace. Using scissors, cut up the underside of the tail and then through the top of the shell also. The cray meat should fall or pull easily away from the shell.

Slice the cray meat into hearty chunks. The tails should have natural segments in them and these are great to follow.

Return all discarded shells (including heads) to the boiling water. Keep an eye on these. After a couple more minutes in the boiling water, you can remove the heads and legs again for a delicious snack while you continue to cook. Make sure you put the shells back in after the nibbling session.

Add all the stock ingredients—chicken stock powder, paprika and garlic and leave to simmer (occasionally stirring), while you get on with the rest of the recipe.

In a small saucepan over medium heat, simmer ½ cup of water, chopped garlic cloves and thyme.

Lower the heat and begin to whisk in cubes of butter one at a time until completely dissolved. The idea is to not let the butter boil and emulsify, but it's not the end of the world if it does.

Once all the butter is dissolved, add the cray chunks and continue to stir, as this will poach the meat. Turn the heat off once the meat turns white.

In a large wok/fry pan, add a generous dollop of the crayfish butter (avoid transferring the meat). Once it starts to sizzle and coat the pan, sauté the french shallots until they have softened.

Add the arborio rice and stir through until slightly toasted.

Your stock should still be bubbling away and you can now add a ladle of it to the rice and stir through, along with the white wine.

Continue to stir and add stock a ladle at a time. As the rice absorbs the stock, continue this process.

After 15-20 mins and having used most of the stock, your rice should be mostly cooked. At this step, add the remainder of your crayfish chunks, along with the rest of the butter, parmesan and stir through. Taste and season with salt and pepper.

Serve with chopped spring onions or chives, with some more grated parmesan.

SPEARO CHEF

Jordan McComb
@jordan_kiwi

ALTERNATIVE SPECIES

Any lobster/crayfish species or red rock cod

MIXED BAG

After a long day spearfishing, you may not have shot that target species, but you didn't come home empty. You brought home that mixed bag of fish that know you can make a delicious meal from.

This section represents that mixed bag. Recipes that don't exclusively fit within the other categories. These recipes lend well to various species, so get creative and checkout our alternative species suggestions in the glossary.

From Japanese seafood pancakes to the humble burger, this section is for you.

YELLOWTAIL KATSU SANDO

While it may just be seen as bait to some, the humble yakka is incredible eating. Smaller specimens lend themselves to butterflying and grilling while larger ones can even be used in sashimi dishes, much the same as trevallies as they are actually in the same family of fishes (*Carangidae*). Shooting yakka makes for some awesome target practice as well. Dialing your aim in for headshots is the key to not ruining your fillets. Save your bone scraps to make stock or ramen.

COOK TIME 20 MIN | SERVES 2
2 yellowtail yakka's

INGREDIENTS

Butterflied yakka
Lemon for zest and juice
Dill pickles
Capers
Dill or chives
Whole egg mayonnaise
½ cup flour
1 egg per yakka
Panko crumbs
Oil for shallow frying
Milk bread (any soft, fluffy white bread is good)
Chinese cabbage

METHOD

BUTTERFLY THE YAKKA

Slice in through the belly on either side of the spine working towards the head. Slice the meat off the spine working from belly to topside of fish. Stop before you reach the very top of the fish under its dorsal fins.

Separate the meat down to the tail on each side. Use a heavy bladed knife and crack the head in half from the chin side.

Grab your kitchen scissors and cut the spine of the fish near the base of the tail. Snip your way to the head of the fish breaking the spine bones just below the skin.

Cut through the spine just behind the head. Remove the spine and flip fish over, use your palm to flatten out the head.

Again, flip your fish and find the belly area. Slide your knife in behind the tiny rib bones that come down each side behind the wings and follow them to the belly. Save all your offcuts for stock or ramen.

SAUCE

Zest the lemon. Cut a lemon in half and put it aside. Rough chop a pickle, a few capers and a bunch of dill or chives, whichever you prefer.

Slap a tablespoon of whole egg mayo into a small bowl and add a pinch of lemon zest, a small squeeze of lemon juice and a sprinkle of the chopped pickles, capers and dill.

Mix it through and give it a try. Add more ingredients however you see fit.

CRUMB

Chuck some flour on a plate. Beat the egg(s) and pour them into a shallow dish. Cover another plate with panko crumbs.

Cover the yakka with flour and spread the butterfly out to ensure everything has been dusted.

Put the yakka into the egg wash for a quick dip. Once all sides are covered, lay the yakka in the panko crumbs and flip it over making sure crumbs coat the whole fish.

For aesthetics and presentation, I like to wipe crumbs off the head at this point. Repeat this process for each yakka.

FRYING

Add a couple cm (½ inch) oil into the pan, enough that the fish is ¾ submerged when laid out.

Heat the oil until stray panko crumbs sizzle and bubble on impact. Give the pan another minute or two, we need it hot to make a crust quickly.

Lay the fish skin side down away from yourself in case there's any splashes (that's a painful lesson).

Once the crumbs around the edges have started to colour, flip the fish with a pair of tongs being careful not to snap off the crispy tail or head.

Another minute and take the fish out to cool on some paper towel on a drying rack. This will stop any of the crumbs becoming soggy. Salt and rest.

SANDO

Cut the crusts off white bread. Thinly slice Chinese cabbage. Dollop some sauce onto a slice of bread and spread.

Drop the butterflied yakka on top and stack on some cabbage. Dollop of sauce on the other slice and place it on top.

Grab your serrated knife and cut the sando into strips, careful not to squash the soft bread.

Lay each section sideways and stack across a plate. Enjoy!

SPEARO CHEF

Josh Bollen
@bosh.jollen

"LARGER ONES CAN EVEN BE USED IN SASHIMI DISHES, MUCH THE SAME AS TREVALLIES AS THEY ARE ACTUALLY IN THE SAME FAMILY OF FISHES"

Josh Bollen

ALTERNATIVE FISH

Whiting, small mackerels, other small fish

LOBSTER CAESAR SALAD

Lobster is what I use in this recipe and we catch them diving in shallow water by hand in winter, spring and early summer. This salad is very easy to make and is a fantastic lunch in warm weather.

COOK TIME 30 MIN | SERVES 2
Lobster

INGREDIENTS

1 boiled lobster
2 boiled eggs
2 rashers bacon
6 slices sourdough bread
1 tbsp olive oil
100g (3.5oz) parmesan cheese
1 cos lettuce
1 bottle (250-350ml/8-12oz) caesar salad dressing

METHOD

Remove the meat from the lobster and slice into medallions.

Boil the eggs until hard. Allow to cool and peel. Cut each egg into six segments.

Cut bacon into 25mm (1in) pieces and shallow fry until crispy. Drain on paper-towel and put aside.

Brush the sourdough slices with olive oil and bake in an oven, preheated to 180°C (356°F), until crispy.

Break into 25 mm (1in) pieces if you want to add them to the salad, or serve whole on the side.

Shave the parmesan cheese.

Tear the lettuce into pieces.

Combine the lobster, lettuce, cheese, egg and bacon in a large bowl.

Pour in half the bottle of salad dressing and combine with your hands.

Add the sourdough pieces.

Toss well and serve on a large plate.

LOBSTER TIP

Lobsters are great fun to hunt and a good way to learn to dive for kids. Lobsters will go to the same holes every year so try to remember good holes as they will be more productive.

SPEARO CHEF

James Sakker
Catch it Grow it Cook it

ALTERNATIVE SPECIES

Crab or prawns

LOBSTER COCKTAIL

Back in the 1970's the prawn cocktail was all the rage. This is my twist on that old classic. It's a simple, easy, lobster recipe that is great for summer. It can serve as an entree or makes an awesome light lunch. Very healthy and tasty with minimal ingredients letting the fresh seafood shine. So let's get retro.

COOK TIME 30 MIN | SERVES 2
Lobster

INGREDIENTS

1 small to medium eastern or southern rock lobster, boiled
1 large avocado
6 leaves cos lettuce

COCKTAIL SAUCE
2 tbsp quality mayonnaise - I prefer Thomy brand
2 tbsp tomato sauce
½ lemon, juiced
Splash of hot sauce - I prefer Tapatio or Cholula
Ground black pepper

METHOD

Fill a large pot with water and when the water is boiling, carefully lower your lobster into the water.

For a large lobster (1.5kg/3lbs) boil for approx 8-10 minutes.

For a smaller model 6-8 minutes is ample.

You want the meat cooked through but not overcooked! If it is undercooked and the meat is still translucent in the middle, don't panic.

Detach the tail, cut longways through the tail and pan fry the insides for an extra few minutes.

When the lobster is cooked, immediately chill your lobster in ice water. Rest for 2 minutes.

Remove the meat and cut the tail into medallions.

Make the cocktail sauce by mixing the mayonnaise, tomato sauce, hot sauce, lemon and some ground black pepper.

Cut the avocado in half, remove the stone. Place it on a bed of cos lettuce.

Place some cocktail sauce in the centre of the avocado and top this with the lobster meat. Add some more sauce as a topping.

Serve with some crusty bread, more of the sauce and a wedge of lemon on the side.

SPEARO CHEF

James Sakker
Catch it Grow it Cook it

ALTERNATIVE SPECIES

Crab or prawns

LOBSTER RICE PAPER ROLLS

Fresh herbs, tangy sauce and delicious eastern rock lobster make this dish a summertime favorite. It's very easy to make with fresh herbs from my garden and lobsters from the nearby ocean. I serve these versatile, tangy rolls as a starter, snack or light meal. You can make these rolls in advance of your meal, or for added fun, make them at the table.

COOK TIME 30 MIN | SERVES 2
Lobster

INGREDIENTS

Rice vermicelli noodles
Eastern rock lobster, boiled then chilled
Fresh herbs (e.g. thai basil, italian basil, cilantro, mint, sawtooth coriander)
Carrot, julienne
Cucumber, julienne
Vietnamese rice paper sheets

SAUCE

2 tbsp kewpie sesame mayonnaise
1 tbsp tamarind puree
½ lime, juiced

PREPARATION TIP

Rice paper rolls can dry out very quickly, ensure you serve immediately to get the best results.

METHOD

Soak the rice vermicelli noodles in hot water until tender, then rinse in cold water and drain.

Cut the cooked lobster meat into small pieces (5cm or 2in) and put it in a bowl.

Add the herbs to the bowl and mix well.

Cut the carrot and cucumber into julienne, or slice them with a peeler—the thinner the better.

Prepare the sauce by mixing the sesame mayonnaise, tamarind puree and lime juice.

Soak a sheet of rice paper for 60 seconds in warm water before adding the ingredients to it.

Prepare the roll by placing some noodles, vegetables, lobster and sauce in the centre of the rice paper sheet.

Fold in the sides and roll it up but be careful not to overfill each roll or it will fall apart!

Serve immediately.

SPEARO CHEF

James Sakker
Catch it Grow it Cook it

ALTERNATIVE SPECIES

Crab or prawns

CHICK-FIL-A COPYCAT BURGERS

Everyone told me that herring cale was a trash fish and not worth eating. I then came across a Ryan Myers video of him making Chick-Fil-A copycat burgers, and I planned to test just how trash these fish were. This dish will serve 4 people with 4 pieces of fish fillet the size of a burger patty, we serve with a side of chips and you're sure to win over any friends or family.

COOK TIME 20 MIN | SERVES 4
Herring cale

INGREDIENTS

BURGERS

4 brioche buns
4 burger patty-sized chunks of fish fillets
Iceberg lettuce
1 large tomato
6-8 medium gherkins sliced
Pickle juice (leftover juice from the jar of gherkins)
1 cup milk
1 egg
500ml (2 cups) peanut oil (don't substitute any other oil)
⅔ cup plain flour
1 tbsp caster sugar
1 tsp sea salt
½ tsp cracked black pepper

SAUCE

¼ cup of mayonnaise
¼ cup of bbq sauce - (I used Sweet Baby Ray's hickory and brown sugar)
2 tbsp of honey
1 tsp of lemon juice
1 tsp of mustard
¼ tsp of smoked paprika

METHOD

Take your burger-sized fish fillet pieces and place into the jar of pickle juice or into a large zip-lock bag and pour in the pickle juice. Place into the refrigerator for 30-45 mins.

Mix all the sauce ingredients in a bowl and store in the fridge. Slice up the gherkins and tomato.

Heat the peanut oil in a deep sided pan, or deep fryer. In a bowl, combine the milk and the egg until they are well mixed.

In a separate bowl, add your flour, caster sugar, sea salt and pepper, and mix together with a fork.

Remove the fish fillets from pickle juice and dunk into the bowl of milk and egg, then into the flour bowl and coat well. Re-dunk the fillet into the milk and egg and add a final coat of flour.

Place the fish into the oil and fry. Turn the fish, once the edges of the batter start to turn golden.

Cook till golden brown, remove from oil and place on a plate lined with a paper towel.

Cut the burger buns in half and place under the grill so the inside of the burger is facing up. Remove from the grill once they are lightly toasted.

Spread a generous layer of the imitation Chick-Fil-A sauce on the base of the bun. Place your beautiful, crispy fish piece on top of that followed by the gherkins, tomato and lettuce.

Serve with chips or waffle cut fries. Tell your friends and family what fish it was after they've eaten it so they can't pre-judge it before trying it if you are using something they would usually avoid!

SPEARO CHEF

Ben Hohnke
@hohnkeoutdoors

ALTERNATIVE SPECIES

Almost any fish with large white firm fillets, kingfish, jobfish (uku), mackerel, drummer, almost any fish

COASTAL OKONOMIYAKI

This savory pancake from Osaka, Japan is a perfect way to use up miscellaneous cuts from most things that you will catch in the ocean. After the base of the pancake, the possibilities for ingredients and toppings are endless. Using squid, cuttlefish or octopus cuts are some of my favourites. This recipe does not strictly follow Japanese cuisine, it is my own interpretation for a diver in a pinch. All you will need are a few extra pantry items that have multiple uses. Always experiment and try new ingredients!

COOK TIME 20 MIN | SERVES 2
Squid, cuttlefish or octopus

INGREDIENTS

PANCAKE

¼ Chinese cabbage (wombok)
Bunch of spring onions
½ cup all purpose flour
1 egg
Bonito flakes (katsuobushi)
Salt
Choice of protein (eg. cuttlefish, squid, crab, lobster, abalone, boneless fish trimming, octopus, tempura pieces, etc).

Note: Any meat products should be half cooked prior to cooking the pancake!

½ cup broth. This can be a dashi or fish stock, water from poached octopus, or tap water if nothing is available.

TOPPINGS

Okonomiyaki sauce (commonly found in asian supermarkets, can be substituted with kecap manis).
Kewpie mayo
Spring onions

Optional: seaweed (nori), bonito flakes, fried squid head, fried fish wing, pickled ginger etc.

METHOD

Remove stem from the cabbage and discard. Chop cabbage coarsely.

Chop spring onions thinly, up to where they start to turn a darker green.

Put cabbage in a large mixing bowl with flour, egg, spring onions and any other fillings.

Roughly stir to mix flour through.

Add the broth slowly while stirring through until you get a thick batter. Add flour if needed.

Pan fry the mix on a medium heat, scraping into the center.

Once a golden crust forms, flip the pancake on to other side—see note below.

Remove the pancake from the pan after another few minutes.

Drizzle sauces in a criss cross pattern. Sprinkle with spring onion and finish with any other ingredients you like.

Note: Flipping the pancake can be easier to do out of the pan between two plates sometimes. The crust will hold the pancake together so you can slide it back into the pan raw side down.

SPEARO CHEF

Josh Bollen
@bosh.jollen

ALTERNATIVE SPECIES

Crab, lobster, abalone, boneless fish trimmings

BONNIE BURGERS

This burger recipe is relatively simple but always a winner. I have found bonnie (bonito) or other types of tuna best for this recipe. The darker meat seems to lend itself better to the process. The key is cooking these burgers fast and hot to sear the outside while leaving the centre still juicy. Tuna can dry out extremely quickly and I always prefer to cook the burgers more under than overdone. If you are looking for an even juicier burger, you can experiment with mixing in ground pork fat to your patties.

COOK TIME 20 MIN | SERVES 2
Bonito

INGREDIENTS

BURGER

1 boneless, skinned bonito fillet
2 spring onions
4 tsp Chinese 5 spice
Brioche or other burger buns
Sliced cheese (processed cheeses work best for a classic smash burger)
Lettuce leaves (little gem variety is my favourite for the size of its leaves)
2 tbsp neutral oil for frying (e.g. rice bran oil, canola etc)
Salt

SAUCE

6 tbsp kewpie mayonnaise
2 tbsp tomato ketchup
1 dill pickle
1/2 white onion
1 tsp mustard

METHOD

SAUCE

Finely dice onion and pickle. Mix through kewpie mayonnaise, ketchup and mustard.

BURGER

Mince bonito meat—chop with a sharp knife until you can no longer see any chunks.

Finely chop spring onions, up to where the stems start turning a dark green.

Mix spring onions into tuna and slowly add the Chinese 5 spice. Portion mix for servings and roll into balls.

On a piece of parchment paper, squash each ball to form your burger patties.

Heat oil in a pan. You want to cook these burgers on a high heat. The tuna will overcook quickly so err on the side of caution!

Toast your burger buns in the pan or you can do them under the grill.

After 3 minutes check for a crust on the underside of the burger patties. Flip the patty and add a slice of cheese on top.

Let the patties cook for 1 more minute then add 1 tbsp of water to the pan and cover. This will melt the cheese. Take the patties out of the pan and rest.

Spread sauce on bottom half of burger bun, add lettuce and follow with the burger patty. I also like to put a little sauce on the top of the burger. Chuck the top on and enjoy!

SPEARO CHEF

Josh Bollen
@bosh.jollen

ALTERNATIVE SPECIES

Crab, lobster, abalone, boneless fish trimmings

BBQ MUSHROOM FISH BURGERS

For this recipe, any good eating fish you can spear will do fine. I have used one of our favourite Western Australian fish—the baldchin groper, aka blue bone, baldy or if you want to sound like you know something about latin, then *Choerodon rubescens*. We love easy, quick and tasty meals and as my wife is vegetarian and my son is a meatatarian, this meal covers all bases. For a vegetarian option, use the stuffed mushroom in place of the fish on the roll.

COOK TIME 20 MIN | SERVES 2-4
Baldchin groper

INGREDIENTS

1kg (2lb) fish fillets
6 large mushrooms
200g (7oz) haloumi cheese
2 handfuls baby rocket/spinach leaves
2 small sliced tomatoes
4 tbsp extra virgin olive oil
Salt flakes and cracked black pepper
Minced garlic
Mixed Italian herbs, to taste
BBQ spice, to taste
Smoked paprika, to taste
Vegeta or vegetable stock powder, to taste
3 tbsp of red pesto
2 handfuls of salted pistachios
Fresh seeded bread rolls
2 tbsp of butter

VEGETARIAN OPTION

Use the stuffed mushroom in place of the fish on the roll for a Vegetarian option.

METHOD

Fillet fish and remove skin. Prepare salad and other ingredients before commencing cooking.

Place in bowls ready for cooking and/or table. Heat the bbq for both the fish fillets and large stuffed mushrooms.

Remove stems from the large mushrooms and chop the stems into small pieces. Place in a bowl.

Dice up the haloumi into cube sized pieces and place in another bowl.

Take all the shells off the salted pistachios and place pistachios in a bowl.

Add soft butter, red pesto and minced garlic to a bowl and mix well.

Then, add the mushroom stems, haloumi cheese and pistachio nuts and mix together.

Add a small pinch of smoked paprika for extra taste.

Fill all the large mushrooms with the mixture and place on the bbq to start cooking 5 minutes before you start on the fish fillets.

Drizzle olive oil over fish fillets on both sides and then season with Italian mixed herbs and your favourite bbq spice. Let this sit for 5 minutes then place on the bbq.

Once cooked, remove from the heat and place on a fresh seeded bread roll. Top with tomato slices and rocket.

Serve the fish with one or two of the stuffed mushrooms.

SPEARO CHEF

Bert Keulder
@oldmanbluedive

ALTERNATIVE SPECIES

Any good eating fish

MATSO'S
BROOME BREWERY
MATSO'S
ALCOHOLIC
GINGER
BEER

SQUID INK PASTA WITH SQUID, CHORIZO, TOMATOES & BASIL

I still get a kick out of creating dishes from something I caught myself or picked with my own hands. Here is my squid ink pasta with fresh squid, cured chorizo, cherry tomatoes and basil. The perfect dish to share with family and friends.

COOK TIME 30 MIN | SERVES 4
Squid

INGREDIENTS

½ red onion, large, diced
1 lemon, finely grated zest and juice
Squid, large with tentacles, finely sliced
3 garlic cloves, finely sliced
Basil, leaves picked and torn
250g cherry tomato
Long red chilli, finely sliced
Extra virgin olive oil
400g squid ink pasta
1 spicy cured chorizo, halved lengthways, finely sliced
Salt flakes and freshly ground pepper, to taste

METHOD

Bring large saucepan of water to the boil and add enough salt so that it tastes like the ocean.

Depending on the cooking time of your pasta, add it to the water with enough time for it to cook and steam dry in the colander for a couple of minutes before the sauce is ready — this will allow more of your sauce to be absorbed into the pasta, giving it a richer flavour.

Add oil, onion, garlic and chilli.

Add 3 tablespoons of the oil and the onion, garlic and chilli to a large saucepan over high heat and cook until softened.

Add the chorizo and fry until caramelised. Add the tomatoes and cook for about 5 minutes until soft.

Add the squid and reduce to a medium heat—we're looking to gently poach the squid, which will stop it from becoming tough.

Add basil, remaining oil and lemon zest and juice.

After 2-3 minutes, add the basil, remaining oil and lemon zest and juice. Stir to combine. Season the sauce well with salt and pepper and tip into the pasta pan with the drained pasta.

Lastly, Toss gently to combine and serve immediately.

SPEARO CHEF

Mark LaBrooy
@markthreeblueducks

ALTERNATIVE SPECIES

Cuttlefish

LOBSTER ORECCHIETTE

I created this recipe to give people a simple and fail safe to enjoy the lobster they just dropped some serious cash purchasing. I really enjoy making this dish for my family, its bloody tasty and something that everyone can enjoy, even my 18 month old daughter. I think to have a good understanding on how to cook a variety of seafoods is paramount to becoming a good cook, lobster requires a soft touch and good observation skills and this dish really demonstrates that.

COOK TIME 20 MIN | SERVES 4
Lobster

INGREDIENTS

1 lobster, 1kg
400g cherry tomato, roughly chopped
1 brown onion, finely diced
5 garlic cloves, finely chopped
2 tsp lemon zest
Long red chilli, deseeded and finely chopped
Extra virgin olive oil
Basil leaves, leaves picked
400g orecchiette, cooked al-dente
Chives (handful), very finely chopped
1 tbsp bottarga, grated with a microplane

METHOD

Using your bbq or grill plate on your stove, place your lobster on the grill for a few mins on each side. This will release the lobster meat from the shell, so we can remove the meat without cooking it. Look for the lobster to turn slightly red before removing from the heat. Don't cook the lobster too much, as we want to do most of the cooking in our pasta sauce.

Fill a large pot with water and place on the boil, season so it tastes like the ocean.

In a heavy-set pan on low heat, softly sauté 1/2 a finely diced brown onion, 5 finely chopped garlic cloves and one finely chopped deseeded long red chilli in 3 tablespoons of olive oil.

Add your tomatoes and cook until they are soft.

Take your kitchen shears and cut the tail away from the head. Then cut down each side of the underside of the tail. Once the underside is pulled back, use your fingers to pull out lobster meat.

Roughly dice the lobster flesh and put it aside.

Boil your orecchiette pasta for 6-7 minutes. Make sure not to overcook it.

Place the lobster into your sauce and then the basil, and cook for 2 minutes until the lobster is cooked and the basil starts to wilt.

Add the orecchiette pasta and adjust the consistency of the sauce with the pasta water, stirring the pasta through the sauce. Take off the heat.

Top the pasta with your chives, lemon zest, bottarga and cracked black pepper.

SPEARO CHEF

Mark LaBrooy
@markthreeblueducks

ALTERNATIVE SPECIES

Crab

SAUCES & ACCOMPANIMENTS

When you set foot into the kitchen, you become the conductor of an orchestra. You are responsible for composing and directing a delicious meal, something that you can be proud to share around a table.

It is much like music where the timing needs to be right, the instruments in tune, the melodies and harmonies should layer on top of each other, and you can't help but tap your foot to the final product.

If a plate of delicious food is a well-practiced band, then the sauce definitely plays the role of lead guitarist. Sauce is what adds the style and completes the meal. It can be used to soften textures, highlight ingredients, add moisture, but most importantly it creates a meaningful pop of flavor that unites the plate.

Sauce can be as simple as a few blended ingredients like oil, lemon, cream, and parsley, or as punchy as a slow stewed curry paste, or as complex and deeply flavorful as a 3-week cold-brewed ponzu. Sauces can be used as an accompaniment on the side of the dish, like ketchup, or a spread on a sandwich, such as herb aioli, or as an agent for retaining moisture like when you cook a fillet that is buried in mayonnaise, butter, and fragrant herbs.

Sauce is responsible for making the whole mouth happy and ensuring that all your tastebuds are dancing.

HOW TO MAKE YOUR OWN SEA SALT

Humans have used sea salt for thousands of years to preserve and season food. The earliest known salt harvesting dates back to around 6000 B.C. in China. It is crazy to think about how these tiny grains were such a valuable commodity and have such a rich history. Salt was even used as currency in some cultures. And right down the street from where we live is the main ingredient for us to make our own!

Making your own salt is very simple but can take a full day, while you leave the saltwater on the stove to boil down. Of course it's simpler to buy sea salt from the market but it's so much more rewarding to add your homemade salt to a meal

INGREDIENTS

1 gallon (3.75l) of clean seawater

METHOD

SALTWATER COLLECTION

1 gallon (3.75l) of seawater will yield about ½ cup of salt. Avoid areas near rivers, sewage runoffs or in stagnant tidal pools.

FILTER IT

Filter the ocean water into the pan with a coffee filter, dish towel or cheesecloth folded over on itself.

BOIL IT DOWN

Assuming you started with a gallon, boil it down until about an inch (2.5cm) of seawater remains in the pan. At this point, turn the heat down to medium-low and start stirring every 10 minutes. If you used more than a gallon, try using several large pots on the burners.

STIR IT UP

When it begins to look like sand and there is more salt than liquid, turn the heat down to low and keep stirring. Do not let the salt scorch or harden.

DRY IT OUT

When the salt is the consistency of wet sand, transfer it to a plate lined with several paper towels. Let it sit for a few hours or overnight. Finally, flip the salt off the paper towels and onto a glass pan or baking sheet.

The larger the sheet, the thinner you can spread it out. Place near a window with sun for four more days (or longer) until the salt is completely dry. Once dry, you can store it in a mason jar.

EXTRA SEASONING

- Smoked paprika and chilli powder
- Basil, oregano, parsley, thyme, garlic
- Rosemary with edible colourful flower petals
- Dried and crushed bacon
- Habanero peppers with pineapple
- Lime zest

To further elevate your salt, try adding the above seasoning combinations. Remember the ingredients must be dry and crushed/minced before mixing into the salt.

SPEARO CHEF

Eric Keener

@finandforage

HOW TO MAKE SUSHI RICE

When I first tried my hand at making sushi many years ago, I was shocked to learn that it wasn't just white rice! There are actually several extra (easy) steps that I wasn't aware of, but boy oh boy was that first bite of homemade sushi delicious!

While this could serve as a general recipe, I think it's more of a process that you need to learn if you plan on making sushi with your catch. We make sushi almost monthly at our house!

INGREDIENTS

1 cup uncooked white sushi rice (or any short grain sticky rice)
2 cups cold water
½ cup rice vinegar
¼ cup fine grain white sugar
1 tbsp sesame oil
1 tsp salt

METHOD

Place the rice in a fine mesh colander and run under cold water, mixing it until the water runs off the bottom totally clear. This is important (otherwise your rice will be chewy and sticky when cooked).

Combine the rinsed rice with 2 cups of cold water in a medium pan and bring to a boil. As soon as it boils, reduce to a very low heat.

Place a cover on the pan and let it cook for 15-20 minutes until all the water is absorbed. Let it cool until you can handle it without burning yourself.

While the rice is cooling, put a small saucepan on medium heat. Add in the oil, sugar, salt and rice vinegar and stir until everything dissolves.

Slowly pour the mixture over the rice while stirring until it is totally coated. It will seem very wet at first but as you stir the rice it will absorb the liquid and get sticky.

Note that if left overnight in the fridge, it becomes very hard to work with for sushi rolls but still tastes delicious.

This is easier with a helper.

ADDITIONAL INFORMATION

Sushi can be an amazing meal, especially when you have quality ingredients, fun friends and some time to play with food.

Some of my best food memories are of a table piled with sushi ingredients, sauces and veggies surrounded by a group of people who are ready to try to make sushi.

See who can come up with the best flavour or prettiest plated roll!

SPEARO CHEF

Eric Keener
@finandforage

LOBSTER OIL

This is a great way to make the most of your leftover lobster heads and shells. The oil is a beautiful addition to sashimi, pasta or even scrambled eggs. You can use cooked tail shells. However, for best results, I prefer to remove the tail meat and cook separately. The recipe uses two lobsters as this is the catch limit for eastern rock lobster in NSW, Australia. If you're lucky enough to find some different species or live elsewhere you can add more shells and concentrate the flavour further.

INGREDIENTS

2 lobster head and tail shells (including legs)
Half a head of garlic
1 tbsp olive oil
Approx 1 cup of canola oil (or similar with little flavour)

METHOD

Remove tail from the lobster by inserting a knife under the carapace around the tail and then twisting.

Using kitchen or other sturdy scissors, cut down the top of the tail. Peel out the tail meat and put aside.

Remove the poo-tube.

Do not wash the heads as it reduces the flavour.

Crush garlic cloves and add to a medium saucepan with a splash of olive oil.

Heat the saucepan to a medium temperature and add the remaining lobster.

When the garlic becomes fragrant and shells begin to turn orange, crush the shells.

Use a wooden spoon or similar utensil to open up the legs and head. Expose as much of the lobster as you can.

Cover with canola oil and reduce the heat to a gentle simmer.

Turn down to a low heat for an hour.

Allow to cool. Strain the oil from the shells through a fine mesh strainer, muslin cloth or even a new chux cloth (rinse this thoroughly before using).

Place in a jar or container. Store in the fridge for up to 6 weeks.

SPEARO CHEF

Josh Bollen
@bosh.jollen

ARIKI REMOULADE WITH FRIED FISH

Danish-style remoulade is the perfect accompaniment for fried fish. Crusty crumbed and juicy white flesh, slightly tangy sweet curried sauce, cold frothies... it doesn't get any better.

This is an interpretation, so there are a few key differences if you are a Danish remoulade purist. It should be finely chopped or blended in a processor but I have no such luxuries on a boat. Even more glaring is that over the years I've forgotten the actual ingredients so I make do with what I have!

INGREDIENTS

REMOULADE

½ carrot
½ onion
½ apple
1 gherkin
15 capers
1 tsp basic curry powder
3 tbsp whole egg mayonnaise

CRUMBED FISH

Oil for frying
1 fillet of white fleshed reef fish
Egg
Cornflakes crumbs
A dash of lemon

METHOD

Finely chop the carrot, onion, apple, gherkins, and capers.

Add the finely chopped ingredients to a bowl and mix the mayonnaise and curry powder through.

Preheat your pan and oil.

Dip the fillet into the egg wash ensuring it is well coated.

Drip off any excess.

Transfer the egg-washed fish into the crumbs and cover well.

Shallow fry until golden brown.

Serve your fish with the remoulade, your choice of side dishes and squeeze that lemon (not in your eye though!).

PREPARATION TIP

Match your sauce to your meal. Ensure it develops the flavour profile you want by tasting it as you add ingredients or as it reduces. It shouldn't overpower the main ingredient's flavour, but it should also not get lost on the plate.

@finandforage

SPEARO CHEF

Henry Hunter
@henbomb86

PONZU

Traditional ponzu is a popular Asian condiment that is made with citrus juice. It's easy to make, fun to modify and has a massive variety of uses; such as fish marinade, salad or noodle dressing, sushi dipping sauce or finishing sauce. Typically, the citrus in the recipe is an Asian variety called yuzu, but real yuzu juice can be difficult to find in stores or grow yourself. Below is a traditional version of a stock ponzu recipe made with ingredients that should be easy to find, no matter where you live. This recipe, by itself, is mouth wateringly delicious. However, we encourage you to try it with a few meals, and I've also included some additional ways to "sex it up" and really start developing your own flavour pairings.

INGREDIENTS

¾ cup of soy sauce
1 large strip of dried kombu kelp (about 8x2in/20x5cm)
⅓ cup of dried bonito flakes (katsuobushi)
1 tbsp fish sauce
3 tbsp sweet sake or mirin
2 tbsp rice wine vinegar
1 tsp fresh ginger, peeled and grated
2 limes, juiced
1 lemon, juiced

METHOD

Add all the ingredients (except the citrus juice) to a small saucepan over medium heat. Turn off the heat just before it gets to boiling and let it cool all the way down to room temperature.

In a sterilised canning jar (to sterilise: boil it in water with lid off for 10 minutes), add the citrus juice, then strain the contents of the pan into the jar.

Screw the lid on tightly and place in the refrigerator.

Gently shake the jar in the morning and the evening. Let it sit for at least 24 hours, but 3 days or more is preferable. This will keep for several weeks in the refrigerator.

"SEX IT UP" SPICY GRAPEFRUIT

Add 1 tsp of fresh grated ginger and 2 spicy dried peppers with seeds in, during the first step. Add juice and zest from a red grapefruit and then add the peppers back into the jar for the marinating process.

MEZCAL SPIKED SMOKEY CITRUS

In the original recipe, replace the citrus for 3 oranges, 3 limes, 3 lemons that have been cut in half and charred on the grill (cut side down until deep brown sear lines appear), then juiced. Add 2 tbsp of mezcal to the juice. Instead of straining the ingredients, leave them all together in the jar to marinate in the refrigerator for 5 days, gently shaking it twice a day, then strain and it is ready to get saucy.

SWEET GARLIC

Use less citrus juice and more sweet rice wine or mirin. Include 2 tbsp crushed fresh garlic cloves and 1 small spicy dried pepper. Leave all ingredients in the jar in the refrigerator to marinate for 3 days, then strain.

SPEARO CHEF

Eric Keener
@finandforage

GARNISHES TO ELEVATE AND IMPRESS

The most important factor in a good meal is that the flavours and textures work together. The last piece of the puzzle is making sure it looks beautiful. Garnishes and presentation can be the factors that take a great meal and make it extraordinary. Here are some very simple recipes for making impressive and tasty additions to your dishes. You'll get major points from your dinner guests for these.

Squid Ink Tuile – Dainty, unique, complex, crunchy and tasty. They look like fan coral and add an ocean feel to almost any dish.

Parmesan Crisps – Parmesan crisps are as versatile as they are easy to make. They can be very strong in flavour, so use smaller pieces to garnish. They can be shaped, cut and flavoured to match your creativity.

Flavoured "Caviar" Pearls – A stunning way to enhance the flavour, texture and appearance of your dish. Think caviar or tobiko but with a flavour you control. They are the consistency of grapes without the skin on, are pretty durable and they're packed with flavour. For this example, I used balsamic vinegar, but you can use things like yuzu, soy sauce, or lime as well.

INGREDIENTS

SQUID INK TUILE

Water
Flour
Squid ink (or food coloring)
High heat oil

PARMESAN CRISPS

½ cup parmesan cheese, thickly shredded (more may be required depending on the size and number of crisps required)
Italian herbs, crushed red pepper, truffle powder, garlic salt
Salt and pepper

FLAVOURED "CAVIAR" PEARLS

⅔ cup (160ml/6fl oz) olive oil
⅔ cup (160ml/6fl oz) balsamic vinegar
2g (a pinch) agar-agar
3 cups (700ml/25fl oz) water

METHOD

SQUID INK TUILE

Add oil to a clean, small, frying pan. Just enough to fully coat the bottom.

Heat oil over high heat.

In a small mixing bowl, thoroughly mix 1 part flour to 9 parts water (make at least 1 cup or 250 ml of batter). The consistency will be very watery but if you keep the ratio correct, it will turn out well.

I add about ½ teaspoon of squid ink so that my lace tuile turns black, but you can use a few drops of food coloring to change the color as desired (red tuile looks like beautiful ocean coral).

Once you're ready to add the batter to the oil, give the batter a quick stir in the bowl and then using a large spoon or small ladel, pour an amount of batter in the pan. Start by trying 1 tbsp of batter–there is a little trial-and-error in this step (see note at end) but thankfully, it is quick and easy to try again with slightly more batter or slightly less oil.

When you first pour the batter in, it looks like black, boiling sludge. This is just the water starting to boil and evaporate. It will definitely splatter, so have a splatter guard handy. Make sure not to stir the batter or move the pan while it bubbles and pops. You will see the sludge start to form holes where the bubbles come through and then you will see the tuile will start to crisp up and harden. This generally takes about 1 minute.

Keep the tuile crisping until the edges are matte and starting to lift from the pan. Most of the oil should be absorbed into the tuile but some left in the pan is normal.

Very gently, remove from the pan and place on a paper towel to dry. It's crazy fragile so lift and place carefully.

Add more oil to the pan, let it heat and repeat the process until your batter is gone or until you have enough tuile.

Depending on your plating creativity, it looks really neat when the tuile is broken into angular chunks about 2 in (5cm) in length and placed at the top of the food on the dish. If using a smaller dish or bowl, consider leaving the tuile whole and placing it as a "lid" to the dish. Sometimes the element of mystery is a fun addition to the dining experience. Note that it will absorb moisture and become soggy if left touching moist food or broth.

The tuile should be used the day it was made as it will generally become less crunchy the longer it sits out in the open air.

Note: The trial and error part is getting the right ratio of batter to depth of oil in the pan. You will need to figure out how much batter to add for how deep your oil is.

METHOD

PARMESAN CRISPS

Preheat your broiler (overhead grill).

Place a baking sheet or parchment paper in a baking tray.

Loosely grate some parmesan cheese in a pile. The desired size and amount of crisps that you're making will determine how much cheese you use. For this example, start with about ½ cup of grated cheese.

Spread the mix evenly on the paper or baking sheet—aim to have very small holes speckled all over where you can see the baking sheet below (think of it as making a mesh sheet)—if the mixture is too thick in spots, it won't crisp up and will stay oily and soggy.

You can choose to include additional (dry ingredient) flavours here as well by lightly sprinkling a pinch of Italian herbs, crushed red pepper, truffle powder, cracked pepper or garlic salt over the top of your cheese layer.

Place the baking tray in the broiler, keeping a very close eye on the parmesan mixture. Cook times will vary based on heat, thickness of cheese, etc, however it shouldn't take more than a couple minutes. You want as much moisture and oil to come out of the parmesan as possible, but you also don't want to let it burn.

When the edges are starting to dry, take it out and immediately cut it into strips or triangles with a circular pizza slicer or knife (press down, don't slice or it will tear) or use a cookie cutter to cut it into circles. You can also cut it into long strips, immediately lay it over something round like a rolling pin (while it's still warm and pliable), and then put it in the freezer—it will harden in the shape you've set it in.

If cooked until the cheese is nearly dry, you can make the crisps a day in advance to help save time for cooking your dish but they should generally be enjoyed the day they are made.

METHOD

FLAVOURED "CAVIAR" PEARLS

Pour olive oil into a pint glass or medium carafe. The thinner and taller the vessel the better so you don't use as much oil, but wide enough to still draw out pearls with a spoon once they are set.

Place oil into the freezer for 30 minutes.

Begin heating the balsamic vinegar in a saucepan over medium heat.

Add agar-agar and stir constantly while bringing to a boil. As soon as it starts boiling, remove it from the heat.

Remove oil from the freezer.

Using a syringe or pipette, draw up the balsamic mixture and begin to slowly drop into the cold olive oil. The larger the droplets, the larger spheres they will form. A good size to aim for is about the diameter of a peppercorn.

Using a spoon, gently transfer the balsamic pearls to a bowl filled with water. Give them a good stir to rinse the oil off of the pearls.

The pearls will last up to a week in the refrigerator and you can reuse the olive oil afterward so there is no waste!

SPEARO CHEF

Eric Keener

@finandforage

The Team

Every person who has had a hand in this project from start to finish, in a voluntary or paid capacity, I'd like to thank and express my gratitude to. You've helped make this special book!

Jason Harris
Editorial Design & Creative Director

Livia Cruz
Chief Administrative Officer

Alasdair Lean
Editor & Proofreader

Martin Hing
Fish Glossary Director, Editor & Proofreader

Samuel Phillis
Fish Glossary Director, Editor & Proofreader

Capt. Dan Walsh
Recipe recreation & Proofreader

Brandon Swanepoel
Social Media Manager & Proofreader

Mark Cronier
Design & Marketing Consultant

Jason Wagnon
Editor & Proofreader

Steven Keegal
Fish Glossary Team & Proofreader

Edward Bodkin
Editor & Proofreader

Eric Keener
Project Consultant & Contributor

John Wood
Proofreader

John Beard
Proofreader

Andrew Bleakley
Proofreader

Harry Foster
Recipe Consultant

Daniel Mann
Recipe Consultant

Nicole Donaldson
Editor

Acknowledgments

I'd like to acknowledge the extraordinary support of my best friend and wife Krystle, who always encourages, listens and loves me and our boys Ben, Troy and Ben.

On an even more personal level, I'm grateful to my Lord and Saviour Jesus Christ who helps me to do all things in Him. My life has been forever marked by His grace and mercy.

I'd like to thank the Noob Spearo Community for their inspiration, encouragement and involvement in all our efforts. This project has been from start to finish, a community project to make our broader spearfishing community more intentional stewards of the seafood we forage and spear.

This entire project fills my heart with gratitude and I'm proud of what we've made.

- Isaac 'Shrek' Daly
Crowd Coordinator

SPECIAL MENTIONS

This book is dedicated to spearos who never made it home to their friends and families. Spearfishing was what they loved doing and they left this world doing it. This book honours their memories.

Special mention to Didrik Thorén Hurum who never resurfaced off North Stradbroke Island on the 23rd June 2021 and is missed by family, Damian Wiremu Mckay, Brad Corbett and the many other friends he made in South East Queensland.

> *"We miss him so deeply, nothing would please us more than honor him this way as we know he loved spearfishing and cooking the fish he caught. He always said he looked forward to cooking for us one day when he came back to Norway".*
>
> **- Didriks Mum and Dad (Nina Thorén Hurum and Bjørn P. Hurum)**

Acknowledgments

KICKSTARTER BACKERS

The 99 Spearo Recipe project was brought to life by 330 backers on Kickstarter in December, 2021 who pledged $26,000+. Without their support, this book would not have been possible. Huge thanks to;

Raelyn & Brynlee Adams	Andrew & Koa	Keith Marshall	Jeremy Hoffing	Alejandro Umansk	James Stewardson
Kelly Kemp	Ethan Nash	Mpmangion	Eboni Rowlands	Mike Mcguire	Captain Miik
Matt Dwyer	Australian Hunting Podcast	Lauren Smith	Paul Bevis	Ed	Krystle Luscombe
Julian Dallmeier	Daniel Walsh	Hayden Boulton	Philby	Isaac Morgan	Anton Beletsky
Alby & Kenzie Roger	Jed	Wet Whale Social Club	Captain Eli	Brendan Coates	Michael Oeberg
Chef Du Pastis	Jason Harris	Ash Clark	Nicholas	Matthew	Jack
Spearsey	Lacramioara Trifu	Samuel Wilson	Deep Down Under	Keith Hinde	Trent Bradshaw
Jodie	Philip van Zijl	Shane Ribovich	Josh Funke	Lee Dobson	Betsy Bothell
BackerKit	Duncan Henderson	David Hallamore - SCORKL	Dani	Nick Thiemann	Oli Sandstrom
Gilles	Cam & Liz	Pav Tryfon	Roger Moore	James Hamman	Dominic Griffin
Mark Rakicic	Craig & Stinks	Tim Hall	Tyler Caudle	Cainit	Chris E Hardy
Dusty Schofield	James	Luke Housefield	Stephan Whelan	Jessie	Nick Ryan
John Millstead	Tom Cornell	Robertson's	Cory	Sarah Wiebe	Filip Jakubiak
Ben & the Brisbane Bullsharks	Kate	James Dixon	Herman Victor	Louis Cummings	Kiran Thapa
Mikey	Cameron Gall	JD Singleton	Jamie Maxted	Adventureman Dan	Tom Tyquin
Washo	Andrew	Lisa	Adam Hempenstall	Lars H Almås	Nathan C
Robbiepocket	Kerri-Lee & Liam	Patrick Gallagher	Cody B	Milen Spasov	Daniel Mann
Campbell Ahsam	Schuey	Bootie Juice Crew	Patrick	Mike Jones	Bradley Pirman, SB Freedivers
Trent Sullivan	Exhale Adventures	Jake Chambers	Ed Murphy	Camielle Donsghey	Ben Leeson
Thomas	Adam Price	Russell Moody	John Gillis	Sailing Vessel Singularity	James A
Duncan Skinner	Will Nasio	Mitchell Larkman	Joanne Stuckey	Frankie Maduro	Zhoel
thetomclarkimpact	Dale	Caryl Jongedyk	Nick Bradish	Sam Mei	Josh Humbert
Bloomy	Mitchell McCluskey	Adrien Simon	Moira	Andrew Mee	Andy MacBride
Josephine	Alasdair Grant	Tate Leckie	Adam Chan	Kevin Guck	Derrick Oscar Cruz
Frederic Flanet	Old Man Blue	Deryck Tan	Jason	Jacob Necaise	Mike Pooler
Chris Wrightson	Hohnke Outdoors	C J Gillespie	Eli Daniel Ravines	Ideazman	Bright Idea Labs
Nick Johnson	Guilherme Rosado	Ben Vittino	Jurg	Raziel Acosta	Joy Miyatake
Daan De Coster	Matt Bond	Ryan Springall	Rexy	Jake Hewitt	Justin turner
Renee Taylor	Ryan	Ryan Hancock	Caspar Noden	DK	Jarrid Plows
Jack Radcliffe	Tiffany Levesque	Jay Wheeler	Linton Hayes	Taygan Ortlepp	Nicholas
Mark Cronje	H2O By Motorcycle	Matthew Cornish	Tasman Cranney	Callum	David Mills

'In memory of Dejan Sverko, may your Spearfishing dream live on in Indonesia'
- Russel Foyle (Noob Spearo Community Member)

'Our life orientates around sustainability and our hearts orientate around the ocean. Spearfishing is a big deal on our island state, and therefore, we are so incredibly proud to see this project successfully backed, and hope everyone that grabs a copy has a taste for the magic that is being a Spearo.'

- Eb and Jack in Tassie

Michael Duff	Red Dear	River Mungall	Dr Specific	Adam Duster	Mickey T
Hamish McMillan	Campbell Tebbutt	Nathan Loch	Jon	Davidb	Simon Turbett
Tony Brookbanks	Spearoms	Steve Pogonowski	Matt Worley	Team Tandy	Marc De Labry
Brad Evans	Edward Dawe	David Hyde	Steven jumisic	Amanda Chiu	J Taylor
Jacob Bonfield	Hinatea Bdec	Aaron Robinson	Tristan	Ryan Robson	Chassaint
Campbell Allen-Craig	Tim Flack	Alby Cooke	Nicholas Grawich	Carl	Gwyn
@Clarence_Bowen	Victor Meng	Stacey Hadsell	Corey Kent	Kraig Thornton	Zaki
The Wongslayer	CaveMan	Flo Raider	Washo	Fonzy S.	Niklas Kerssenfischer
Danny Dyson	Catherine Neidhardt	Ian Mallett	Steven McCloghry	@chris._lambert	Damian McKay
SY Tequila	Campbell McArthur	Nick	Sebastian Basso	Matt McKay	Armando Axel Herrera
Justin Russell	Angelo	Peter	Ethan Storey	Son Dang	Andrew & Liz Bleakley
Chloe Darkson	David Grant	Russel Foyle	Bryan Russell	Kevin Lopeman	Stuart Harwood
Joseph	Luke Colys	JB Spearo	Alex Lord	Mike K	Sam the waterman
Jarrad, Jason, Neil, Andreas	S&K Designs	Tom Moore	Alina	Dayne	Damian Mckay
Ben Osgood	Tuna Slayer	Daniel Wigen	Albi Liversidge	Chee Ooi	Chris
Peter Deas	Meruw	John Varco	Michael Buttigieg	Louey Yen	Graham & Tristan
Callum Provan	Meatloaf	John Varco	Brandon Hendry	George Yacoub	Simon Biggs
Riley Jones	Nikolas	Tayls	Alen Van Rooyen	Rob Harrison	Cambo
Pierce & Cat	Ken Williamson	James Peak	Tron Congdon	Alessia & Olivia Pusceddu	Andrew Moulder
Sven Franklin	Tony Rear	MagicMickMaaate	Tron Diggity	Vaughan Merryfull	The Clay Family
Ant Kowalczyk	Jerwin Cuason	Daniel Vallis	Jason Alma	Sam	The Harris Family
Brian McComb	Alaska Freediver	Justin C. Townsend @Harvesting Nature	Michael Cruse	Carl Morandi	Linton Hayes
Todd Kautz	David McGowan	Brandon Swanepoel	Tissysbaby	Axelle	**+ Many more!**

Fish Glossary

ONE SPEARO'S SNAPPER IS ANOTHER SPEARO'S SEABREAM

In the 99 Spearo Recipes Fish Glossary, we refer to each species used throughout this book by their scientific name, as well as their common name(s). This ensures there is no confusion regarding which species is being referred to, as common names can be used interchangeably around the world. A good example of this is the Australasian snapper (*Chrysophrys auratus*) or silver seabream. Although it is almost universally known in Australia and New Zealand as "snapper", it does not belong to the snapper family, *Lutjanidae*, but to the seabream family, *Sparidae*.

We will be listing the family that each species belongs to, as many of the species we commonly catch are related at a family level, and may be interchangeable in certain recipes. We will also use the genus and species classifications. Genus is the next, more related level in classifying organisms and species is the most related level. Think of it like brands and models of spearguns – they're all spearguns, but they're not fins, so you could think of "speargun" as the "family".

The genus would be like the different brands – all the Rob Allen spearguns are more similar to each other than they are to all the Aimrite spearguns.

We can then break it down into models within each brand–The Rob Allen Sparids could be thought of as the species in our analogy and are all very similar to each other. They're fairly similar to the Rob Allen Tuna and the Rob Allen Scorpia (other 'species' of the "genus" Rob Allen), but quite distinct from the Aimrite Venom.

Knowledge of the scientific classification of different fish species will help us gain an understanding of the species we commonly catch, what they are related to, and importantly what we can substitute them with in the recipes found in this book.

Understanding the relationship between certain species not only allows us to be better cooks, but also helps us become better stewards of the ocean. This ensures we remain aware of how best to work with, and protect this resource which provides us with so much.

SPECIES SIMILARITY DIAGRAM

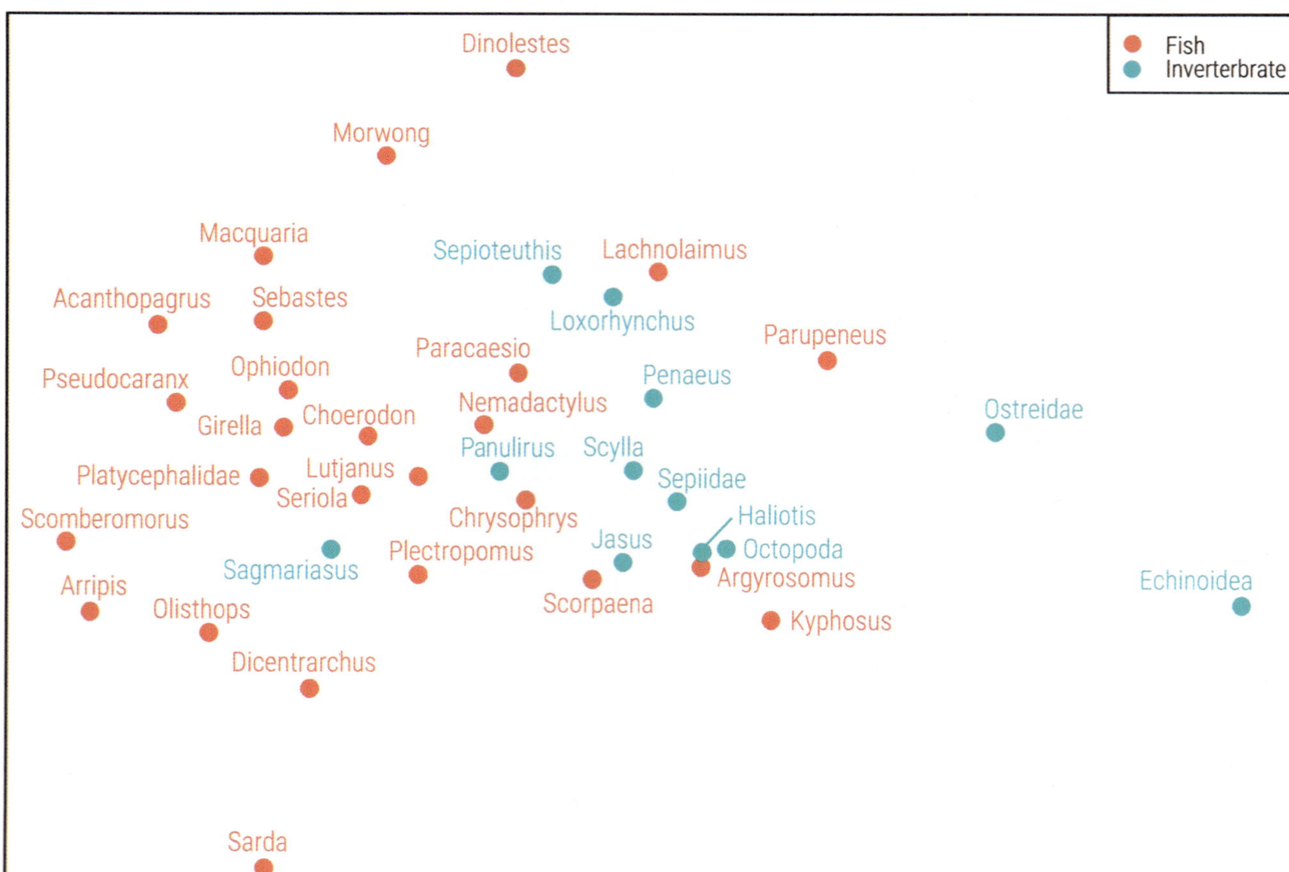

I WANT TO TRY SHREKVICHE, BUT I CAUGHT A LUDERICK

To help you noobers out in this situation, we created the Species Similarity Diagram, to be used alongside the recipes and the Fish Glossary. You may have noticed that each recipe has a list of alternative fish species.

If the species you caught isn't in the alternative fish list, don't despair–it might still work. This is where the Species Similarity Diagram may come in handy.

The Species Similarity figure shows how similar each genus is to every other genus in flesh profile. Points close together are more similar than those further apart. For example, sea urchins (*Echinoidea*) are not very similar in flesh profile to any other fish or invertebrate.

On the other hand, kingfish, samsonfish and amberjack (*genus Seriola*) are reasonably similar to snappers (*Lutjanus*), flathead (*Platycephalidae*), luderick, black drummer (*both Girella*) and tuskfish (*Choerodon*). These species are likely to be good alternative species if you haven't got a kingfish in the esky.

This figure should be used alongside the Fish Glossary and "Alternative Fish" listed in each recipe to find dishes that will likely work well for different species. So in the situation that you want to try Shrekviche, but have caught a luderick instead of the suggested sawtail surgeonfish.

While this process may seem a little tedious at first, as you become more comfortable with the scientific naming and more familiar with your local species you will find this process much easier.

Like anything, it gets easier with practice. Before you know it you'll be nerding it up with the local fish biologists at the nearest uni bar.

1. Check the Alternative Fish in the recipe. You'll find these are parrotfish, trevally and tuskfish- Boooooooo! No luderick.

2. Go to the Fish Glossary and familiarise yourself with the genus names of the alternative fish species and the species you have collected-in this case, Parrotfish, Trevally and Tuskfish are family *Scaridae*; family *Carangidae* and genus *Choerodon*, respectively. While Luderick is in the genus Girella.

3. Look at the species similarity figure (following page) and find Girella.

4. Rejoice! You can see that *Girella* is quite similar to *Pseudocaranx* (a genus of trevally) and *Choerodon* (tuskfishes). As such, we now know that luderick would be a fine substitute species for Shrekviche!

FIRMNESS

Firmness could range from delicate to leather boot (I'm looking at you abalone). Delicate fish and seafood require gentler handling and cooking methods to achieve the best results. On the other hand, firmer flesh typically requires more prep work and seasoning to bring their flavours forward.

They are often described as "meatier" and may require different cooking methods.

FATTINESS

Lean fish tend to be milder in taste because of lower fat content and are an excellent source of protein. They may require some moisture, fat or oil to supplement the cooking process in order to bring out the flavours.

Steaming, poaching and frying are likely to be good cooking methods for these kinds of fish. Fatty fish sometimes have a buttery texture. These fish are well suited to cooking methods like grilling or baking as they don't tend to dry out as easily.

OILINESS

Oily fish tend to have a very strong 'fishy' flavour. These fish are rich in vitamins (A and D) and omega-3 fatty acids. They're also very flavoursome, though not everyone enjoys this flavour. These species are great for the smoker as oil tends to soak up the smoky flavours.

MOISTURE CONTENT

Moisture content is quite important for selecting the cooking method. Dryer flesh is best suited to wet cooking methods like boiling or steaming.

On the other hand, moist flesh lends itself to dry cooking methods like baking or grilling.

COLOUR

The colour of seafood flesh generally ranges from clear to white to pink to deep purple. Some dark coloured fish like tuna are very good for sashimi. But don't let that fool you–many pale coloured species also sashimi very nicely.

Darker colours generally indicate stronger 'meatier' flavours, however, some lightly coloured fish still have strong robust flavours.

FLAVOUR

Flavour profiles are incredibly complex and probably beyond the scope of this book. We could wax lyrical ad nauseam on the various notes and subtleties of the different species but for simplicity, we will deal with the strength of flavour which is a bit more straightforward.

Some fish have very strong flavour and will not need much in the way of seasoning to bring out the flavours. However, some fish have a very strong 'fishy' flavour (this is often related to the oiliness of the fish) that not everyone is a fan of.

These 'fishy' fish are often great candidates for smoking or pickling. Very lightly flavoured fish on the other hand, may require some seasoning or additional flavours (herbs, spices etc) to supplement the mild flavour just be sure to avoid overpowering the subtle taste of these fish.

Mild flavoured fish often have a sweetness in their flavour profile and are an excellent starting point for those new to eating seafood.

A

Abalone (*Haliotidae - Haliotis sp.*) aka. Paua
Black lip (*Haliotis rubra*)
Green lip (*Haliotis laevigata*)
Abadabas, 76
Abalone schnitzel, 77
Green lipped abalone in a teriyaki sauce, 187
Slow fried Tasmanian black lip abalone, 78

Also does well in...
Bottom Scratchers Cioppino, 96
Coastal Okonomiyaki, 242
Lobster Fettuccine, 227
Turban Taco aka Snail Choy Bao, 190

Amberjack (*Seriola* - multiple species)

Also does well in...
The Mango King, 85
Zesty Parsley Kingfish, 84

Australian Salmon (*Arripidae - Arripis sp.*)
Refer to Kahawai

B

Bald Chin Grouper (*Labridae - Choerodon rubescens*)
Refer to Tuskfish

Barramundi (*Latidae - Lates calcarifer*)

Also does well in...
Crispy Skin Fish with Salsa Verde, 122
Super Simple Mexican Bream, 101
Thai Green Mango Salad Fried Whole Fish, 79

Black Drummer (*Girellidae - Girella elevata*)
Crispy skin black drummer, 146
Thai Inspired Fish Sausage Rolls, 164

Also does well in...
Chick-Fil-A Copycat Burgers, 241
Whole Charred Fish with Peanut Curry Sauce, 72

Black Grouper (*Epinephelidae - Mycteroperca bonaci*)
Refer to Grouper

Black Sea Bass (*Serranidae - Centropristis striata*)

Also does well in...
Bonfire Grilled Mahi Mahi with Garlic Cilantro Lime Slaw, 71

Blacksaddle Goatfish (*Mullidae - Parupeneus spilurus*) aka **Blackspot Goatfish**
Refer to Goatfish

Blackspot Tuskfish (*Labridae - Choerodon schoenleinii*)
Refer to Tuskfish

Bluefin Tuna (*Scombridae - Thunnus sp.*)
Refer to Tuna

Blue Moki (*Latridae - Latridopsis ciliaris*)
Refer to Trumpeter

Blue Morwong (*Latridae - Nemadactylus douglasii*) aka. **Grey Morwong**
Refer to Morwong

Bream (*Sparidae* - multiple species)
Note: Bream may refer to a number of species from the *Sparidae* (Seabreams) or *Lethrinidae* (Emperor Breams) Families. Only Sparidae is referred to below as no Lethrinidae recipes are included in this book.

Black Bream (*Acanthopagrus butcheri*)
Gilt-head (*Sparus aurata*)
Yellowfin (*Acanthopagrus australis*)
Crispy skin black drummer, 146

Also does well in...
Crispy Skin Fish with Salsa Verde, 122
(Yellowfin) Mid-Spear, 2 Min Fish Ramen, 212
Passionfruit Ceviche, 33
Popcorn Crayfish, 90
(Yellowfin) Super Simple Mexican Bream, 101
Thai Green Mango Salad Fried Whole Fish, 79

Bonito (*Scombridae* - multiple species)
Australian (*Sarda australis*)
Leaping (*Cybiosarda elegans*)
Bonito and Urchin Tostadas, 31
Bonito Poke Bowl, 30
Dry Aged Bonito, 32
Smoked Fish Pâté, 137

Buffalo Bream (*Kyphosidae - Kyphosus sp.*) aka **Chub, Silver Drummer**
Western (*Kyphosus cornelii*)
Southern Silver Drummer (*Kyphosus sydneyanus*)
Sweet and Sour Buffalo Bream, 107

Also does well in...
Fish Karaage, 80

Butterfish (*Odacidae - Odax pullus*) aka **Greenbone**
District 6 Curry Fish, 197

Bug (*Scyllaridae* - multiple species)
Refer to Slipper Lobster

C

Cabrilla Grouper (*Epinephelidae - Epinephelus labriformis*)
Refer to Grouper

Calamari (*Order Myopsida or Order Oegopsida*)
See Squid

Calico Bass (*Serranidae - Paralabrax clathratus*)
Calico Poke Bowl with Jicama Roses, 50

California Rockfish (*Sebastidae - Sebastes miniatus*)
Refer to Rockfish

California Sheephead (*Labridae - Semicossyphus pulcher*)
Refer to Sheepshead

California Spiny Lobster (*Palinuridae - Panulirus interruptus*)
Refer to Lobster

California Yellowtail (*Carangidae – Seriola lalandi ssp. dorsalis*)
Refer to Yellowtail Kingfish

Clam (*Class Bivalvia* - multiple species)
Note: Clam is often used to describe a wide range of bivalve species.

Also does well in...
Bottom Scratchers Cioppino, 196

Crab (*Infraorder Brachyura* - multiple species)
Blue Swimmer Crab (*Portunidae – Portunus armatus*)
Dungeness (*Cancridae – Metacarcinus magister*)
Mud Crab (*Portunidae – Scylla serrata*)
Sheep Crab (*Epialtidae – Loxorhynchus grandis*)
Red Rock Crab (*Cancridae - Cancer productus*)
Spider Crab (*Majidae* - multiple species)

Also does well in...
Bottom Scratchers Cioppino, 196
(Mud) Chilli Mud Crab, 108
Coastal Okonomiyaki, 242
Crab Mac n Cheese, 165
Lobster Caesar Salad, 238
Lobster Cocktail, 239
(Blue Swimmer/Mud) Lobster Fettuccine, 227
Lobster Rice Paper Rolls, 240
Seafood Chowder, 201
(Sheep) Sheep Crab California Rolls, 192
Spider Crab Linguine, 230

Cod (*Gadiformes* - multiple species)
Note: Cod is sometimes used as an abbreviation for Rockcod.

Also does well in...
Crispy Skin Tom Kha Pla, 142
Gravlax on Aussie Salmon, 42
Marinated Flathead Skewers, 110

Coral Trout (*Serranide - Plectropomus sp.*)
Arctic Freediver's Fried Fish, 100
Ariki Ceviche, 38
Ariki Remoulade with Fried Fish, 260
Coral Trout & Mango Ceviche, 37
Coral Trout Laksa, 206
Coral Trout Wing in a Tempra Sauce, 106
Lime Coconut Ceviche, 34
Trout bombs, 145
Trout Crack, 96
Whole Charred Fish with Peanut Curry Sauce, 72

Also does well in...
Whole Steamed Coral Trout, 185

Crayfish (*Palinuridae* – multiple species)
Refer to Lobster

Cuttlefish (*Sepiidae* – multiple species)
Cephalopod Bolo, 210
Cuttlefish Tomato Kway Tiaw, 103

Also does well in...
Grilled Tako, 207
Octopus Tom Yum, 125
Sotong Bakar (Barbequed Squid), 118

D

Dolphinfish (*Coryphaenidae – Coryphaena hippurus*)
Refer to Mahi Mahi

Drummer (Multiple families)
For Silver Drummer refer to Buffalo Bream.
For Black Drummer refer to Black Drummer.

Dusky Morwong (*Latridae - Dactylophora nigricans*)
Refer to Morwong

E

Eastern Rock Lobster (*Palinuridae – Sagmariasus verreauxi*)
Refer to Lobster

European sea bass (*Moronidae – Dicentrarchus labrax*)
Refer to Robalo

F

Flat Head (*Platycephalidae* - multiple species)
Blue Spotted (*Platycephalus caeruleopunctatus*)
Dusky (*Platycephalus fuscus*)
Southern Blue Spotted (*Platycephalus speculator*)
Tiger (*Platycephalus richardsoni*)
Apple Cider Battered Fish Wraps, 88
Cam's Breaky Wrap, 119
Crispy Fish Wings, 68
Grandma Eiko's Karaage, 120
Marinated Flathead Skewers, 110

Also does well in...
Crispy skin black drummer, 146
Passionfruit Ceviche, 33

G

Goatfish (*Mullidae* - multiple species) aka **Kumu**
Blacksaddle (*Parupeneus spilurus*)
Kumu (*Parupeneus porphyreus*)
Bonito and Urchin Tostadas, 31
Charcoal Grilled Goatfish with Kombu Butter, 118
Garlic Thyme Bamboo Steamed Kumu, 182
Goatfish Ramen, 198
Lobster Spanakopita, 152

Also does well in...
Moqueca (Brazilian Fish Stew), 200
Stinky Pike Sashimi, 55
Super Simple Mexican Bream, 101

Greenbone (*Odacidae - Odax pullus*)
Refer to Butterfish

Green Jobfish (*Lutjanidae - Aprion virescens*) aka. **Jobfish**

Also does well in...
Chick-Fil-A Copycat Burgers, 241
Crispy Skin Fish with Salsa Verde, 122
Spanish Mackerel Poke Bowl 2 ways, 40

Grouper (*Epinephelidae* - multiple species)
Black (*Mycteroperca bonaci*)
Cabrilla (*Epinephelus labriformis*)
Gag (*Mycteroperca microlepis*)
Red (*Epinephelus morio*)
Also does well in...
(Black, Red, Gag) Bacon wrapped grouper cheeks, 74
Bonfire Grilled Mahi Mahi (*Cabrilla*), 71
Crispy Skin Tom Kha Pla, 142
Filipino Grandpa's Steamed Fish & Beans, 191

Goldspotted Sweetlips (*Haemulidae - Plectorhinchus flavomaculatus*)
Smoked Sweetlips, 132

H

Halibut (*Pleuronectidae - Genus Hippoglossus and Genus Reinhardtius*)

Also does well in...
Zen's Baja Tuna Tartare, 57

Hāpuku (*Polyprionidae - Polyprion oxygeneios*) aka. **Hapuka**

Also does well in...
Roasted Kingfish Belly w/ Eggplant Kasundi, 162

Herring Cale (*Odacidae – Olisthops cyanomelas*)
Smoked Fish Pâté, 137
Chick-Fil-A Copycat Burgers, 241

Hogfish (*Labridae - Lachnolaimus maximus*)
Simple Ceviche, 51

J

Jewfish (*Sciaenidae - Argyrosomus japonicus*) aka **Mulloway**
Refer to Mulloway

Jobfish (*Lutjanidae - Aprion virescens*) aka **Green Jobfish**
Refer to Green Jobfish

Jolthead Porgy (*Sparidae - Calamus bajonado*)
Quick and Dirty Whole Fish, 115

K

Kahawai (*Arripidae* - multiple species) aka **Australian Salmon**
East Aus. Salmon (*Arripis trutta*)
Kermadec Kahawai (*Arripis xylabion*)
West Aus. Salmon (*Arripis truttacea*)

Also does well in...
Bonito Poke Bowl, 30
Butterflied Baitfish Beauty - more than just a livie, 75
Gravlax on Aussie Salmon, 42
Roasted Kingfish Belly w/ Eggplant Kasundi, 162
Smoked Fish Pâté, 137
Spiced Kingfish Cutlet, 86
Trevally Carpaccio, 43

Kingfish (multiple families)
Note: Kingfish in the USA may refer to *Scomberomorus* (e.g. King Mackerel) or *Seriola* species (e.g. Yellowtail Kingfish). In Australia and New Zealand, Kingfish usually refers to *Seriola* Species.
For *Scomberomorus* species refer to Mackerel
For *Seriola* species refer to Yellowtail Kingfish

Kina (*Class Echinoidea* - multiple species)
Refer to Sea Urchin

Kumu (*Mullidae - Parupeneus porphyreus*) aka **Whitesaddle Goatfish**
Refer to Goatfish

L

Leather Jacket (*Monacanthidae* - multiple species)
Six Spine (*Meuschenia freycineti*)
Moqueca (*Brazilian Fish Stew*), 200
Six Spine Ravioli, 222

Also does well in...
Grandma Eiko's Karaage, 191
Winter Kingfish Belly Satay, 83

Ling Cod (*Hexagrammidae - Ophiodon elongatus*)
Lebanese style Ling Cod, 156

Lionfish (*Scorpaenidae - Pterois volitans*)
South of the Border Lionfish Ceviche, 54

Lobster (multiple families) aka **Cray, Crayfish, Rock Lobster, Spiny Lobster, Spiny Cray**
Spiny Lobsters (*Family Palinuridae*)
California Spiny Lobster (*Panulirus interruptus*)
Eastern Rock Lobster (*Sagmariasus verreauxi*)
Painted Cray (*Panulirus versicolor*)
Southern Rock Lobster (*Jasus edwardsii*)
Western Rock Lobster (*Panulirus cygnus*)
True Lobsters (*Family Nephropidae*)
American Lobster (*Homarus americanus*)
European Lobster (*Homarus gammarus*)
(Cray) Ariki Ceviche, 38
(Lobster) Bottom Scratchers Cioppino, 196
(Lobster) Coastal Okonomiyaki, 242
(Eastern RL) Crayfish Risotto, 233
(Cray) Creamy Garlic and Chilli Pipi Fettuccine, 224
(Southern RL) Karaage crayfish, 95
Lobster Caesar Salad, 238
Lobster Cocktail, 239
Lobster Fettuccine, 227
Lobster Oil, 256
Lobster or Scallop Mornay, 153
Lobster Rice Paper Rolls, 240
Lobster Spanakopita, 152
Lobster Tagliatelle with Champagne and Vanilla Cream, 92
Lobster with Miso Butter, 154
Luxury Lobster Rolls, 180
(Spiny) Millionaire's Miso Soup, 205
Mule's Sure Fire Grilled Lobster, 89

Lobster (multiple families) aka **Cray, Crayfish, Rock Lobster, Spiny Lobster, Spiny Cray**
(Lobster) Old Man Blue Tacos, 93
OMG you did what to Crayfish?!, 144
(Lobster/Cray) Sheep Crab California Rolls, 192
Southern Cray Spaghetti in Bacon and
(California Spiny) Taiwanese Popcorn Spiny Lobster, 90
Tomato Cream, 232
Spearo Crayfish Pasta, 228
Thai Lobster Cakes, 94

Long Finned Pike (*Dinolestidae - Dinolestes lewini*)
Stinky Pike Sashimi, 55

Luderick (*Girellidae - Girella tricuspidata*) aka **Parore, Blackfish**
Thai Inspired Fish Sausage Rolls, 164

M

Mangrove Jack (*Lutjanidae - Lutjanus griseus*)
Quick and Dirty Whole Fish, 115

Also does well in...
Crispy Skin Fish with Salsa Verde, 122
Honey Buffalo Fish Wings, 117

Mackerel (*Scombridae* - multiple species)
Spanish (*Scomberomorus commerson*)
Grey (*Scomberomorus semifasciatus*)
King (*Scomberomorus cavalla*) aka Kingfish
(Grey or Spanish) Ariki Boat Curry, 211
Yellow Tail Katsu Sando, 236

Also does well in...
Ariki Ceviche, 38
Chick-Fil-A Copycat Burgers, 241
Dry Aged Bonito, 32
Smoked Fish Pâté, 137
Bonito and Urchin Tostadas, 31
Grandma Eiko's Karaage, 120
Hot Smoked Spanish Mackerel, 134
Smoked Mackerel Carbonara, 133
Spanish Mackerel Poke Bowl 2 ways, 40
Stinky Pike Sashimi, 55
The Sergeants Ramen, 202

Mahi Mahi (*Coryphaenidae – Coryphaena hippurus*) aka **Dolphinfish**
Bonfire Grilled Mahi Mahi with Garlic Cilantro Lime Slaw, 71
My oh My Mahi, 69

Also does well in...
The Sergeants Ramen, 202
Military Turban Snail (*Turbinidae - Turbo militaris*)
Turban Taco aka Snail Choy Bao, 190

Morwong (*Family Cheilodactylidae and family Latridae*)
Banded (*Cheilodactylus spectabilis*)
Blue (*Nemadactylus douglasii*) aka. **Grey Morwong**
Dusky (*Dactylophora nigricans*)
Red (*Morwong fuscus*)
Crispy Fish Wings, 68

Also does well in...
(Blue/Grey) Crispy skin black drummer, 146
(Blue/Red) Crispy Skin Fish w/ Salsa Verde, 122
(Red) Garlic Butter Pasta in a hurry, 229
(Red) Parcel steamed fish, 184
(Blue/Grey) Passionfruit Ceviche, 33
(Blue/Red) Super Simple Mexican Bream, 101
(Dusky) Sweet and Sour Buffalo Bream, 107
(Blue/Red) Thai Green Mango Salad Fried, 109
Whole Charred Fish with Peanut Curry Sauce, 72

Moses Perch (*Lutjanidae - Lutjanus russellii*) aka. **Moses Snapper**

Also does well in...
Crispy Skin Fish with Salsa Verde, 122
Salt baked sea bass, 149

Mud Crab (*Portunidae – Scylla serrata*)
Refer to Crab

Mulloway (*Sciaenidae – Argyrosomus japonicus*) aka. **Jewfish**
Mulloway Steak Assam Pedas, 112

Mullet (*Mugilidae - multiple species*)

Also does well in...
Kingfish Botarga, 49

Mussels (*Mytilidae - multiple species*)
Campfire Mussels, 209

O

Octopus (*Octopodidae* – multiple species)
Cephalopod Bolo, 210
Greek Octopus Salad, 181
Grilled Tako, 109
Octopus Dumplings (*Takoyaki*), 97
Octopus Tom Yum, 207

Oyster (*Ostreidae* - multiple species)
Oyster Omelette, 111

P

Parore (*Girellidae - Girella tricuspidata*)
Refer to Luderick

Parrotfish (*Scaridae* - multiple species)

Also does well in...
Shrekviche, 52

Prawns (*Suborder Dendrobranchiata* - multiple species)
Note: Shrimp and prawn are often used interchangeably despite their differences.
Eastern King Prawn (*Penaeus plebejus*)
Western King Prawn (*Penaeus latisulcatus*)

Also does well in...
(King) Assam King Prawns, 102
Bottom Scratchers Cioppino, 196
Lobster Caesar Salad, 238
Lobster Cocktail, 239
Lobster Fettuccine, 227
Lobster Rice Paper Rolls, 240
Lobster Tagliatelle with Champagne and Vanilla Cream, 92
Seafood Chowder, 201
Sheep Crab California Rolls, 192

Pearl Perch (*Glaucosomatidae - Glaucosoma scapulare*)

Also does well in...
Crispy Skin Fish with Salsa Verde, 122

Perch (Multiple families and species)
Note: "Perch" may refer to a number of species. Some of the more common ones are listed below.
Blue Perch (*Scorpididae - Medialuna californiensis*)
Black Perch (*Embiotocidae - Embiotoca jacksoni*)
Barred Surfperch (*Embiotocidae - Amphistichus argenteus*)

Also does well in...
Filipino Grandpa's Steamed Fish & Beans, 169

Pipi (*Psammobiidae* - multiple species) aka **Beach Pipi, Clam, Cooron Cockle, Eugarie, Goolwa Cockle, Pippie** and **Ugari**
Creamy Garlic and Chilli Pipi Fettuccine, 224

R

Red Morwong (*Latridae – Morwong fuscus*)
Refer to Morwong

Red Rock Crab (*Cancridae - Cancer productus*)
Refer to Crab

Red Rock Cod (*Scorpaenidae - Scorpaena sp.*) aka **Red Scorpionfish**

Also does well in...
Crayfish Risotto, 233
Six Spine Ravioli, 222

Red Mullet (*Mullidae* - multiple species)
Refer to Goatfish

Red Vermillion Rockfish (*Scorpaenidae – Sebastes miniatus*)
Refer to Rockfish

Robalo (*Moronidae - Dicentrarchus labrax*) aka. **Sea Bass, European Seabass**
Steamed Sea Bass with Green Sauce, 183
Crispy Skin Fish with Salsa Verde, 122
Salt baked sea bass, 149

Rockfish (*Scorpaenidae* - multiple species)
Red Vermillion (Sebastes miniatus) aka **California Rockfish**
Crispy Skin Tom Kha Pla, 142
Ruby Red Vermillion Rockfish Ceviche, 48
Seared and Basted Lemon (*Red Vermillion*) Parsley Butter Rockfish, 62
Vermillion Rockfish Provençal, 158

S

Salmon (*Arripidae* - multiple species)
Note: Salmon in this book refers to Arripidae species, not 'Atlantic Salmon'.
Refer to Kahawai

Sawtail Surgeonfish (*Acanthuridae - Prionurus microlepidotus*)
Shrekviche, 52

Scallop (*Pectinidae* - multiple species)
Commercial Scallop (*Pecten fumatus*)
Rock Scallop (*Crassadoma gigantea*)
Cream mustard drunken scallops, 186
Friday Fish Pie, 166
Rock Scallop Watermelon Aguachiles, 47
Scallop Bake, 163

Also does well in...
Lobster or Scallop Mornay, 152
Creamy Garlic and Chilli Pipi Fettuccine, 224

Sea Bass (*Moronidae - Dicentrarchus labrax*)
Refer to Robalo

Sea Urchin (*Class Echinoidea* - multiple species) aka **Kina, Uni**
Bonito and Urchin Tostadas, 31
Cured Urchin Butter, 59
Kina Craybonara, 226
Uni Linguine, 225

Sergeant Baker (*Aulopidae - Latropiscis purpurissatus*)
The Sergeants Ramen, 202

Also does well in...
Six Spine Ravioli, 222

Sheep Crab (*Epialtidae – Loxorhynchus grandis*)
Refer to Crab

Sheepshead (*Labridae – Semicossyphus pulcher*)
Yuzu Ponzu Dressed Sheepshead Sashimi, 45
Grilled Stuffed Burrito, 14

Shellfish (multiple families and species)
Note: the term "shellfish" is used very broadly to describe many hard bodied invertebrates e.g. Clams, Cockles, Mussels, Oysters, Pipis, Scallops, Shrimp, Crabs etc.
Seafood Chowder, 201

Also does well in...
Vermillion Rockfish Provençal, 158

Shrimp (*Suborder Pleocyemata* - multiple species)
Note: Shrimp and prawn are often used interchangeably despite their differences.

Also does well in...
Bottom Scratchers Cioppino, 196
Lobster Fettuccine, 227
Sheep Crab California Rolls, 192

Silver Drummer (*Kyphosidae* - multiple species)
Refer to Buffalo Bream

Silver Trevally (*Carangidae - Pseudocaranx georgeanus*)
Refer to Trevally

Six Spine Leather Jacket (*Monacanthidae – Meuschenia freycineti*)
Refer to Leatherjacket

Skipjack Tuna (*Scombridae - Katsuwonus pelamis*)
Refer to Tuna

Slipper Lobster (*Scyllaridae* - multiple species) aka **Slipper Cray**

Also does well in...
Crayfish Risotto, 233
Creamy Garlic and Chilli Pipi Fettuccine, 224
Lobster Spanakopita, 152
Lobster Tagliatelle with Champagne and Vanilla Cream, 92
Lobster with Miso Butter, 154

Snapper (multiple families)
Note: Snapper may refer to several species of Sparidae or Lutjanidae.
Pink (*Sparidae – Chrysophrys auratus*) aka Australasian snapper
Grey (*Lutjanidae - Lutjanus griseus*)
(*Grey*) Quick and Dirty Whole Fish, 115
(*Pink*) Soy Sauce Steamed Snapper Fillet, 188
Baked white fish, 58

Also does well in...
Bonfire Grilled Mahi Mahi with Garlic Cilantro Lime Slaw, 71
Bonito and Urchin Tostadas, 31
Calico Poke Bowl with Jicama Roses, 50
Crispy skin black drummer, 146
Crispy Skin Fish with Salsa Verde, 122
Eiko's Simmered Snapper, 189
Lobster Spanakopita, 152
Salt baked sea bass, 149
Super Simple Mexican Bream, 101
Thai Green Mango Salad Fried Whole Fish, 79

Snook (*Sphyraenidae - Sphyraena novaehollandiae*) aka Pike, Australian Barracuda
Stinky Pike Sashimi, 55

Southern Crayfish (*Palinuridae – Jasus edwardsii*)
Refer to Lobster

Southern Rock Lobster (*Palinuridae – Jasus edwardsii*)
Refer to Lobster

Spanish Mackerel (*Scombridae – Scomberomorus commerson*)
Green Thai Fish Cakes, 89
Hot Smoked Spanish Mackerel, 134
Smoked Fish Pasta, 136
Smoked Fish Pie, 135
Smoked Mackerel Carbonara, 133
Spanish Mackerel Poke Bowl 2 ways, 40

Spider Crab (*Majidae* - multiple species)
Refer to Crab

Squid (*Order Myopsida or Order Oegopsida*) aka. **Calamari**
Chorizo Stuffed Squid, 105
Coastal Okonomiyaki, 242
Garlic Butter Pasta in a hurry, 229
Sotong Bakar (Barbequed Squid), 103

Also does well in...
Ariki Ceviche, 38
Bottom Scratchers Cioppino, 196
Cuttlefish Tomato Kway Tiaw, 113
Cephalopod Bolo, 210
Greek Octopus Salad, 181
Octopus Tom Yum, 207

T

Tailor (*Pomatomidae - Pomatomus saltatrix*)
Tailor Pie, 160

Also does well in...
Smoked Fish Pâté, 137

Tilapia (*Cichlidae - Oreochromis mossambica*)

Also does well in...
Filipino Grandpa's Steamed Fish & Beans, 191

Trevally (*Carangidae* - multiple species) aka **Jacks**
Bigeye (*Caranx sexfasciatus*)
Bluefin (*Caranx melampygus*)
Giant (*Caranx ignobilis*)
Silver (*Pseudocaranx georgeanus*)
White (*Pseudocaranx dentex*)

Also does well in...
(Silver) Mid-Spear, 2 Min Fish Ramen, 212
Hot Smoked Spanish Mackerel, 134
Shrekviche, 52
Trevally Carpaccio, 43
Zesty Parsley Kingfish, 84

Tuna (*Scombridae* – multiple species)
Bluefin (*Thunnus sp.*)
Dogtooth (*Gymnosarda unicolor*)
Skipjack (*Katsuwonus pelamis*)
Yellowfin (*Thunnus albacares*)
Mediterranean Style Tuna Collar, 141
(Bluefin) Tuna Tartare in Sesame Ginger Sauce, 57

Also does well in...
(Skipjack) Bonito Poke Bowl, 30
Ariki Ceviche, 38
Bonito and Urchin Tostadas, 31
Smoked Mackerel Carbonara, 133
Spanish Mackerel Poke Bowl 2 ways, 40

Tuskfish (*Labridae - Choerodon* species)
Bald Chin Grouper (*Choerodon rubescens*)
Bluespotted Tuskfish (*Choerodon cauteroma*)
Blackspot Tuskfish (*Choerodon schoenleinii*)
Venus Tuskfish (*Choerodon venustus*)

Also does well in...
(Bald Chin Grouper) BBQ Mushroom Fish Burgers, 132
(Blackspot) Honey Buffalo Fish Wings, 117
Shrekviche, 52
Whole Steamed Coral Trout, 185

Trumpeter (*Latridae* - multiple species)
Bastard Trumpeter (*Latridopsis forsteri*)
Blue Moki (*Latridopsis ciliaris*)
Striped Trumpeter (*Latris lineata*)

Also does well in...
Crispy Skin Fish with Salsa Verde, 122
District 6 Curry Fish, 197

U

Uni (*Class Echinoidea* - multiple species)
Refer to Sea Urchin

V

Vermillion Rockfish (*Sebastidae – Sebastes miniatus*)
Refer to Rockfish

W

Wahoo (*Scombridae - Acanthocybium solandri*)

Also does well in...
Smoked Mackerel Carbonara, 133
Spanish Mackerel Poke Bowl 2 ways, 40

West Australian Dhufish (*Glaucosomatidae - Glaucosoma hebraicum*)

Also does well in...
Mulloway Steak Assam Pedas, 112

White Sea Bass (*Sciaenidae - Atractoscion nobilis*)

Also does well in...
Filipino Grandpa's Steamed Fish & Beans, 191

Whiting (*Sillaginidae* - multiple species)

Also does well in...
Super Simple Mexican Bream, 101

Y

Yakka (*Carangidae - Trachurus novaezelandiae*)
Yellow Tail Katsu Sando, 236

Yellowfin Bream (*Sparidae - Acanthopagrus australis*)
Refer to Bream

Yellowfin Tuna (*Scombridae – Thunnus albacares*)
DIY Canned Tuna, 58

Yellowtail Kingfish (*Carangidae - Seriola lalandi*)
California Yellowtail (*Seriola lalandi ssp. dorsalis*)
(California) Filipino Grandpa's Steamed Fish & Beans, 191
Baked Kingfish, 151
Baked Orange and Yellowtail, 159
District 6 Curry Fish, 197
Kingfish Botarga, 49
Roasted Kingfish Belly w/ Eggplant Kasundi, 162
Spiced Kingfish Cutlet, 86
The Mango King, 85
Winter Kingfish Belly Satay, 83
Yellowtail Kebabs, 82
Zesty Parsley Kingfish, 84

Also does well in...
Bonito and Urchin Tostadas, 31
Bonito Poke Bowl, 30
Chick-Fil-A Copycat Burgers, 241
Grandma Eiko's Karaage, 120
Hot Smoked Spanish Mackerel, 134
Smoked Mackerel Carbonara, 133
Spanish Mackerel Poke Bowl 2 ways, 40
Stinky Pike Sashimi, 55
The Sergeants Ramen, 202

Terms Glossary

TERMS AND DEFINITIONS

Abs - Abalone, Paua (New Zealand), Ormer (UK), Perlemoen (South Africa).

aka - Also known as.

Al-dente - To cook food until just firm, usually referring to pasta, but can include vegetables.

All purpose flour - Bread flour is a close alternative.

Agar-agar - algae-based gelatin derived from seaweed.

Bake - Cook using an oven or other type of dry heat, like hot stones or coals. Generally refers to cakes, pastries, tarts, and also savoury items like bread, quiche or meat pies. Interchangeable with "roasting".

Banana pepper - Medium-sized member of the chilli pepper family that has a mild, tangy taste. While typically bright yellow, it is possible for them to change to green, red, or orange as they ripen. It is often pickled, stuffed or used as a raw ingredient in foods. Alternative: pepperoncini.

BBQ - Can be gas, hard wood or charcoal/briquettes.

Braai - A South African BBQ that is fueled by hardwood or charcoal/briquettes that is reduced to coals for cooking. The temperature is regulated by adjusting the height of the grid that contains the fish/meat/sausage/bread or vegetables.

Biomagnification (aka bioaccumulation) - A concentration of toxins (such as pollutants) in the tissues of tolerant organisms at successively higher levels in a food chain.

Biomass - In an ecological sense - a measure of living material. Biomass is sometimes used as a term by fisheries management authorities. e.g. virgin biomass.

Blanch - Scald in boiling water/steam for a short period of time then plunge into ice or running water.

Bleeding - this is the deliberate process of cutting the artery that runs along the bottom of the area between a fish's gills. This is essential for best eating quality.

Bone-whole (butterflied): Scaled fish with removed bones. This cut is excellent for stuffing a fish. Remove pin bones. Leave or remove the tail and head as needed.

Bonito flakes (aka katsuobushi) - Thinly shaved flakes of smoked, dried bonito fish.

Brine - Soak in a salted water solution.

Broil - a caramelised, browning on any dish.

Broth aka bouillon - Often used as a stock and made from boiling water with veg, fish or meat.

Brunoise - is a culinary knife cut in which the food item is first julienned and then turned a quarter turn and diced, producing cubes of about 3mm or less on each side.

Cephalopod - is a class of mollusc - such as octopus, squid, cuttlefish and nautilus.

Ceviche - (aka seviche, cebiche) A dish where raw fish is marinated in citrus juice.

Chilli - In the USA, the preferred spelling is "chili," but other English-speaking countries use "chilli".

Chilli Bin aka Esky aka Cooler or Icebox.

Cooler aka Esky aka Chilli Bin or Icebox.

Coriander - cilantro.

Cornstarch - cornflour.

Crayfish (Cray) - In Australia and New Zealand, salt water lobster species are often called crayfish or crays. Rest assured, crayfish are lobster.

Crème fraiche - a high fat, soured fresh cream.

Crudo - Italian word for raw.

Curing - the process of fermenting, smoking, pickling, salting (or a combination of) fish or meat to preserve it

Deglaze - remove flavour from the bottom of the pan using wine or water.

Deshell - remove the shell.

Drop weight - A weight often attached to a small float on the surface that a diver can use to mark a location on the bottom. Commonly used lobster diving but also for abalone/sea urchin in dirty water where it is difficult to locate bottom structures from the surface.

Dry ageing - a process that reduces moisture in fish which intensifies flavour and increases tenderness over a period of time.

Eschalot - (called shallots in some countries) are smaller than regular onions, and vary in colour from golden brown to deep red. They are harder to peel but are milder and taste great in raw salads.

Esky - Australian slang for chilly-bin or cooler or icebox.

Fillet - a boneless cut of fish or meat.

Flash fry - rapidly fry at temp above 400°F/204°C.

Freediver - An underwater diver who performs their chosen activity on a single breath of air.

Frothies - beers

Galangal - can refer to 4 different types of the ginger family *Zingiberaceae* however commonly refers to greater and lesser Galangal. It is commonly used in Asian cuisine.

Ghee - Clarified butter.

Green Onions aka spring onions - Green onions are sold in bunches and have long, green leaves and no bulb. The flavour is mild, and they can be eaten raw or lightly cooked.

Hāngī - traditional New Zealand Māori method of cooking in a pit oven (umu) over hot stones.

Ice slurry - crushed ice and sea water mix.

Ikejime aka brainspike - a method of killing a fish by inserting a spike directly into the hindbrain.

Kachumber - Kachumber, or cachumber, is an Indian salad dish made from fresh chopped tomatoes, cucumbers, onions, lemon juice, and often, chilli peppers.

Karaage - Japanese technique of lightly coating fish, chicken and other meats with flour, potato or corn starch then deep frying.

Katsuobushi - Bonito flakes.

Kobujime - Japanese technique of curing fish, meat or veg between kombu leaves.

Kombu - edible kelp.

Laksa - is a spicy noodle dish popular in Southeast Asia usually utilising meat or seafood. Laksa is usually prepared with a rich and spicy coconut soup or seasoned broth.

Lekker - South African word for good or pleasant.

Lozenged - cross score.

Miso paste - fermented paste made of soybeans. Has a salty, umami flavour.

Macros aka macronutrients - where we get most of our energy from—proteins, carbohydrates and fats.

Mandolin - slicer.

Marinade - a sauce or liquid used to flavour and tenderise meat and fish.

Mezcal - a spirit made from maguey (agave), similar to tequila.

Noob - borrowed from video gaming, 'Noob' as we define it is someone in the process of learning and mastery of a particular skill. Being self deprecating, allows the person to learn without shame or derision. Calling ourselves noobs also serves as a ward to ego.

Numb ray - species of stingray that can deliver an electric shock to unsuspecting victims.

Old bay seasoning - seasoning mix containing celery salt, black pepper, crushed red pepper flakes, paprika, and many others.

Opprobrium - harsh criticism or censure.

Julienned - sliced thinly into sticks or batons.

Panko - Japanese style of breadcrumbs giving a very crisp texture when fried.

Pico de gallo - aka salsa fresca (fresh sauce) made from red tomatoes, white onion, jalapeño, cilantro, lime and salt.

Pinbone - the fine bones found in the fillet of a fish.

Pizzling - n. A drubbing, a 'hazing' (from the bull's pizzle as an 'instrument of flagellation' 1599 OED) eg. to take a beating.

Ponzu - a citrus based Japanese sauce.

Purslane - edible succulent, can be eaten raw or cooked.

Ramekin - (also spelled ramequin) is a small dish used for culinary purposes.

Raita - an Indian yoghurt sauce often with cucumber, mint and cilantro.

Red Shallots (Allium cepa var. aggregatum) - a smaller type of onion with a red pink colour.

Remoulade - European cold sauce based with mayonnaise. Although similar to tartar sauce, it is often more yellowish, sometimes flavoured with curry, and sometimes contains chopped pickles or piccalilli. It can also contain horseradish, paprika, anchovies, capers and a host of other items.

Roe - ripe eggs or egg mass. e.g shrimp roe, scallop roe, sea urchin roe or squid roe.

Roux - a mixture of equal parts flour and fat, cooked over low to medium heat, to create a thickening agent.

Salted water - ingredient mix as salty as the sea. Approximate ratio should be 35g per l (4.7oz per gallon).

Samphire - an edible succulent, salt-tolerant plant that grows in the wild.

Sashimi - Japanese delicacy of raw fish or meat.

Sauté - fry quickly in a little hot fat.

Score - to cut slits on the surface of a piece of food.

Seeded Mustard - whole grain mustard.

Shiso - The Japanese name for a popular herb (*Perilla frutescens*) known for its jagged leaves and refreshing flavour. A member of the mint family, it has a unique flavour similar to basil and cilantro with subtle hints of cumin and cloves.

Shuck - remove the shell eg. from an oyster.

Smoke/smoking - curing through the use of smoke.

Spearo - someone who loves the lifestyle of spearfishing. Ungendered, spearo can refer to a man or woman ('speara' is sometimes used for women).

Spring onions aka scallions (USA). Spring onions and green onions are both immature onions, but they are often called the same thing. Spring onions have a white, round bulb with long stems, and are also sold in bunches.

Steak - Cut across the backbone, horizontally, leaving a thick round piece with the skin still on. Broil, grill or even pan fry this meaty cut of fish. In some the bone remains and others are boneless.

Steep - To allow dry ingredients to soak in a liquid.

Stone shot - To shoot through the brain or spinal cord of a fish shot with a speargun. Causes instant paralysis or death. This is the preferred shot placement of spearos.

Sushi/Sashimi - A raw dish, usually seafood, expertly cut and served with condiments like wasabi, preserved ginger and soy. Sushi is a similar dish, but the focus is on the rice, with the seafood or other garnish serving to highlight.

Tarspot - sperm packet under the carapace on a female lobster.

Tartare - a raw dish of finely diced fish or meat.

Tartar Sauce - originally a French sauce that was served with fish or meat, à la tartare. Tartar (often spelled Tartare) sauce is a cold sauce composed of mayonnaise, pickles, capers and herbs such as dill.

Tempra: Tempra is a Baba-Nonya/Peranakan dish not to be confused with the Japanese Tempura. Tempra is a sweet and sour sauce used mostly in fish dishes, whereas tempura is a crunchy batter used to coat seafood and vegetables.

Tempura - Tempura is a typical Japanese dish usually consisting of seafood, meat and vegetables that have been battered and deep fried.

Tomalley - Often referred to as "mustard". Greeny coloured substance found in lobsters and crabs. Considered a delicacy in some areas, it can be eaten on its own or used in sauces or stock to add complexity and flavour.

Toro - the fatty underbelly of tuna.

Tua Tua - *Paphies subtriangulata* is a species of edible bivalve clam known as tuatua in the Māori language, a member of the family *Mesodesmatoidae* and endemic to New Zealand.

Tucker - Tucker is an informal word for food.

Tuile - A baked wafer, French in origin, generally arced in shape, that is made most often from dough, often served as an accompaniment of other dishes.

Umami - Savoury seafood taste.

Wasabi - aka Japanese Horseradish. A spicy green paste.

Wobbegong - 12 species of carpet sharks (*Orectolobidae*) that frequent Australian and Indonesian waters.

Yuzu Ponzu - Japanese citrus dipping sauce made of soy sauce and citrus juice.

Zucchini - courgette.

Special Thanks

PHOTOGRAPHY

A big special thanks to all of the individuals who contributed their photos towards this project.

A special thanks to Erik Keener and the Fin+Forage team for all of the photography submissions to assist with building this book. Visit finandforage.com for more content.

All photography remains the rights of the original contributors.

CORNERSTONE CONTENT GUIDES

A massive thank you to all of the writers who contributed to the cornerstone content guides that are within this book. From caring for your catch, finding lobsters and dry aging techniques, we have you covered.

Our key contributors: Eric Keener (@finandforage), Jai Gibbons (@SpearoChef), Spencer Allen (@el_spencerino), James Sakker (Catch it Cook it Grow it), Michael Isbey (@matakanasmokehouse_nz) & Harry Foster (@hazfos).

DISCLAIMER AND COPYRIGHT

This edition of 99 Spearo Recipes was published in 2022 by Noob Spearo Pty Ltd

Business enquiries:
Noobspearo.com | shrek@noobspearo.com

Disclaimer: Freediving and Spearfishing are inherently dangerous endeavors that can lead to permanent injury or death. Under no circumstances shall Noob Spearo or any of its affiliates, partners, suppliers or sponsors be held liable for any indirect, incidental, consequential, special or exemplary damages arising out of or in connection with your access to or use of the resources, opinions, guides or posts found in this book, web pages or any of our social media outlets. Any action you take upon the information produced by Noob Spearo is strictly at your own risk.

None of the authors, contributors, editors or anyone else connected with Noob Spearo, in any way whatsoever, can be responsible for your use of the information contained in this book or on our web pages.

Printed in Great Britain
by Amazon

21276507R00159